# Beyond Bullets Points:

Using Microsoft® Office PowerPoint® 2007 to Create Presentations That Inform, Motivate, and Inspire

**CLIFF ATKINSON**

PUBLISHED BY
Microsoft Press
A Division of Microsoft Corporation
One Microsoft Way
Redmond, Washington 98052-6399

Library of Congress Control Number: 2007931457

Printed and bound in the United States of America.

1 2 3 4 5 6 7 8 9   QWT   2 1 0 9 8 7

Distributed in Canada by H.B. Fenn and Company Ltd.

A CIP catalogue record for this book is available from the British Library.

Microsoft Press books are available through booksellers and distributors worldwide. For further information about international editions, contact your local Microsoft Corporation office or contact Microsoft Press International directly at fax (425) 936-7329. Visit our Web site at www.microsoft.com/mspress. Send comments to mspinput@microsoft.com.

**Acquisitions Editor:** Juliana Aldous
**Developmental Editor:** Sandra Haynes
**Project Editor:** Valerie Woolley
**Editorial Production:** Waypoint Press
**Technical Reviewer:** Andrew Cohen
**Cover:** Tom Draper Design

*Cover Photo by Bradford Rogne*

Body Part No. X13-92839

*To my family: Andrew, Reuben, Hildegund, Reuben Jr., Vicki, Tripp, Jenna, Christina, Jeremy, Bobby, and Stanley.*

—Cliff Atkinson

# Contents

**What do you think of this book? We want to hear from you!**

Microsoft is interested in hearing your feedback so we can continually improve our books and learning resources for you. To participate in a brief online survey, please visit:

**www.microsoft.com/learning/booksurvey/**

## On the CD

**What do you think of this book? We want to hear from you!**

Microsoft is interested in hearing your feedback so we can continually improve our books and learning resources for you. To participate in a brief online survey, please visit:

**www.microsoft.com/learning/booksurvey/**

# Acknowledgments

**MY SPECIAL** gratitude to Juliana Aldous Atkinson (no relation) and the team at Microsoft Press, who graciously provided me with the opportunity to revise this book and make it even better the second time around. Thanks to my editing team of Sandra Haynes, Valerie Woolley, Steve Sagman, and Jennifer Harris for working so patiently with me—I count myself lucky to have had such a talented team at my side again. Thanks to Rob Nance for many of the illustrations used in the book, and to Garth Johnson and the iStockphoto community for the stock photography used in many of the presentation examples.

Thanks to those who inspired the foundation of the BBP approach most profoundly: Richard E. Mayer's important work on multimedia learning, Barbara Minto's revolutionary critical-thinking methodology, Jonathan Pryce's insights on structuring and outlining information, the engineers who developed the STOP proposal-writing method at Hughes Aircraft, and the media producers who practice their craft here in Los Angeles.

Thanks to those whose embrace and application of BBP has matured and deepened the approach you see in this book. A special thanks to the early advocates of BBP—especially Mark Lanier, for presenting the approach on a national stage, as well others in the legal profession, including Lisa Blue and Jaine Fraser—and to the early adopters at organizations including Toyota, Nestlé Waters Group, Amgen, Sony, Intel, and Noel-Levitz. Thanks to the many BBP readers and workshop participants—your insights made this revision better, and your courage in applying BBP often against great odds gives me hope that BBP will continue to make a difference in the world.

—Cliff Atkinson

# About the Author

**Cliff Atkinson** is the leading expert on using PowerPoint software effectively in high-profile legal trials and just about every other context. His Amazon.com Top 5 bestselling book Beyond Bullet Points (Microsoft Press, 2007) expands on a communications approach that is transforming the way people communicate around the world. He designed the presentations that helped persuade a jury to award a $253 million verdict to the plaintiff in the nation's first Vioxx trial in 2005, which *Fortune* magazine called "frighteningly powerful." He consults on legal trials and teaches BBP at many of the country's top law firms, government agencies, business schools, trade associations, and corporations, including Sony, Toyota, Nestlé, Amgen, Bristol-Myers Squibb, Intel, Microsoft, the American Association for Justice, and the American Bar Association.

Cliff received his B.A. in English and journalism from Baylor University in Texas and his M.B.A. from Richmond, The American International University in London. After serving as a captain in the U.S. Air Force, he held marketing and consulting positions for several start-up companies in San Francisco. Cliff currently serves as president of BBP Media, LLC, in Los Angeles.

# Introduction

**I ORIGINALLY WROTE** *Beyond Bullet Points* to offer a new way for
people to create Microsoft® Office PowerPoint® presentations more effectively. I never imagined that shortly after the book's publication, the impact of the
Beyond Bullet Points (BBP) approach would make headlines in the *New York
Times*, the *Wall Street Journal*, and the *Los Angeles Times*. Since then, interest
in BBP has elevated the first edition of this book to bestseller status, at one
point reaching the #4 sales rank out of all books at Amazon.com. It turns out
that BBP is striking a chord with people who have a simple desire—to move
beyond the bullet points that keep both presenters and audiences trapped,
frustrated, and alienated from one another.

People are finding that BBP really works for them and that once they try this
approach, they can't go back to the old way of using PowerPoint. Since the
first edition of this book was published, BBP has been even more thoroughly
road-tested and resoundingly audience-approved. Individuals report a
process that is practical, orderly, focused, and disciplined, and organizations
are finding a methodology that is attainable, effective, efficient, and scalable.
BBP is working today across an incredible range of professions and purposes.
It will help you frame and facilitate a conversation with your audience, and
it will guide you on how and where and why to use PowerPoint. Lately,
questions about BBP have shifted from "How do I do this?" to "How does my
organization do this?" which indicates that the approach is taking hold at a
deeper level and setting the stage for a broader movement of people who
support and use BBP every day.

The underlying system of BBP in this book is the same as in the first edition,
offering a way to turn general theories about communication into the practical
things you do when you open a new PowerPoint presentation tomorrow
morning. But there are also a number of significant improvements in this
edition. After teaching, testing, and applying BBP with groups and individuals

for the past two years, I saw firsthand what was working and what needed improvement. In this book, I highlighted more prominently the things you need to know most, expanded on material that needed more explanation, and replaced all of the examples with new and improved versions.

I have added significant new resources and materials to help people get through the most difficult hurdles in structuring and designing BBP presentations. Based on feedback from groups and individuals, I simplified the terms used in the key tools and streamlined the process to remove roadblocks to easier understanding and faster implementation. People asked for more specific examples of BBP in action, so Chapter 1 describes a headline-making BBP presentation, Chapters 4 through 8 use a new example to demonstrate how to apply BBP step by step, and Chapter 9 shows more examples. People asked for more ways to explain to others the why and the how of BBP, so Chapter 2 shows why BBP works so well in terms of three "research realities," Chapter 3 shows step by step how the process will unfold, and Chapter 11 on the companion CD shows a quick exercise you can conduct to introduce BBP to your team. People asked for a community they could join to learn more about BBP and to collaborate with others, so a new companion Web site at *www.beyondbulletpoints.com* now fulfills that need.

This book focuses on applying BBP with PowerPoint 2007 and using the software's new features to accelerate the graphic design process and eliminate the guesswork for those who are not designers or technical experts. As before, this book assumes that you are not a graphic designer and do not know graphics software beyond PowerPoint 2007. There is, however, a new hardware tool that I wholeheartedly recommend you adopt if at all possible as you work with BBP—a Tablet PC. This special type of computer allows you to write directly on the screen and will help you sketch your storyboard faster and more efficiently, and it will open up new opportunities to interact with your audience. Tablet PCs are now widely available and are a must-have tool for presenters today. I started using one after the first edition of the book was published, and it has now become central to my own practice of BBP—I would not consider creating or giving a presentation without one.

As in the previous edition of this book, I will take you step by step, chapter by chapter, through the BBP process. Chapters 1 through 3 provide an overview of the reasons why you should try BBP and how the process looks, and

Chapters 4 through 10 explain specifically the detailed steps of how to use BBP. A new companion CD includes Chapter 11, copies of key tools described in the book, and PDF versions of several appendixes, including the *BBP Ground Rules* and *BBP Checklists* that you can use as a desktop reference. This book is designed to be a practical guide that you keep close at hand while you work on PowerPoint presentations, as well as a source of ongoing inspiration.

To run the PowerPoint 2007, your computer needs to meet the following minimum requirements:

- 500 megahertz (MHz) processor

- 256 megabytes (MB) RAM

- CD or DVD drive

- 1.5 gigabytes (GB) available hard disk space

- Monitor with 800x600 screen resolution; 1024x768 or higher recommended

- Keyboard and mouse or compatible pointing device

- Internet connection, 128 kilobits per second or greater

- Windows Vista or later, Microsoft Windows XP with Service Pack 2 (SP2), or Microsoft Windows Server 2003 or later.

- Windows Internet Explorer 7 or Microsoft Internet Explorer 6 with service packs

For many people, BBP turns the conventional thinking about PowerPoint presentations upside-down and unlocks the potential that has always been available in the software tool, as well as in the people who use it. The heart of this book is really about people communicating with people. By using a commonly available software tool to help you to do that, you can find focus, clarity, and engagement. I hope you'll find that and much more in this book, as you make and tell your own presentation stories *beyond bullet points*.

# Making Headlines Beyond Bullet Points

**IN THIS CHAPTER, YOU WILL:**

- Witness a Beyond Bullet Points (BBP) presentation that made headline news.
- See how BBP works in a real-world practical application.
- Get a sense of the potential impact you can make with BBP.

**THERE ARE** at least 253 million reasons why you should try the Beyond Bullet Points (BBP) approach. At least that's what one presenter believes, after he used BBP in a courtroom to help persuade jurors to award a $253 million verdict for his client in a major legal trial. His story is just one of the many that tell of the impact BBP is making on presentations far and wide, and it is also an example of the impact you can make on your next presentation with the book you hold in your hands right now.

## Can I Really Change the World with a PowerPoint Presentation?

If you were to see a newspaper headline that read, "PowerPoint presentation changes the world!" you would probably laugh because the very concept sounds absurd. Who could believe that a software tool that is associated more with boredom than brilliance could possibly produce an experience so powerful that it would make headlines? Yet, believe it or not, that's exactly what happened with the Microsoft® Office PowerPoint® presentation described in this chapter. And it's something you have the potential to do when you use BBP—you really can create PowerPoint 2007 presentations that can change the world.

In short order, the chapters of this book will take you through the nuts and bolts of why BBP works, how you can apply it to your next presentation, and what you can do to deliver it. But first, the best way to learn about BBP is to see how it plays out in the real world—on one particular day, in one specific room, with one presenter and his audience. That was the day when BBP was put on trial and received a stunning verdict.

## The Perfect PowerPoint Storm

Every summer, the residents of Angleton, Texas, brace themselves for the possibility that a fearsome hurricane might bear down on their Gulf Coast town near Houston. But nothing could prepare them for the hot and humid July day when a different kind of storm hit this quiet town of 18,000 people. The doors of the old gray county courthouse in the town square opened to a flood of television crews who crowded the hallways looking for a place to film. A group of newspaper reporters surged into the main courtroom, squeezing into uncomfortable wooden benches and tapping updates on their laptops to the newsrooms of the *New York Times*, the *Wall Street Journal*, the Associated Press, *Fortune*, and Reuters.

The journalists were in Angleton to cover the news event of the day: the opening statements of a major legal trial that would begin with the delivery of a PowerPoint presentation. Everyone in the courtroom stood when the jurors filed into the room and settled into their seats. The room was silent, here at the eye of the storm, when a man stood up to face the jurors. Little did anyone know that this lawyer was about to unleash a storm of his own from his laptop computer. After all, this was no ordinary PowerPoint presentation he was about to give—it was a Beyond Bullet Points presentation. Like many of the hurricanes that have passed through Texas, this presentation would make headlines for its devastating force.

It might come across as odd to you that PowerPoint would take center stage in a Texas courtroom, but it's just one more venue this ubiquitous software tool has transformed in its relatively brief 20-year history. Originally introduced as a tool to help businesspeople present their ideas in meeting rooms, today PowerPoint is everywhere. You are probably one of the millions of people who use PowerPoint, and one of the billions who have been in the audience at other people's presentations. Teachers use PowerPoint in classrooms to present their course materials, and researchers use PowerPoint in conference rooms to present their data and analyses. Hollywood designers use PowerPoint in studios to storyboard creative concepts for films, and ad agencies use PowerPoint in board rooms to pitch major campaigns. Military leaders use PowerPoint in the field to present strategic plans, and politicians use PowerPoint on the campaign trail to communicate their themes. And more and more lawyers are using PowerPoint to present their cases in courtrooms like this one in Angleton.

The lawyer who was about to speak was no stranger to PowerPoint, or to the courtroom. Born and raised in Texas, Mark Lanier specializes in representing plaintiffs in personal injury trials, winning a long list of verdicts in favor of his clients. Early on, he had worked as a lawyer in large law firms, but then he started up his own firm and eventually moved it to the outskirts of Houston. Although he didn't have all the resources of a large law firm in one of Houston's downtown skyscrapers, Mark would soon demonstrate that these days anyone with a laptop computer and PowerPoint software—and an effective way to use them—can make as great an impact as anyone with unlimited resources.

Mark turned to his client, the plaintiff in this case, who was sitting in the first row with her family. "Your Honor," Mark said, "if I may begin by introducing to the jury and to the Court my client." As Carol Ernst stood, Mark introduced her and her daughter. Carol's husband, Bob, had died of a heart attack, and she suspected that a painkiller her husband had taken, Vioxx, was a cause of the heart attack. So she filed a lawsuit against the defendant, the drug's manufacturer, Merck & Co., Inc. Mark would represent Carol throughout the trial.

As Carol sat down, Mark walked toward the jury box past the row of lawyers sitting at the defense table. These lawyers were from two internationally recognized law firms hired by the defendant. With billions of dollars in their war chest, the company could afford the best. Facing such a formidable opponent with deep pockets, Mark knew that he would need to be at the top of his game and that he would need to use the tools and techniques he had to the best of his ability to make the greatest impact.

Mark paused at the jury box and made eye contact with each of the 12 jurors. Before the jurors arrived, Mark had wheeled the lawyers' podium to the side of the courtroom because he didn't want a piece of furniture, or anything else, to stand between him and his audience. Mark had a reputation for a folksy style when he talked to jurors in the courtroom, speaking with a Texas drawl, colorful language, and a conversational manner. But by now, any of Mark's legal opponents would know that to misinterpret his simple style as unsophisticated would be a big and expensive mistake, because of his strong track record of successful verdicts in jury trials.

The jury would be Mark's audience for the next six weeks of the trial, and as any presenter knows, he would need to quickly make a strong impression on them. He would have the opportunity to do that today with his opening statement, a presentation in legal trials that introduces the case to the jurors and lays out the key evidence. This presentation is extremely important to lawyers because they assume that many jurors make up their minds about the outcome of the case by the end of the opening statement. Mark had his work cut out for him as he faced the jurors—you might be able to relate to his situation if your own presentations must make an immediate educational and persuasive impact on your audiences.

## KNOW YOUR AUDIENCE

It is essential that you know your audience well before you start planning your presentations. Mark knew some things about his audience in the jury box—the legal teams from both sides had prepared a written questionnaire for the jurors, in which they found that the jurors were in their 20s and 40s, high-school educated, and from a range of professions, including electrician, a college student, a construction worker, a product technician, a homemaker, a secretary, and a government employee. The lawyers also had an opportunity to ask jurors questions in person during a Q&A session. In your own presentations, the better you know your audience, the better you'll be able to customize your material to them.

The judge had instructed the jurors earlier that when they took their oath, they had become court officials like himself and the lawyers. The jurors were charged with administering justice in this case, by listening to all the evidence in open court and then making a decision based on the facts and the judge's instructions and reading of the law. Like any audience, they sat ready to hear what the presenter would say.

As you might be able to relate to, most experienced speakers say they get nervous before a big presentation, and likewise Mark must have felt some nervousness, but not just because the jurors were watching him closely. Plaintiffs' attorneys like Mark can spend upward of $1 million to bring a case to trial on behalf of their clients, and if they lose, they literally have lost everything they put into the case. The defendant had a great deal to lose as well, because this was the first case to go to trial against the pharmaceutical company. Beyond any negative media coverage the case might bring, a verdict against the company might have a big impact on its bottom line—it could lose millions of dollars in an unfavorable verdict, and possibly lose billions of dollars in market value if its stock price dropped on the news.

**NOTE** Mark Lanier discovered the first edition of *Beyond Bullet Points* at an online bookseller as he was preparing for this trial, and he invited me to fly to Texas to help him use the BBP approach to create his opening statement. We followed the approach in this book step by step as we structured his presentation, and I selected the graphics and designed slides similar to the ones that appear in this chapter. By following the detailed descriptions of the BBP approach through the examples in the rest of this book, you'll be able to apply the same effective approach to your own presentations.

The fact that PowerPoint would play an important role in this trial was a sign not only of how much the software has changed many professions but also of the increasingly high-stakes contexts in which it is used. If you're like many people, you see PowerPoint mostly in the context of selling products or teaching information, but increasingly, the most senior members of organizations use this software tool to communicate the most important work they do. CEOs commonly use PowerPoint today to decide company strategy, consultants use it to recommend restructuring organizations, lobbyists use it to influence legislation, and executives use it to build important relationships. Based on what the plaintiff and defendant had at stake in this trial, today's courtroom presentation was about as high-stakes as a PowerPoint presentation can get.

## Stepping onto the Media Stage

Mark glanced down at his laptop computer, which sat facing him on a small table below the jury box, out of sight of the jurors. What he saw on his laptop screen was a feature in PowerPoint called Presenter view, similar to the screen shown in Figure 1-1, which gave Mark a special view of the presentation that only he could see. Like the teleprompter that broadcasters use to present their speaking notes, this sometimes-overlooked PowerPoint feature gives you the ability to see additional information that does not appear on the screen the audience sees. For example, on the upper left on his screen, Mark could see the blank blue slide that the jurors currently saw. But he also could see his speaker notes on the upper right, reminding him of the points he planned to make while each slide was displayed on screen, as well as a row of small previews of his upcoming slides at the bottom of the screen, helping him to make a smooth transition from one slide to the next.

**See Also** To learn how to use Presenter view for your BBP presentations using PowerPoint 2007, see Appendix B on the companion CD.

**FIGURE 1-1** A feature in PowerPoint called Presenter view gave Mark a view of the current slide the jurors saw on screen, along with his own speaker notes and thumbnail views of upcoming slides.

As he began speaking, Mark's thumb pressed the button on a remote control device like the one shown in Figure 1-2, which he cupped in his hand at his side where the audience would not notice it. This remote would be his constant companion for the next couple of hours, as he used it to advance the PowerPoint slides while he spoke, giving him flexibility to slow down or speed up to match his narration and ensure that the experience appeared seamless to the jurors.

**FIGURE 1-2** Remote control devices offer presenters the ability to advance the slides of a PowerPoint presentation without using the keyboard.

"It's extremely important to me that you hear what this case is about," Mark said, "so I've put together...different exhibits to try and help it stick in your brain and help you focus on what we think are critical points." When Mark clicked the remote control button, it signaled his laptop computer to advance to the first image in the PowerPoint presentation. Although the jurors could not see the laptop below the jury box, they did see an image of Carol and Bob appear on the 10-foot screen directly behind Mark, as illustrated in Figure 1-3. From where the jurors sat, it appeared that Mark was in a giant television set, as the images on the screen would soon start dissolving and changing behind him in a seamlessly choreographed media experience.

**FIGURE 1-3** The images from Mark's PowerPoint presentation filled the 10-foot screen behind him, creating a persuasive backdrop.

## REMOTE CONTROL

One of the biggest distractions you can create during a presentation is to return to the keyboard every time you need to advance a slide. This creates a visual distraction, disrupts the natural flow of your delivery, and leaves the impression that the computer is controlling you rather than you controlling the computer. Like Mark did in the Angleton courtroom, free yourself from the computer by using a small remote control device to advance the slides in the presentation. Many of these devices are designed specifically for PowerPoint presentations and are attached to a computer using a USB connection with no installation software needed. Some models feature a simple interface with only advance and reverse buttons, and some even include a laser pointer along with a button that allows you to black out the screen during the presentation.

The projected colors, images, and words were so thoroughly integrated into the presentation experience that turning off the projector would have been like eliminating the set of a theater production or the screen in a movie theater. This innovative media stage transformed the courtroom into something new—an absorbing media experience that would engage the jurors through the next 2½ hours of the presentation. Never breaking eye contact with the jurors or looking back at the screen, Mark now began to tell a gripping story that would lay out the evidence of the plaintiff's case.

## A Singular Story

What was notable about Mark's PowerPoint slide, shown on its own in Figure 1-4, was not so much what was on it, but rather what was not on it. You would probably expect the slides of a PowerPoint presentation to be filled with bullet points, but here the jurors saw only the visual power of a single, simple photograph. Such full-screen images are rare in PowerPoint presentations, but this image fit in perfectly with what Mark would do next.

**FIGURE 1-4** A family photo of Bob and Carol showed the happy couple after they were married.

With a photograph of the couple on the screen as his backdrop, Mark began telling an anecdote to introduce Bob and Carol to the jurors. "But let me tell you a little bit about Bob," Mark said. "Bob was a great fellow who always took [Carol] to wonderful, interesting places. They went to the kite festival in Washington State. They went to the balloon launch in Albuquerque. They had a lot of fun. He got her into tandem bike racing. They weren't the winning kind of athletes. They just did it to be together, and it was a good, fun way for them to live together."

Mark knew that telling the details of an anecdote like this one about Carol and Bob is an effective and efficient way to introduce a new and complicated topic to an audience. With a simple story of a tandem bike race, the jurors could quickly imagine what Carol and Bob's relationship and lives were like. And seeing the family photograph would make it easier for jurors to relate to the plaintiff, perhaps reminding the jurors of similar photos they have taken or seen in their own families. The photo and specific details of the couple's life together would work powerfully to quickly introduce Carol and Bob to the jury and to make an emotional connection with them. This slide worked much more effectively than a list of bullet points ever could, because we don't live our lives in bullet points—we live in images and stories.

"They did get married after being together for a number of years," Mark explained. " Interestingly enough, they were introduced over exercise. And you'll hear Carol talk about her...daughter...being the matchmaker between Carol and Bob." Here Mark added a detail informing the jurors that they would hear from Carol herself on the stand, establishing a sense of anticipation that they would get to hear from her firsthand. Mark knew that hinting at events to come is an effective way to engage any audience's interest. And by using the specific details about Carol and Bob while the photograph was displayed on screen, he connected the audience's emotions to the image.

Mark clicked the remote control again and displayed the same photograph, except now the background behind the photograph had disappeared, as shown in Figure 1-5. As the new photograph appeared, Mark said, "They had a wonderful time together. But ultimately...the picture starts to fade and things start to go different. And let me tell you why." People are not used to seeing family photographs where the background suddenly disappears, so this visually set the stage that something unexpected was about to happen to Carol and Bob. The emotions of the audience that Mark had associated with the photograph suddenly were stripped away.

**FIGURE 1-5** The next slide shows the same photograph with the background stripped away to indicate that something unexpected had happened.

Clicking again, Mark displayed a new version of the photograph, except in this one, Bob was missing from the photograph. In his place was a thick black line like the chalk outline from a crime scene, as shown in Figure 1-6. "You see, Bob Ernst is dead today," Mark said. "One of my witnesses that I want to bring in the case I cannot bring you. Bob Ernst cannot come in here today. He is no longer here. He didn't know he was going to need to be here. He didn't leave us anything in video. He didn't leave us anything in writing that would talk about the issues that we need to talk about." This striking photograph visually communicated to the jurors that the worst had happened—that Bob and Carol's happy marriage ended abruptly and unexpectedly when Bob died of a heart attack. The black outline where Bob had been in the photo visually brought home the point that Bob's death suddenly had left a hole in Carol's life, and in her heart.

**FIGURE 1-6** This slide shows Bob missing from the photograph, with only a thick black line to indicate where he once was.

Mark knew that his audience came from a part of Texas that was growing increasingly conservative and that the jurors might not be predisposed to award a big verdict to a plaintiff in a product liability case like this. But with the thick black outline that indicated where Bob had been, Mark also introduced a powerful new outline for his presentation. If the jurors were not going to be friendly toward a product liability case, Mark was now visually reframing his opening statement to a new story line that the conservative jurors would find more engaging—a murder mystery. In this third photograph, the black outline subtly communicated a familiar story setting that the jurors immediately would understand—a crime scene from a television show. This unexpected use of this familiar convention from TV would surprise the jurors and make the idea stick in their minds. This slide would then thematically transition to the next, pivotal, slide in the presentation.

Mark clicked the remote again, and this time a black slide appeared with the phrase *CSI: Angleton* on it, similar to the slide shown in Figure 1-7, as he said, "If we were going to put it into a TV show, this would be 'CSI: Angleton.' ...What you're going to do is...follow the evidence, like any good detective would."

**FIGURE 1-7** Next the words CSI: Angleton appeared on the screen as Mark told jurors that they would be like crime scene investigators, sorting through the evidence to figure out what caused Bob's death.

This simple slide would help Mark deeply engage his audience. If you're a presenter these days, audiences usually expect you to interact with them in some way, at least by posing a question and asking them to raise their hands with their response. But in court, Mark could not interact with the jurors, making his task to engage them that much tougher. The solution to the problem would be for him to promote the jurors to the leading role of this presentation, as CSI detectives.

In an entertaining fictional story, the main character is someone an audience observes from a distance. But in a nonfiction presentation, making the audience the center of the action can dramatically increase the involvement any audience feels. You'll learn how you can always make your audience the main character of your presentation story when you plan your first five slides in Chapter 4.

In keeping with classical storytelling form, Mark's next step would be to present the main characters with a problem that they would have to face.

## The Heart of the Problem

Mark clicked the remote control to advance to the next slide, showing an image of a headquarters building, similar to Figure 1-8, as he said, "The evidence is going to lead you to one place"—the front steps of one of the largest pharmaceutical companies in the world. Mark explained that he would show a great deal of evidence from many sources that all proved that the company's drug was a cause of Bob's heart attack. But then he added, "There are lots of different ways it can be painted," and jurors would have to eventually weigh the evidence against everything else that they would hear.

**FIGURE 1-8** Next Mark showed a photo of the headquarters building of the pharmaceutical company similar to this and told jurors that the evidence in the case would lead to the company's doorstep.

Mark clicked the remote button to show the next slide, a photograph of a gavel and flag, similar to Figure 1-9, as he said, "You're going to hear all of this evidence because...your job to do is to get us to justice...Nobody else has this power. A judge can't do it...Politicians can't do it. Nobody else can do it. This is where you can make a difference in the world." The image of the gavel along with Mark's narration reinforced the problem the jurors faced: they will see the evidence against the company, but now they will have to sort through it and bring the situation to justice. You'll learn how to create dramatic tension in your presentations in Chapter 3, when you plan the two specific slides that present your audience with an unresolved problem that your presentation will help them to solve.

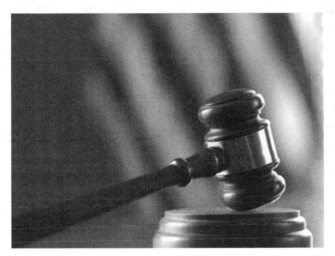

**FIGURE 1-9** With a gavel and flag displayed on screen, Mark explained that the jurors could bring the situation to justice.

Next, as Mark began to click through a sequence of images similar to those shown in Figure 1-10, he said, "How are you going to do it? My suggestion to you is, again, you've got to follow the evidence." This statement and the images Mark displayed clearly defined the story thread that would pull the entire presentation forward and focus every piece of information to come. You'll learn more about story threads and how to choose one for your next presentation in Chapters 3 and 4.

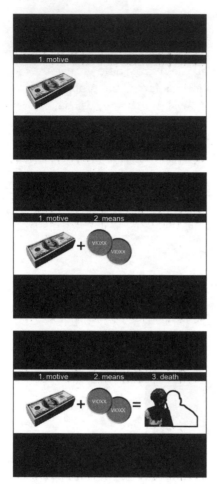

**FIGURE 1-10** All the jurors needed to do was follow the familiar formula of a murder-mystery story structure: motive + means = death.

Here Mark used a *motif*—a recurring visual or verbal theme—in the form of a murder mystery to make the story coherent and memorable. "First of all, I'm going to show you a motive." The word *motive* appeared on the screen (top) along with a picture of a stack of money." I'm going to show you the means," he said, as the word *means* and an image of pills similar to this one appeared on the screen (middle). "I'm going to show you the death," he said, as the word *death* and the familiar outline of Bob appeared next to Carol on the screen (bottom).

With these slides, Mark asked the jurors to follow the simple formula that underlies every murder-mystery story: *motive + means = death*. Even jurors who don't watch TV would know this familiar structure from books, board games, or stories in the news. Earlier, Mark hinted at a murder-mystery motif with the black outline and again with the CSI reference, and now at the most important part of the presentation, he fully established the murder-mystery motif as the structure for the entire presentation to come. You'll learn more about how you find your story thread and integrate verbal and visual motifs into your own presentation starting in Chapter 4.

# Distilling the Essence

When Mark clicked his remote and displayed a slide similar to the one shown in Figure 1-11, he accomplished something dramatically simple yet powerfully effective. This single slide distills the essence of the entire story into a single image—you'll create a similar slide in Chapters 7 and 8. Although the slide appears simple, it is was extremely sophisticated in its effect because it reduced a very complex case into something very easy to understand and follow.

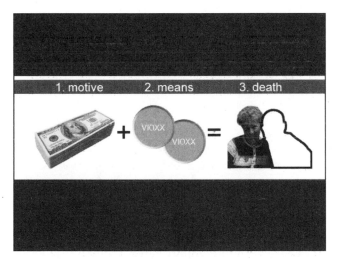

**FIGURE 1-11** This summary slide visually distills the entire case into a single image. The horizontal bars above and below the icons are red to indicate that this slide stands out as the most important in the presentation.

As he was in the planning stage of his presentation, Mark faced a vast amount of information that he could have potentially presented to his audience, as you certainly do in your own presentations. For Mark, it would be tough to explain the complex science behind how the drug worked, how it was developed, and how it was reviewed and studied. It would be confusing to recount the details of every event, every person involved, and the sequence in which the case unfolded. It would be daunting to select the most important evidence to explain the case from more than 3 million documents and countless hours of videotaped depositions from witnesses.

On top of the vast amount of information to choose from, Mark faced the constraints of a limited amount of time to communicate to his audience, as you do in your presentations. In no more than 2½ hours, he had to present the jurors with an overview of the case, educate them about key concepts, and equip them with a framework to understand the six weeks of testimony to come. And he had to do all this while keeping jurors interested and engaged.

Just as you'll do in Chapter 5, Mark solved the problem of potentially overwhelming his audience by distilling his presentation into three roughly equal parts that he would spend equal amounts of time explaining. With his three key points identified, and using the murder-mystery motif as a familiar structure, Mark verbally and visually introduced the enormously complex case to jurors as being "as easy as 1-2-3" to understand, using this summary slide as he spoke.

Next Mark clicked the remote to show the slides containing his key points, similar to the images shown in Figure 1-12, as he introduced each of the three sections of the presentation. Instead of overwhelming jurors with 3 million documents, Mark now guided them along what appeared to be a very simple story as he introduced the three most important parts of the case, which he then explained in more detail as his presentation moved forward. Now the jurors could relax as they listened and watched the story unfold.

In any presentation, the audience can't possibly remember all the information they see and hear, but it helps if you give them graphical cues to the presentation's organization and the slides' relative importance. The look of these three slides was based on the style of the earlier summary slide, carrying forward the story visually to complement Mark's verbal explanation. The simple split-screen layout of the slides, the use of the striking red color, and the consistent graphical style ensured that when these slides appeared, they would stand out as the most important among all of the other slides. You'll learn more about how to apply these techniques when you sketch your own storyboard in Chapter 7.

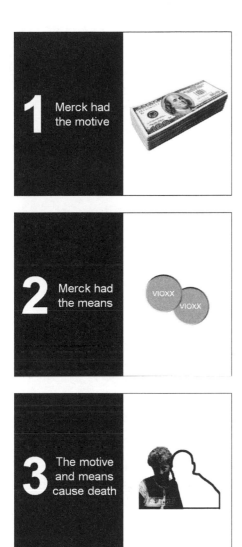

**FIGURE 1-12** As he introduced each of the three sections of the opening statement, Mark displayed slides that carried forward the theme from the earlier summary slide, including the red backgrounds on the left half of each slide.

## Mixing Mediums

With this simple yet clear and engaging introduction to his opening statement, Mark had succeeded in presenting a framework that would be easy for jurors to follow. He continued to integrate the story seamlessly through the remaining slides over the next few hours. Although your own presentations will likely not last as long, the same BBP approach will give you the ability to quickly scale down any presentation from 45 to 15 to 5 minutes.

As Mark continued through the presentation, many of the slides in the presentation looked similar to the ones shown in Figure 1-13. The slides were designed so that the jurors' attention would first go to the most important information at the top of the screen—a headline that summarized the main point at hand, like a newspaper headline. Next the jurors would see a simple graphic that illustrated the specific headline. Last the jurors' attention would now shift from the screen to Mark, who explained the point of the slide in more detail. The range of visuals used on the slides included a wide variety of photographs, medical illustrations, documents, screen captures, timelines, and more.

**FIGURE 1-13** The slides within each section of the presentation used a similar layout style, which helped the jurors quickly understand the information.

Mark clicked through the 153 slides of this presentation at a pace of less than one minute per slide, which allowed his audience to digest the information on the screen before moving forward to the next slide and the next part of the story. This pace kept the jurors visually interested. As shown in Figure 1-13, at the bottom of each slide, a navigation bar displayed the major sections of the presentation to keep the story theme and structure continuously present in the jurors' minds. You'll see how to create a similar navigation bar in Chapter 8.

Conventional PowerPoint slides can overwhelm audiences with too much information on the screen, but Mark's presentation contained only one idea per slide, giving jurors time to digest each point as they listened to Mark's verbal explanation. Instead of reading bullet points from the screen, Mark used his slides as visual cues to prompt him on the next point he would make, allowing him to speak with a natural and spontaneous style that came from the depth of his knowledge and authority on his topic. And instead of looking at the screen to see what was on it, Mark kept his attention focused on the jurors, making eye contact with each person throughout the presentation.

Beyond the PowerPoint slides, Mark also used a range of other media and physical props to engage with the audience over the course of the presentation. At times, he switched the screen to a special document projector, where he displayed physical paper documents and highlighted passages on the pages with a yellow marker as he explained the significance of the evidence. Later he used a large paper flip chart that he calls a "double-wide," where he wrote out key terms and concepts with large markers. Sometimes he switched from the slides to a brief video that illustrated a point. Other times he used physical props such as a plastic model of a heart held up in his hand to teach jurors the science behind heart attacks.

Mark used different types of media to keep things varied and interesting throughout the presentation and to keep the experience from feeling too slick and produced. But after using each type of media, Mark always returned to the PowerPoint presentation on the 10-foot screen because it was a visually unifying tool he could use to tie everything together and move the story forward. The shifting and dissolving images holding the audience's interest on the large screen seamlessly came together with Mark's physical presence, and his voice tied everything together. In the Angleton courtroom, PowerPoint had taken on a new role—it was now a powerful, persuasive backdrop that would have a major impact on the jurors in the eye of the PowerPoint storm in this Angleton courtroom.

# Fade to Gray

After Mark finished his presentation, the judge allowed a break, and the jurors left the courtroom. Now it was the defense team's turn to present its opening statement. They got their PowerPoint presentation ready on their own laptop computer, and they rolled back the podium to where it had been before Mark moved it, in front of the jury box. When the jurors returned, the defense lawyer walked up to the podium, looked down at his printed notes, and began to read his opening statement to the jurors.

In the crucial first few minutes of the presentation, when it is essential to make an audience feel like the presentation is all about them, the lawyer recited the details about the admirable history of the company. Instead of making the presentation human by telling an anecdote about a real person, he cited dry data about the millions of people the company aims to reach with its various drugs. As he read the prepared script in formal and impersonal language, someone else on his team advanced the PowerPoint slides forward on the computer, sometimes missing a cue and leaving a disconnect between what the lawyer said and what the jurors saw. The lawyer occasionally turned back at the screen behind him to point at a complicated chart or a long passage of text.

Rather than display a dynamic and engaging visual experience, the lawyer next showed a slide with a formal photograph of the company's former CEO in a coat and tie as he talked about the CEO and his family, his biography, his public service, and his civic involvement. Missing the chance to connect with the everyday people in the jury with color and character, the defense lawyer continued on with slides that showed formal photographs of other corporate executives, their Ivy League educations, detailed biographies, and long lists of accomplishments. Missing the point that less is more, later the lawyer displayed the familiar bullet points, charts, and long passages of text that the jurors strained to read.

The defense lawyer's relationship with the jurors never warmed up with the chilly and formal tone of the prepared talk. The podium that was now in front of the jurors had erected a wall between the presenter and his audience, the prepared script took away the lawyer's natural voice and spontaneity, and the PowerPoint slides on the screen became a 10-foot distraction from the lawyer who was speaking.

At the end of the defense's presentation, everyone stood as the jurors left the courtroom, and then the court adjourned for the day. If what lawyers believe is true, the presentation the jurors had just experienced would play a significant role in the verdict they would reach at the end of the trial. Whatever the jurors thought that day, the journalists in the room wasted no time in pronouncing their verdict about how they thought the two PowerPoint presentations had gone.

# Stark Choices

The news media cover opening statements of legal trials every day, but it's unusual when the topic of the coverage is the presentation style itself. According to the coverage of this opening statement the next day, something exceptional had happened in the Angleton courtroom. According to *Fortune*'s account, Mark "gave a frighteningly powerful and skillful opening statement," speaking "without notes and in gloriously plain English" and taking on the defendant "with merciless, spellbinding savagery" (Roger Parloff, "Stark Choices at the First Vioxx Trial," *Fortune*, July 15, 2005). The reporter had not noticed that Mark did have a form of notes—his PowerPoint presentation in Presenter view on his laptop below the jury box. The *New York Times* reported that in comparison with Mark's opening, the defense lawyer's presentation was "staid" and that "he read portions of his statement and illustrated his talk mostly using blue-and-yellow PowerPoint pie charts and long excerpts of letters from the Food and Drug Administration" (Alex Berenson, "Contrary Tales of Vioxx Role in Texan's Death," *New York Times*, July 15, 2005).

The difference between the two approaches presented jurors with a choice that day, according to *Fortune:* "The trial offers jurors a stark choice between accepting Lanier's invitation to believe simple, alluring and emotionally cathartic stories" and the defense's "appeals to colorless, heavy-going soporific Reason. Lanier is inviting the jurors to join him on a bracing mission to catch a wrongdoer and bring him to justice." In contrast, the *Fortune* article continued, the defense "is asking the jurors to do something difficult and unpleasant like—well—taking medicine."

Six weeks later, the trial ended, and the jurors entered the jury room to deliberate. After a day and a half of discussion, the jurors made a decision, and the journalists and lawyers filled the courtroom again to hear what they would say. The jurors awarded the plaintiff a stunning $253 million verdict. Amid the storm of international headline news, the pharmaceutical company's market capitalization fell $5 billion (Alex Berenson, "Jury Calls Merck Liable in Death of Man on Vioxx," *New York Times*, August 20, 2005).

After the verdict was announced, the *Wall Street Journal* reported one juror as saying "'Whenever [the defense] was up there, it was like wah, wah, wah,' . . . imitating the sounds Charlie Brown's teacher makes in the television cartoon. 'We didn't know what the heck they were talking about'" (Heather Won Tesoriero, "Merck Loss Jolts Drug Giant, Industry," *Wall Street Journal*, August 22, 2005).

The impact of the PowerPoint presentation in Mark's opening statement proved to last long after the trial. Six months later, Mark met with the Angleton jurors during a focus group to see what they remembered about the trial, and the jurors vividly recalled the specific story and images that Mark presented in his opening statement.

## Winds of Change

Although using PowerPoint helped win the day in Angleton for the plaintiff, that particular story is not yet over. The $253 million verdict would be reduced to $26.1 million according to caps on such verdicts placed by Texas law, and the case is under appeal. Later the pharmaceutical company's market capitalization recovered. But what was unlocked in Angleton that July day was an example of the dramatic results an effective PowerPoint approach can have on a single presentation in a single room with a single audience.

The BBP approach had never been used in a courtroom before the Angleton trial, but since that day, its impact is still reverberating through the legal profession. Today, if a legal team faces a courtroom opponent who is using BBP, they know that they have to somehow respond and raise the bar of their own presentations. Legal teams that have faced opponents using BBP in the courtroom have started to adopt the story themes and graphics that the other side uses. For example, in trials against the pharmaceutical company that followed the Angleton verdict, the defense lawyers began using the "CSI" theme in their presentations. When Mark faced them again, he used techniques to counter what the defense lawyers did, raising the bar even higher.

The same sorts of impacts are being felt in other professions as well, as BBP begins to transform the status quo for presenters everywhere. As you consider applying BBP to your own presentations in this book, it might seem hard to imagine how to apply these types of techniques to your specific profession. But beyond lawyers and law firms, many people in many other professions and organizations are accomplishing significant results with this new approach, including presenters in major corporations, governmental agencies, universities, research firms, and nonprofit organizations. Within these groups, people use BBP in a wide range of functions such as marketing, sales, training, and education. In this book, you'll find examples of presentations from different fields and for different purposes so that you can see how you can apply BBP to your own situation.

Everything Mark and many others have accomplished using the BBP approach is explained in detail in this book. In Chapter 2, you'll learn the underpinnings of BBP along with the key research findings you need to know, and in Chapter 3, you'll see an overview of the three steps of the BBP approach. Then you'll get right to work on planning your first five slides in Chapter 4 and the rest of your slides in Chapter 5. In Chapter 6, you'll set up your storyboard and narration; in Chapter 7, you'll sketch the storyboard; and in Chapter 8, you'll add graphics. You'll see how BBP plays out through a wide range of presentation contexts and purposes in Chapter 9, and Chapter 10 offers advice on delivering BBP presentations. The companion CD included with this book provides a bonus chapter that shows you how to administer a 5-minute test of BBP with your team and provides other tools and resources that you can start using immediately. The companion Web site to this book, at *www.beyondbulletpoints.com*, offers advanced resources to the fast-growing community of people using BBP. By the end of this book, you should be well-equipped with the knowledge and tools you need to start applying BBP to your own presentations.

## The Power of BBP in Your Hands

Mark's presentation in Angleton is only a sample of how you can use BBP to unblock the engaging, compelling stories locked inside of you. When Mark entered the Angleton courtroom that hot July day to present his opening statement, he had the same Power-Point software that you have. He just used it in an innovative way that produced dramatic results and made headline news. Every one of us has the power in our hands to teach an old dog new tricks. Even if you can't fully adopt BBP today, you can at least begin to sow the small seeds of change that will one day lead to a presentation revolution of clarity, effectiveness, and positive cultural change.

CHAPTER 2

# Teaching an Old Dog New Tricks

**IN THIS CHAPTER, YOU WILL:**

- Learn why Beyond Bullet Points (BBP) gets the results it does.

- Review key research principles that every presenter needs to know.

- Compare the research principles with BBP and the conventional approach.

**BEYOND BULLET POINTS** (BBP) is making headlines because it gets dramatically better results than the standard bullet point approach that most people use with Microsoft® Office PowerPoint®. But it's no accident that BBP gets these results, because beneath the simple, clear, and compelling visual stories is a sophisticated foundation that determines everything you say, show, and do during a presentation. This chapter will explain why BBP works so well and why the conventional approach so often falls short of expectations.

## Three Bedrock Tools of PowerPoint

Throughout its 20 years of existence, PowerPoint software has always offered the ability to work on your presentation in three key views: Normal view, Notes Page view, and Slide Sorter view. Although the rest of the PowerPoint features added since then are nice to have, these three views continue to be the bedrock tools you need to manage the images and narration of your presentations.

**See Also** This chapter focuses on the three views you use when you prepare your slides in advance of a PowerPoint presentation. For more information about the two views you can use when you present your slides to an audience—Slide Show view and Presenter view—see Appendix B on the companion CD.

Normally when you create a text slide in PowerPoint with the standard bullet point approach, you first start in Normal view, as shown on the left in Figure 2-1, where you click to add a title to the title area and then click to add text in the content area below. If you have more to say verbally about the slide but can't fit the extra words in the content area, you might be one of a few people to visit Notes Page view, shown in the middle in Figure 2-1, where you can see the slide area at the top and an adjacent text box in the notes area at the bottom that does not appear on screen during a presentation. And after you've created your slides, you might visit Slide Sorter view, shown on the right, to take a look at all of your slides together as small thumbnails.

FIGURE 2-1 The three working views in PowerPoint: Normal, Notes Page, and Slide Sorter.

This sequence of using PowerPoint in Normal, Notes Page, and then Slide Sorter views is the norm today, and it defines the standard for PowerPoint approaches. The secret to unlocking the power of BBP is to flip this sequence and always work in PowerPoint in Slide Sorter view first, then in Notes Page view, and finally in Normal view. As this chapter explains, when you discover this new order for using the same features that have been around for two decades, you will teach an old PowerPoint dog new tricks. And when you apply the new sequence to your own presentations, you'll see how BBP taps into the powerful potential of PowerPoint that has been waiting for you all along.

| NOTE | The Ribbon has been minimized throughout the figures in this book to make the graphics more visible. If you ever need to minimize your Ribbon, click the Customize Quick Access Toolbar button next to the Quick Access Toolbar on the upper left in the PowerPoint window, and then select Minimize The Ribbon. |
| --- | --- |

## Trick 1: Use Slide Sorter View to Manage the Volume

Open a new, blank PowerPoint presentation, and on the View tab, in the Presentation Views group, click Slide Sorter, as shown in Figure 2-2. Although you might be used to looking at Slide Sorter view only occasionally, if ever, the first trick of BBP is to always begin working in PowerPoint in this view. You'll do that starting in Chapter 6 after you finish writing the outline for your presentation. If you're wondering why it's so important to bump up the status of this little-used view to the most important way to look at your presentations, you need to step out of the PowerPoint mindset altogether for a bit and ask some uncommon questions first.

**FIGURE 2-2** Slide Sorter view, displaying all of your slides as small thumbnails.

## In Search of "Research Reality"

When you talk about PowerPoint, you'll usually discuss which size font to use, how to insert a video clip, and whether the background of a PowerPoint template should be blue or black. One thing you never hear is a conversation about any research related to PowerPoint presentations. Despite the widespread use and influence of PowerPoint software in many professions, you would be hard pressed to find research that demonstrates that the underlying theory, impact, or effectiveness of the conventional PowerPoint approach is better than any other approach.

For example, you won't find research indicating that presenting with bullet points on a PowerPoint slide is more effective than presenting without them, or studies showing that using a PowerPoint design template to make every slide background the same produces better learning than not using a design template, or a quantitative justification and rationale for commonly accepted PowerPoint design guidelines such as the 6-by-6 rule, which states that every slide should have six lines of text with six words per line. This lack of comparative studies on PowerPoint approaches has created a void in terms of research-based guidelines on how best to use the software, and this void has been quickly filled with popular myths and cultural habits. In other words, the main reason we approach PowerPoint the way we do is simply because that's the way that we've always done it, and not because any research says it's better than any other way.

Although there is little research specifically comparing PowerPoint approaches, there is a significant body of research that has direct relevance to those who use spoken words and projected images to communicate. Researchers in the fields of cognitive science and educational psychology have been studying for decades the best ways to help people learn new information using narration and images. Their work is a treasure trove of information that is directly relevant and applicable to you when you use PowerPoint to create presentations. The only problem is that currently the research dots are not connected to our PowerPoint bullet points. That is what you'll do now as you apply three key parts of this research to the three views of PowerPoint. As you do that, you'll see how these three "research realities" quickly dispel the myths and break the habits that stand in the way of effective presentations. These three research realities also will show clearly why BBP works so well and why the conventional approach to PowerPoint does not deliver results as effectively.

## THE MULTIMEDIA RESEARCH

This chapter is inspired by the work of Richard E. Mayer, Ph.D., a professor of psychology at the University of California, Santa Barbara. Ranked as the most prolific researcher in the field of educational psychology, Mayer is the author of 18 books and more than 250 articles and chapters and has been researching multimedia learning and problem solving for 15 years. In his books and related articles and papers, Mayer proposes a way to understand the use of multimedia that promotes meaningful learning and lays out a set of principles for designing any multimedia experience based on his own research and that of others. For more information about the research on multimedia learning and its implications for PowerPoint presentations, see:

- Richard E. Mayer, Ed., *The Cambridge Handbook of Multimedia Learning* (Cambridge University Press, 2005).

- Cliff Atkinson, "The Cognitive Load of PowerPoint: Q&A with Richard E. Mayer," *www.beyondbulletpoints.com* (March 2004).

## Research Reality 1: You Have to Respect the Limits of Working Memory

Whether or not you think about it consciously, you probably accept fundamental assumptions about communication that literally shape your thinking in ways large and small. If you commonly talk about communication in terms of a "sender" who transmits a "message" to a "receiver," you might assume that you can "send" information through an unobstructed channel, like a pipeline, and the audience will "get it," fully intact, at the other end of the pipeline, as shown in Figure 2-3.

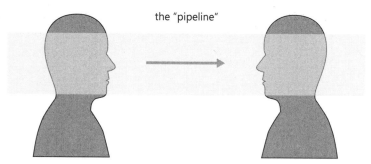
the "pipeline"

**FIGURE 2-3** The pipeline concept assumes that there is an unobstructed channel between you and your audience.

With the pipeline in mind, you assume that you can produce a PowerPoint presentation in whatever way you like, as shown on the left in Figure 2-4. After you send this PowerPoint presentation through the pipeline, you assume that its receivers will "get it" on the other side, as shown on the right. Your work is then done. The only criterion for success is that you "delivered" the PowerPoint presentation through the pipeline. If for some reason the audience didn't get what you delivered, of course, it's not your fault as a presenter—after all, you delivered the PowerPoint presentation, and what they did with it is their problem, not yours.

The pipeline assumption is at work when people make statements like, "We showed them the facts, but they just didn't get it," or, "The presentation went right over their heads." When a verdict in a legal trial goes against one party, it is common for people to say the jury just didn't "get" the evidence, or when a sales presentation does not succeed, the presenter might say the audience just didn't "get" the benefits of the product or service. It is hard to separate the pipeline metaphor from our thinking because it is woven into the words and expressions we use commonly every day.

What you present to your audience          What you assume the audience learns

**FIGURE 2-4** With the pipeline in mind, you assume that your audience will "get" whatever you "deliver" to them.

Although the pipeline metaphor is convenient, in practice it does not deliver what you might assume it does. According to leading educational psychologist Richard E. Mayer, if you give a multimedia presentation to an audience, there are three possible outcomes, as shown in Figure 2-5. The first possible outcome is that your audience experienced *no learning* (upper right). This is the worst-case scenario—in spite of your work in preparing your presentation and your audience's time and effort in showing up and paying attention, no learning happened to make the experience worthwhile.

**FIGURE 2-5** In reality, audiences do not automatically get what you send through the pipeline.

A second possible outcome is that your audience remembered perhaps the bullet points on slides 12 and 33 and the diagram on slide 26—but that's all they remembered. In this scenario, they remember only bits and pieces of the presentation because they experienced *fragmented learning* (middle right). In fragmented learning, the audience members remember at least some things; but from a presenter's perspective, you have no control over what they learned because the fragments could be *any* pieces of information among many, and you don't know which ones.

The third possible outcome is that the audience remembered exactly what the presenter intended—they experienced *meaningful learning* (lower right). Meaningful learning is what any group wants to achieve in their time together—the people in the audience understand what the presenter intended, and they are able to apply the information after the meeting. Audiences routinely report that PowerPoint presentations today are "Forgettable!" and "What's the point?" It's rare to hear an audience and a presenter agree that meaningful learning has occurred. In order to turn the situation around, you literally need to change the shape of the metaphor that guides the way you think about human communication.

During a PowerPoint presentation, the memory of an audience member is the critical human element that determines how well new information is received, processed, and stored in the human mind. Researchers who study the mind generally accept that there are three types of human memory, as shown in Figure 2-6. The first type is *sensory memory*. Sensory memory is the part of the mind where your audience members briefly store the initial impressions of sights and sounds as they look at and listen to the environment around them. Sensory memory is potentially unlimited in capacity, although sights and sounds might persist in sensory memory for less than a second.

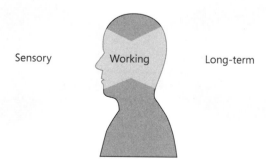

**FIGURE 2-6** The three types of human memory: sensory memory, long-term memory, and working memory.

The second type is *long-term memory*—the part of the mind where your audience members store information over an extended period of time, from as little as 30 seconds to as long as a lifetime. In a presentation context, this is where you would like your audience to store the new information you intend to communicate to them. Beyond just remembering the new information, you also would like them to be able to access and apply the information from long-term memory when needed. Like sensory memory, long-term memory is also potentially unlimited in its capacity.

The third type is *working memory* (sometimes called *short-term memory*)—the part of the mind where your audience members hold their attention. The theories underlying working memory are complex, but essentially, working memory is a temporary holding area for information. As sensory memory briefly holds sights or sounds, working memory then pays attention to some of them and holds them for a matter of seconds while it works to integrate them into long-term memory.

While sensory memory and long-term memory each have unlimited capacity, working memory is severely limited in its capacity to process new information. In an influential paper published in 1956, George A. Miller observed that people could hold a small number of "chunks" that they mentally form in what we now understand as working memory. Although the capacity of chunks was thought to be around seven for most people, depending on the type of information, working memory expert Nelson Cowan recently revisited Miller's classic work and now estimates the capacity of working memory for new information at three or four chunks.

**See Also** For more information about the capacity of working memory, see:

- George A. Miller, "The Magical Number Seven, Plus or Minus Two: Some Limits on Our Capacity for Processing Information," *Psychological Review* **63**, 81–97 (1956).

- Cliff Atkinson, "The Science of Making Your PowerPoint Memorable: Q&A with Nelson Cowan," *www.beyondbulletpoints.com* (June 2004).

Although the limits of working memory have been acknowledged for 50 years, the concept has never been fully absorbed or integrated into our day-to-day practice and understanding of human communication. The pipeline metaphor has such a strong grip on our collective consciousness that we have effectively resisted the adoption of the research that contradicts it. Yet as much as you might want to believe that there is an unobstructed pipeline between sender and receiver, the reality is that the limits of working memory put a major crimp in that metaphor. In order to align your own assumptions about communication with what researchers accept about the way human memory works, you'll need to drop the old pipeline metaphor and pick up a new metaphor—the *eye of the needle*, as shown in Figure 2-7.

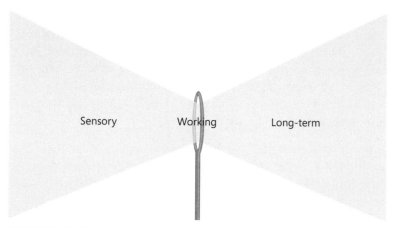

Sensory        Working        Long-term

**FIGURE 2-7** The limited capacity of working memory to process new information creates a narrow passage—much like the eye of a needle—that stands between the information you present sensory memory and the information that is integrated into long-term memory.

Keeping this new metaphor in mind when you create presentations, you know that you have a potentially unlimited amount of new information that you could show some-one's sensory memory (left). You want the new information to be retained in long-term memory (right). But working memory is so constrained in its capacity to process new information that it creates a narrow passage, much like the eye of a needle (center). This extremely small space of the "eye" of working memory constitutes the most formidable challenge you face as a presenter.

This new metaphor visually explains why audiences report either no learning or fragmented learning. If you present working memory with more new information than it can handle, as shown on the left in Figure 2-8, the eye of the needle is easily overloaded and will process and integrate into long-term memory what it can—only bits and pieces out of the entire presentation, as shown on the right. As much as you might want your audience to learn the new information you present, they will never be able to learn it unless you help that information properly pass through the eye of the needle.

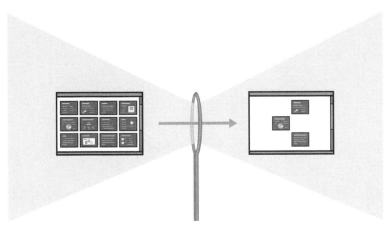

**FIGURE 2-8** When you show more information than working memory can handle, audience members remember only bits and pieces.

The impact of reducing excess load on working memory has been documented by researchers including Mayer, who conducted a study using two multimedia presentations. The first presentation featured interesting but irrelevant graphics, and the second presentation provided the same information, but without the interesting but irrelevant graphics. Mayer measured the impact of the two approaches on audiences in terms of two criteria: *retention*, the ability of the audience to simply recall the information, and *transfer*, the ability to creatively apply the new information. Audiences who experienced the second presentation retained 69 percent more information and were able to apply 105 percent more creative solutions using the information than those who experienced the first presentation. This study offers research-based evidence to support the saying "Less is more"—the less you overload working memory with extraneous information, the more learning improves.

## BBP Respects the Limits of Working Memory

With the eye of the needle metaphor in mind, take a look at how a BBP presentation appears in Slide Sorter view, as shown in Figure 2-9. Studies have found that people learn better when information is broken up into digestible pieces, and here in Slide Sorter view, you can literally see each specific digestible piece—in the form of a single slide that contains only one main idea that is clearly summarized by a headline. This eases your audience through your story and explanation frame by frame, one piece at a time.

A familiar motif relates new information to
existing information in long-term memory.

Information is
presented in
bite-sized segments,
with one idea per slide.

There is clear
guidance to
help the viewer
build a coherent
structure.

Slide layouts and backgrounds call
attention to the most important slides first.

**FIGURE 2-9** Slide Sorter view shows a presentation that is broken up into digestible chunks for easier
handling by working memory.

In the Slide Sorter view of a BBP presentation, your eye immediately goes to the most
important slides because you use layouts and backgrounds to cue your audience to
where they are. This approach draws from the hard work you do when you distill your
complex ideas to the essence and identify your key points, as you'll see in Chapter 5.
These visual cues also indicate the sections of the presentation that explain your key
points, explanation, and backup detail. In Chapters 6, 7, and 8, you'll use consistent
layouts and backgrounds within the individual sections of a presentation to create visual
and verbal continuity, but when you reach a new section of the presentation, the layouts
and backgrounds will change. This orients both presenter and audience to where they
are in the story, and the changing slide layouts and backgrounds offer your audience
visual variety to keep their interest.

You can also see from Slide Sorter view that BBP uses a visual motif through a
presentation. Researchers have found that you can improve the ability of working
memory to process new information by applying familiar organizing structures. This
works because an important quality of working memory is that it is a two-way street.

Although working memory has only limited capacity to handle *new* information as that information arrives, as shown on the left in Figure 2-10, it also has unlimited capacity to pull in *existing* information from long-term memory, as shown on the right.

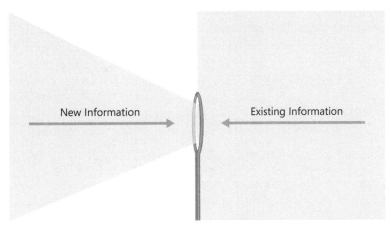

New Information

Existing Information

**FIGURE 2-10** Working memory is limited in its capacity to process new information (left), but it is unlimited in its capacity to process existing information from long-term memory (right).

This plays out in the classic test of working memory, when a researcher presents someone with new information in the form of a series of unrelated numbers, such as *1 2 1 5 1 5 2 3 5 4*. The number of these individual chunks of information that someone can recall is considered the capacity of that person's working memory. However, people can remember more of the same set of numbers when working memory pulls from long-term memory a structure they already know. This organizes the new information into meaningful chunks that hold the same information in a more memorable way, such as 212-555-1234—the familiar structure of a U.S. telephone number. Thus a "chunk" is defined by the *audience* as they apply a meaningful structure from their long-term memory to new information. You help your audience accelerate understanding of new information with BBP by introducing a familiar "chunking" structure to new information you present. For example, in Chapters 4 and 5, you choose a familiar motif that resonates with your audience, and then later in Chapters 7 and 8, you extend the motif visually across the slides.

**See Also**   For more information about using familiar structures to overcome the limited capacity of working memory to process new information, see John Sweller, "Implications of Cognitive Load for Multimedia Learning," in *The Cambridge Handbook of Multimedia Learning*, Richard E. Mayer, Ed., pp. 19–30 (Cambridge University Press, 2005).

# The Old Way Ignores the Limits of Working Memory

For comparison, take a look at a conventional PowerPoint presentation in Slide Sorter view, as shown in Figure 2-11. Audiences might not know about the limited capacity of working memory, but they do know what they're talking about when they say presentations like this are a "Data dump!" and "Overwhelming!" They've been down the road to overload before, and Slide Sorter view shows exactly how the conventional approach takes them there. The new information is clearly not presented in bite-size pieces; instead, it fills every slide, slide after slide, with overwhelming detail.

Information is not presented
in bite-sized segments.

The slides do not
help introduce new
information
with a familiar
structure.

There are no visible
signals to indicate
which slides
are most important.

There is no guidance to help the viewer
build a coherent structure.

**FIGURE 2-11** Slide Sorter view of a conventional PowerPoint presentation reveals no digestible pieces and no cues about the presentation's structure or organization.

What you see here is visual tedium rather than visual organization. As in most PowerPoint presentations, these slides use a design template with a single predesigned background. Using a single background gives all your slides a uniform look, but it also prevents you from using a range of design techniques to visually highlight the most important information on single slides or across slides. It also makes the overall presentation appear visually repetitive, which causes boredom that quickly shuts down attention.

> **MYTH VS. TRUTH**
>
> **Myth:** There's no need for me to use graphical cues to point out the organization of the presentation.
>
> **Truth:** Research shows that people learn better when you use visual cues to highlight a presentation's organization.

**See Also** For more information about the research described in the Myth vs. Truth sidebars in this chapter, see Richard E. Mayer, Ed., *The Cambridge Handbook of Multimedia Learning* (Cambridge University Press, 2005).

Looking at this big-picture view of the presentation, you can't see immediately the location of the most important slides. Instead, every idea has equal visual weight, and there are no cues given by the slide backgrounds about relative importance of ideas. Working memory, with its limited capacity to process new information, has to sort things out on its own and is presented here with the impossible task of holding all this new information while it figures out what's most important to know.

> **MYTH VS. TRUTH**
>
> **Myth:** People will learn more if I show more.
>
> **Truth:** Research shows that people learn better when information is presented in bite-size pieces.

You can also see that there is no structure that ties each of the individual slides together into a coherent whole—this presentation is just a series of bulleted lists, slide after slide. There is no effort to introduce a familiar framework that the audience already has in long-term memory—such as a story structure with a beginning, a middle, and an end— that can guide working memory to make sense of the new information.

## Trick 2: Use Notes Page View to Sync Pictures and Narration

Now that you've sorted out the most important view of PowerPoint for the BBP approach, it's time to move on to another seldom-seen view in PowerPoint. Click the View tab, and in the Presentation Views group, click Notes Page, to switch to Notes Page view, shown in Figure 2-12. As described earlier, Notes Page view lets you see the on-screen slide above, along with an off-screen notes area that the audience does not see. The second trick of BBP is to always work in Notes Page view after Slide Sorter view, which you'll do starting in Chapter 6. There are two specific reasons to do that, as you'll see next.

**FIGURE 2-12** Notes Page view includes the on-screen slide area above and an off-screen notes area below.

## Research Reality 2: You Have to Address the Two Channels

The next research reality, the concept of *dual channels*, states that people receive and process new visual and verbal information in not one, but two separate but related channels. Allan Paivio described his theory of *dual coding* in the 1970s, and during the same decade, Alan Baddeley and Graham Hitch described a similar two-channel structure in working memory. Today, the concept has become a widely accepted standard among researchers. In the dual-channels model, the images someone sees are processed through a *visual channel*, the domain of images including photographs, illustrations, charts, and graphs, as illustrated conceptually in Figure 2-13 (top). What a speaker narrates is processed through the *verbal channel* (bottom), which is the domain of language.

**FIGURE 2-13** The second research reality is that working memory receives information through two channels—a visual channel and a verbal channel.

Although text on a screen is a visual element, working memory quickly verbalizes the words and sends them through the verbal channel. Research over the years has found that the way information is presented to these two channels has a big impact on the effectiveness of working memory.

**See Also** For more information about the dual-channels concept, see:

- Alan D. Baddeley and Graham Hitch, "Working Memory," in *The Psychology of Learning and Motivation: Advances in Research and Theory*, G. H. Bower, Ed., Vol. 8, pp. 47–89 (Academic Press, 1974).

- Allan Paivio, *Mind and Its Evolution* (Lawrence Erlbaum Associates, 2007).

## BBP Addresses the Two Channels

You can see how BBP addresses the reality of dual channels by looking at a typical slide in Notes Page view, as shown in Figure 2-14. A clear headline at the top of the page always summarizes the point—you'll write out these headlines in Chapters 4 and 5. The off-screen text box in the bottom half of the page contains what you will say aloud while the slide is on screen—you'll write out your narration for each slide in Chapter 6. And last you'll add a simple graphic to the slide area that you see in the top half of the page to complement the headline and the verbal narration in Chapter 8.

BBP plans for visuals in the slide area and
spoken words in the off-screen text box below.

Seamlessly integrating visuals and spoken
words ensures that the attention is not split
between screen and presenter.

Using the notes area recognizes the critical
information presented by the speaker's voice.

**FIGURE 2-14** With BBP, you use Notes Page view to manage the visual channel in the on-screen slide area above and the verbal channel in the off-screen text box below.

Writing out the spoken information in the off-screen text box before you add a graphic significantly reduces the amount of information you otherwise would place in the slide area and instead keeps the slide area simple and clear. This helps working memory focus attention on the single point that you explain verbally during this slide. Instead of reading the headline verbatim, you let the audience quickly read and digest it on their own.

BBP uses Notes Page view in this way to tightly integrate screen and narration in order to make the most efficient use of the two channels of working memory. Looking at the visual and verbal areas together in Notes Page view is like looking at a single frame in a filmstrip, which is made up of a sequence of connected visual frames, each with a corresponding chunk of audio. When you design for multimedia such as film, you apply a different set of conventions than the ones used for print because a film model has two coordinated informational tracks—a visual track that contains pictures and an audio track that contains the spoken words.

## AN EFFECTIVE SCREEN AND HANDOUT

By viewing your slides in Notes Page view like the frames in a filmstrip, you align your approach with the dual channels—the information that is presented to the visual channel is in the on-screen slide area, and the information presented to the verbal channel is in the off-screen text box. This approach also creates a well-balanced handout that you can print in Notes Page format, as shown in Figure 2-14. By using PowerPoint this way, you ensure that you produce both an effective live presentation and an effective printed document.

It is no accident that the structure of a filmstrip is conspicuously similar to the dual-channels concept. When you watch a film with sound, your mind coordinates the different information from the soundtrack and the visual frames on screen. Filmmakers have managed to communicate complex ideas to audiences around the world with synchronized images and sound for almost a century, with little if any text on the screen. Likewise, working memory can easily coordinate visual and verbal channels if they are properly coordinated and presented.

With the screen behind the speaker, the audience sees and quickly digests the slide and then pays attention to the speaker and his or her verbal explanation. The entire experience appears seamless to the audience. Using the off-screen notes area in Notes Page view also takes into account the fact that the speaker has a voice during a presentation, which offers a critical source of information that has to be planned and integrated into the experience.

BBP fundamentally changes the media model for PowerPoint from paper to a filmstrip. But the difference between a filmstrip and the BBP approach is *pacing*. In film and television, you commonly view 24 to 60 frames per second. A BBP presentation runs at the speed of conversation—about one frame per minute—allowing time for the audience to digest the new information and then focus next on the presenter. This even and appropriate pacing ensures that your audience experiences only the right things at the right times.

## The Old Way Addresses Only One Channel

If you choose not to address both the visual and verbal channels, you can see from the Notes Page view of a conventional slide shown in Figure 2-15 that you load up the slide area at the top with all of the information you want to communicate both visually and verbally. Because half of the available real estate available for information in Notes Page view is not used—the off-screen text box below is empty—the slide area becomes the single place to hold both spoken words and projected images.

Placing all information on the slide area results in an overwhelming amount of information on the slide.

When the text on screen is the same as what is narrated, it creates redundancy that reduces understanding.

The busy slide splits attention from the speaker's narration.

Not using the notes area ignores a critical source of information, the speaker's voice.

**FIGURE 2-15** The conventional PowerPoint approach does not incorporate the dual-channels concept and instead places both visual and verbal information in the slide area.

When you do not align your PowerPoint approach with the dual-channels concept, you impair learning in a number of ways. For example, ignoring the off-screen text box creates a scarcity of resources in the slide area, which predictably produces overloaded slides. Words will usually take priority over visuals, so you will tend to see slides filled with text. Visuals added to these already crowded slides will usually shrink to the size of postage stamps so that they can be squeezed between the boxes of text. These dynamics produce slides that are overly complex and difficult to understand.

During a presentation, as the audience tries to make sense of the overloaded slide, they are not paying attention to the speaker. When they do shift attention to the speaker, they soon look back at the slide and work hard to try to synchronize the two sources of information. Researchers call this the *split-attention effect*, which creates excess cognitive load and reduces the effectiveness of learning. You can observe similar dynamics when you're watching a film or TV show and the sound is slightly out of sync—it's very noticeable because your working memory has to do the extra work of continually trying to synchronize the mismatched images and narration.

---

**MYTH VS. TRUTH**

**Myth:** I don't need to worry if what I say doesn't match up with my slide.

**Truth:** Research shows that people understand a multimedia presentation better when they do not have to split their attention between, and mentally integrate, multiple sources of information.

---

Another problem with ignoring the off-screen text box in Notes Page view is that you do not recognize and plan for an incredibly rich source of information during PowerPoint presentations—your own narration. The result is that the relationship between your spoken words and projected visuals is not fully addressed. Thinking of the slide area as the piece of paper rather than one frame in a filmstrip ignores this essential element of a live presentation—your verbal narration. You might assume that the information can stand alone, without verbal explanation, but a PowerPoint slide does not exist in a vacuum— you are standing there speaking to your audience while you project the slide. You must effectively plan how your spoken words and projected images relate to each other. And if you write nothing in the off-screen notes area, you will be unable to take advantage of Presenter view, as shown in Figure 2-16 and described in Appendix B on the companion CD, to manage your presentation because nothing will appear in the speaker notes pane on the right to guide you while you cover all the points you want to make.

## AN INEFFECTIVE SCREEN AND HANDOUT

By addressing only one channel in your presentation, as shown earlier in Figure 2-15, you easily create split attention and redundancy in a live presentation. And by not capturing what is said verbally in the off-screen notes area, you also miss the chance to use PowerPoint for an effective handout that you could otherwise create by printing notes pages.

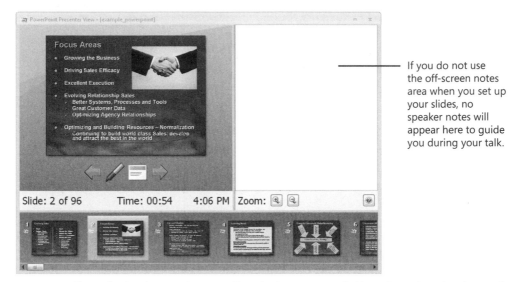

If you do not use the off-screen notes area when you set up your slides, no speaker notes will appear here to guide you during your talk.

**FIGURE 2-16** If you don't write out what you will say in the notes area in Notes Page view, there's no point in using Presenter view, because nothing will appear in the speaker notes pane.

Audiences might not know about dual-channels theory, but they do know how they feel when presenters don't integrate the concept into their PowerPoint approach. When presenters read bulleted text from the screen, audiences complain that the presenter should "E-mail it to me!" or "Just give me the handout!" This frustration has a research basis—writing out the text of your presentation on your slides and then reading it to your audience contradicts the widely accepted theory of dual channels. You might assume that presenting the same information in multiple ways will reinforce your point. But if you present the same information to the two channels, you reduce the capacity of working memory and in turn reduce learning by creating what researchers call the *redundancy effect*.

When someone speaks, you process the verbal information at one speed. When the speaker also displays the text of the speech, you process the information at a different speed—your mind first takes in the text visually and then verbalizes it for processing in the verbal channel. Because the same information is arriving through the same channel at different speeds, working memory has to split attention between the two sources of information as it works hard to reconcile them. This redundancy quickly overloads working memory and impairs learning.

Redundancy also happens when the same information is presented both visually and in text because the same information is entering through two channels and the mind has to exert more effort to reconcile them. This reduces the efficiency of working memory and can lead to the cognitive overload that so frustrates audiences. This inefficient duplication of information is unnecessary, because the verbal channel is perfectly capable of understanding the narration without the display of text to the visual channel.

---

**MYTH VS. TRUTH**

**Myth**: It's OK to read my bullet points from the screen.

**Truth:** Research shows that people understand a multimedia presentation better when the words are presented as verbal narration alone, instead of verbally and as on-screen text.

---

To explore the redundancy effect, Mayer conducted experiments using two multimedia presentations. The first presentation included the same material both narrated and displayed with text on the screen, and the second presentation included the narration with the text on the screen removed. Audiences who experienced the second presentation retained 28 percent more information and were able to apply 79 percent more creative solutions using the information than those who experienced the first presentation. Thus, the dual-channels concept turns one of our core assumptions about PowerPoint upside-down. Contrary to conventional wisdom and common practice, reading bullet points from a screen actually hurts learning rather than helps it. Research shows that when you subtract the redundant text from the screen that you are narrating, you improve learning.

If you choose not to align your PowerPoint approach with dual channels, you diminish the potential effectiveness of your presentations. When you place both verbal and visual material in the slide area, the busy slide splits the audience's attention between screen and presenter, which creates additional load on working memory. And when you present the same information in both visual and verbal form, you create redundancy that overloads working memory. You can easily resolve the situation in BBP by effectively coordinating visual and verbal information in Notes Page view.

# Trick 3: Use Normal View to Guide the Eye and Ear

With two views in PowerPoint, Slide Sorter view and Notes Page view, taken care of, it's time to get back to normal in terms of the way you're used to working in PowerPoint. Click the View tab, and in the Presentation Views group, click Normal to display Normal view, as shown in Figure 2-17. The third trick of BBP is to always work in Normal view last, which you'll do in Chapters 7 and 8. The third research reality will guide you through the reasons why.

**FIGURE 2-17** The most common way to work in PowerPoint is in Normal view.

## Research Reality 3: You Have to Guide Attention

The third research reality confronts the PowerPoint assumption that you can create your slides however you want and your audience will understand them. In the pipeline metaphor, a presentation exists by itself, independent of the people who receive it—a presenter simply pours information into the passive minds of the audience. Yet researchers have long known that the mind is not a passive vessel, but rather it is an active participant in the process of learning. It is the minds of your audience that have to create understanding out of the new information they process in working memory. You play an important role in helping your audience create understanding by designing slides in specific ways that guide the attention of working memory to the most important visual and verbal information, as illustrated in Figure 2-18.

**FIGURE 2-18** The third research reality is that you must guide the attention of working memory.

## BBP Guides Attention

As described earlier, with the BBP approach, each slide has a headline when you start working in PowerPoint. You then write out what you will say verbally in the off-screen text box in Notes Page view and then add a simple graphic in Normal view to produce a slide, as shown in Figure 2-19.

The graphic clearly and simply illustrates the main point of the slide.

The headline summarizes the main point.

After quickly digesting the slide, audience attention turns to the speaker and the narration.

There is no extraneous information to detract attention.

**FIGURE 2-19** A BBP slide, shown here in Normal view, guides the attention of working memory from the headline to the graphic to the person speaking.

The simplicity of this slide belies the sophisticated impact it has as it effectively guides the attention of working memory. It is crystal clear where working memory should focus first—on the headline at the top of the slide. People are used to reading newspaper headlines that summarize the main point of a story in a single sentence, and here the complete sentence headline serves the same function. The audience doesn't have to work hard to figure out the point you want to make—instead, you have cleared the way for them to focus on the idea at hand rather than be distracted by unnecessary cognitive work.

## HEADLINE RESEARCH

Michael Alley, author of *The Craft of Scientific Presentations: Critical Steps to Succeed and Critical Errors to Avoid* (Springer, 2005), conducted a study using two PowerPoint presentations, each with a different headline format. One presentation included only sentence fragments at the top of each slide, and the second presentation included a complete sentence at the top that summarized the most important point of the slide. In tests to measure the knowledge and comprehension of the information in the presentations, the audiences who experienced the slides with the complete sentence headlines saw an average improvement in test scores of 11 percentage points over the audiences who saw the slides with the sentence fragments. When you use the title area of the slide to summarize your point for your audience, you properly guide their attention, and in the process you ease the burden on their working memory to figure out your point.

Research has found that visuals can improve learning, but only if they illustrate the point you are making. In Chapter 7, you will sketch the appropriate graphics for each slide by focusing on the slide headlines, and then in Chapter 8, you will add the specific graphics. Because you choose only graphics that relate to the specific point at hand, the graphics tell a major part of the story as they communicate information through the visual channel in sync with your verbal explanation. This makes effective use of working memory by using both the visual and verbal channels, rather than just the verbal channel alone. It also ensures that working memory is not distracted by graphics that don't relate specifically to the information at hand. Likewise, the slide background contains no extraneous information that would add more cognitive load.

The simple elements of a BBP slide work together to guide the complete presentation experience. First the audience members quickly digest the headline, then they view the simple graphic that illustrates the headline, and then they turn their attention to the verbal explanation of the speaker. The result is an engaging multimedia experience that balances visual and verbal elements and contributes to meaningful understanding.

## The Old Way Does Not Guide Attention

It's not easy to see where the presenter intends to guide attention in the conventional PowerPoint slide shown in Figure 2-20—the slide contains so much information, it's hard to know where to look. Such a busy slide assumes that viewers have the time and the working memory capacity to read through all the material as they might with a written document—all while they are listening to you speak. As described earlier in the discussion of the dual-channels theory, it is easy for too much material on this slide to split the attention of the audience between screen and presenter or to impair learning by using both on-screen text and narration to explain the same information.

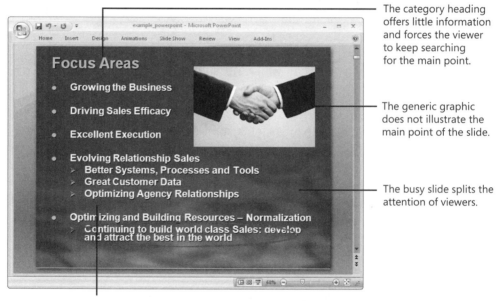

The category heading offers little information and forces the viewer to keep searching for the main point.

The generic graphic does not illustrate the main point of the slide.

The busy slide splits the attention of viewers.

The grocery list approach offers no structure that ties the list items together.

**FIGURE 2-20** The conventional PowerPoint approach does not help working memory to select the most important information.

If you grew up writing essays and reports on paper or as Microsoft Office Word documents, it's a natural transition to think of a PowerPoint slide as a piece of paper where you can start writing out your thoughts. But one of the fundamental assumptions about a piece of paper is that it can stand alone—a presenter normally does not need to be there to explain it. The only problem is that this example PowerPoint slide is accompanied by the narration of a live presenter—yet the slide does not take that fact into account.

Another problem with thinking of the slide area as a piece of paper is that you are much more likely to fill it with text instead of a graphic. Although text on a screen is initially processed through the visual channel, it is quickly verbalized and sent through the verbal channel—thus text-filled slides essentially ignore the capacity of the visual channel to efficiently process information in sync with the verbal channel.

---

**MYTH VS. TRUTH**

**Myth:** Graphics are nice to have, but they're not essential.

**Truth:** Research shows that people learn better from words and pictures than from words alone. This applies when the pictures illustrate what the words say, not when pictures are added for decorative effect.

---

One of the reasons the example slide does not guide attention is that it uses a *category heading*—like those you see in almost all PowerPoint presentations. A category heading like "Focus Areas" can help you quickly brainstorm a list of information, but as you can see here, it does nothing to guide you to a quick understanding of what is the most important information on the slide. Simply categorizing and listing information does not entail the critical thinking it takes to determine the point of the lists in the first place. Category headings don't say anything specific, and to uncover the mystery of what you are trying to communicate when you use them, your audience members need to invest extra capacity of working memory they don't have to connect all the dots of the bullet points below the headings. And these headings put an extra burden on you and your audience as you both struggle to see the focus of your ideas through the sequence of slides in your presentation. As your audience views these headings and their corresponding stacks of bulleted lists, slide after slide, it's no wonder that they find the presentation unfocused, hard to understand, and overwhelmed with unnecessary details.

The background of the example slide offers no visual guidance related to the topic, and although the slide includes a photograph of a handshake, it does not illustrate the specific point of the slide and was likely added to spice it up. This runs counter to the research that shows that the less you overload working memory with extraneous information, the more people learn.

---

**MYTH VS. TRUTH**

**Myth:** People learn more when I wow them with special effects and spice up my presentations with razzle-dazzle.

**Truth:** Research shows that people learn better when extraneous information is removed from a presentation.

Audiences might not know about the research that indicates that you need to guide their attention, but they do know what they are talking about when they frequently say conventional presentations are "incoherent lists" with "no direction" and "a jumble." Instead of guiding working memory through the experience, this example slide creates unnecessary work by not quickly getting to the clear point, by not tapping into the visual channel, and by creating split attention and redundancy with the narration of a live presenter.

## THE MISALIGNED TEMPLATE

Many organizations create a corporate PowerPoint template in an effort to ensure that every presentation created in the organization has a similar graphical style. Although these templates can ensure a similar look across presentations, if they ignore the three research realities described in this chapter, they also diminish the effectiveness of presentations of all the presenters who use them.

# A Well-Trained Tool

In the light of these three research realities, you can see the stark contrast between BBP and the conventional approach to PowerPoint and why BBP gets dramatically better results. Now you can personally connect the dots between this research and the three views of PowerPoint by adopting a new metaphor, the eye of the needle, and by using the BBP approach to guide you through the challenges of creating powerful and effective presentations.

Forget the old tricks of PowerPoint, because as you can see in this chapter, when you ignore the research realities, you use an approach that is broken, ineffective, and frustrating for audiences. Instead you can use an approach that fixes the problems, is effective, and produces experiences that audiences find engaging and meaningful. That's because you have now taught an old PowerPoint dog three new tricks, and with these new ideas in mind, you are ready to unlock the power of BBP in your own presentations as you turn now to Chapter 3.

CHAPTER 3

# Getting Started with BBP

**MAKING A LIVE** presentation with Microsoft® Office PowerPoint® 2007 is complex and difficult from a couple of perspectives. From a presenter's point of view, you have many things you want to say and show during a presentation, including your purpose, your key points, and the many thoughts, ideas, anecdotes, arguments, data, and evidence that back up your key points. You would like your audience to integrate the new information into clear understanding in long-term memory, as shown in Figure 3-1.

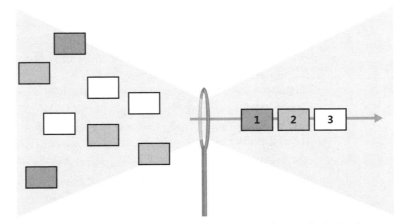

**FIGURE 3-1** The formidable challenge every presenter faces—the limited capacity of working memory.

But as you saw in Chapter 2, you also know what is happening from the audience's point of view in terms of memory. *Sensory memory* can see and hear a potentially unlimited amount of verbal and visual information, but only for a fleeting second. *Long-term memory* can hold a potentially unlimited amount of information from 30 seconds to up to a lifetime. Yet the capacity of *working memory* to handle new information, the eye of the needle, is relatively limited for the few seconds it pays attention to what you are showing and saying.

That means that effectively communicating a message is not as easy as creating a PowerPoint presentation and assuming that you can deliver it through an unobstructed pipeline to the passive minds of your audience. Instead, you have to set PowerPoint myths aside and engage the three research realities you learned about in Chapter 2—finding the right amount of new information to engage the limited capacity of working memory without overloading it, engaging both the visual and the verbal channels, and guiding the working memory of your audience to help them integrate new information into their long-term memory. Some of the Beyond Bullet Points (BBP) techniques you will use to accomplish this are new, some you already know, and some are old techniques used in new ways. If you're new to PowerPoint, you won't have to unlearn old habits; instead, you'll find here a better way to use PowerPoint from the start.

## What Does the Road Ahead Look Like?

This book guides you step by step as you see how BBP is applied in depth to one specific example presentation, using tools and techniques that you can apply to any presentation. People give such a wide range of types of presentations that it's difficult to choose a single type to demonstrate how to apply the approach. The example presentation used in Chapters 4 through 8 features a topic most people can relate to—finance—and shows how BBP handles a challenging topic that would normally use only bullet points along with charts and graphs. The example in this book is intended to be delivered as a 45-minute presentation, so you can get a sense of what it takes to produce a presentation that long. This example topic is very different from the jury presentation in Chapter 1 yet still produces clear communication using the same underlying approach. You can adapt the same BBP process to a wide range of presentation topics, contexts, and purposes—Chapter 9 gives you a tour of more examples that you can review for inspiration.

## WHAT TOOLS DO I NEED FOR BBP?

This book and the companion CD include what you need to get started with BBP. Of course, you'll also need a computer with Microsoft Office Word 2007 and PowerPoint 2007 installed. As you begin or continue to work with BBP, the companion Web site to this book at *www.beyondbulletpoints.com* offers additional resources and a community to help you create BBP presentations smarter, faster, and easier from start to finish. If you have the capability, using a Tablet PC to create and give your BBP presentations will accelerate the process of working with your storyboard and will improve your live presentations by giving you the ability to interact with the audience in ways that are not possible otherwise. Many computer manufacturers offer Tablet PCs—to see what's available, do a Web search for "Tablet PC reviews."

You'll find that BBP is both simple and hard. It's simple because at many levels, it's doing the obvious—like telling a story, getting to the point, or being more visual. And the basic work you do is to fill in the blanks of a Word document, create a PowerPoint file from the document, and then add graphics to the slides. But at many levels, BBP is hard too. BBP is not a quick fix or a patch that you can put over your current approach to PowerPoint. Learning BBP will take you through a sometimes challenging process of letting go of long-standing assumptions, habits, and practices. Especially if you have been using PowerPoint for years, BBP represents a fundamental shift in thinking and action. You won't learn BBP in five minutes or an hour, but you will learn it over the course of a day, two days, a week, or a month as you read this book at your own pace and apply the process to your own presentations. Although there is a steep learning curve at the beginning, be assured that the process will get faster. Over time, with knowledge and practice of the techniques and tools in this book, you'll be producing BBP presentations quickly and building an ever-growing library of resources that you can reuse later.

If you work for yourself or by yourself, you have no choice but to apply BBP on your own, and you'll do just fine. But you'll get the most out of BBP if you unlock the benefits it produces for teams. BBP offers organizations a process where they might not have had one before and often aligns PowerPoint with the group's communications strategy for the first time. If possible, the most-senior people should be in involved in the BBP process along with others such as marketers, graphic designers, and even some of your customers who would be willing to join you. When BBP brings together these separate groups, the efficient process of producing presentations increases the speed of decision making, reduces revisions, and improves the quality and impact of PowerPoint communications for both presenters and audiences. BBP will also reveal that people on your team have unexpected talents that will surprise you—perhaps computer engineers will turn out to be good at graphic design, graphic designers will be good at wordsmithing a logical argument, and statisticians will be good at facilitating the social process of BBP.

# Sewing Up Understanding with BBP

When you face the limited capacity of the working memory of your audience to process new information, a core challenge is not creating the visuals and narration, but rather determining the underlying structure that will shape those elements in the first place. A structure focuses your ideas and helps you figure out what you want to say and how you want to say it. That's where an incredibly powerful structural tool you will use comes into play—the BBP Story Template.

## The Heart and Brain of BBP: The Story Template

With the lessons of the dual-channels theory from Chapter 2 in mind, filmmaking is an appropriate model for designing multimedia presentations because it plans and manages both visual and verbal information simultaneously. Filmmakers know that the best way to start planning a film is with the written word, in the form of a script. A script is much shorter and less detailed than a novel because it assumes that the visuals and dialog will play a major role in telling the story. The best scripts distill stories to their bare essence and strip away anything that does not contribute to a story's singular focus.

When a writer completes a script, the document then becomes a powerful organizing tool that literally puts everyone on the same page. The script is the starting point for planning and producing visuals and dialog, and it serves as a way for everyone involved in the project to be clear on what everyone else is saying and doing. If you were a filmmaker and you started filming before you had a script—similar to working on a PowerPoint presentation without a written structure—you would probably waste time and resources while you changed your focus and figured out the story along the way.

Although putting your thoughts in writing adds a new step to your usual PowerPoint process, doing so will save you time and effort later. When you begin writing your PowerPoint script next in Chapter 4, you won't have to start with an empty page, because you'll use the story template shown in Figure 3-2 to guide you every step of the way.

Title and byline

**Act I:** Set up the story from the audience's viewpoint (*"A to B, what's in it for me?"*)

**Setting** *(Where am I?)*

**Role** *(Who am I here?)*

| **Point A** (*What challenge do I face?*) | **Call to Action** (*How do I get from A→B?*) | **Point B** (*Where do I want to be?*) |
| --- | --- | --- |
| | | |

**Act II:** Develop the action (*"1-2-3, show me only what I need to see"*)

| **Key Point** (*5 minutes*): | **Explanation** (*15 minutes*): | **Detail** (*45 minutes*): |
| --- | --- | --- |
| 1 | | |
| 2 | | |
| 3 | | |

**Act III:** Set up the resolution *(To be completed in the storyboard phase)*

**FIGURE 3-2** The BBP Story Template, which you will complete in Word.

The story template serves as a central organizing tool for the entire presentation. It is a visual interface for the structure of your presentation, helping you see the big picture on a single page or two before you commit to adding a visual and verbal track to individual slides. The story template has roots in many sources, including classical philosophy, contemporary media techniques, and the research described in Chapter 2. It draws from these inspirations and more and interprets them all through the lens of a process you can use to produce your next presentation.

## The Built-In Story Structure

The Greek philosopher Aristotle recorded the classical elements of storytelling 2,400 years ago, including the concept that a story has a beginning, a middle, and an end. When you adapt this timeless idea to your PowerPoint presentations, you will ground your communications in a powerful technique that works.

The story template includes three sections, or *acts*, that form a classical story structure and correspond to the beginning, middle, and end of your presentation. Each act in the template is delineated by a horizontal black bar extending across the page, as shown in Figure 3-3. Act I begins your story by setting up all of the key story elements, including the setting, the main character, a conflict, and the desired outcome. Act II drives the story forward by picking up on the conflict in Act I and developing it through the actions and reactions of the main character in response to changing conditions. Act III ends the story by framing a climax and a decision that the main character must face to resolve the situation, revealing something about his or her character. This time-tested structure keeps your audience interested in your presentation and eager to find out what happens next.

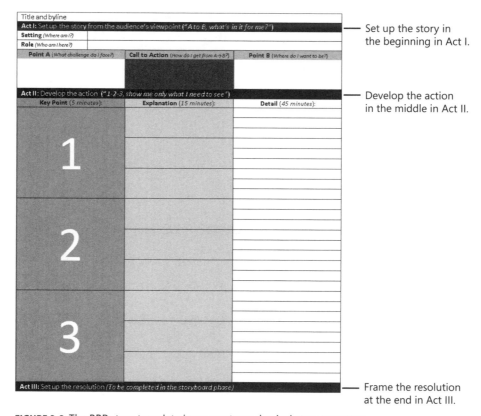

Set up the story in the beginning in Act I.

Develop the action in the middle in Act II.

Frame the resolution at the end in Act III.

**FIGURE 3-3** The BBP story template incorporates a classical story structure.

This three-part story structure follows natural patterns that underlie the way we think and understand. No one needs special training or technology to understand a classical story structure because it's the way humans have been communicating with one another throughout history. Stories frame the context for communication and focus attention by making information specific and relevant to an audience. A story structure literally ties together scattered pieces of information. A story also can help you to focus your ideas, clarify your words and images, and produce an engaging experience for both you and your audiences. By reaching into the past and incorporating these fundamental ideas in your current PowerPoint story, you'll be building on a solid foundation that ensures that your presentation is focused, clear, and engaging.

There is also a research basis for using a story structure. As mentioned in Chapter 2, the long-term memory of your audience already contains existing structures that can help working memory organize and integrate new information. One of the most basic structures is the three-act structure that forms the foundation for countless stories, novels, theatrical productions, films, and television shows. When you tap into this powerful three-part organizing structure that already exists in your audience's long-term memory and apply it to the structure of the new information you present, as shown in Figure 3-4, you are well on your way to creating a clear pathway through the limited capacity of working memory.

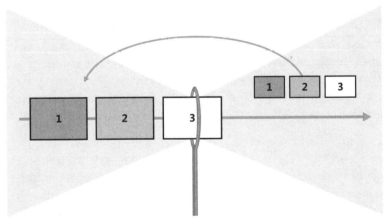

**FIGURE 3-4** Introducing the familiar three-act structure to new information as you present it to working memory.

The research principles described in Chapter 2 have been around as long as 50 years, and the idea of a story structure has been around even longer—for thousands of years. These are proven ideas and techniques that work—the real challenge is how to make the concepts practical as you work on your next PowerPoint presentation. To help get your job done quickly and efficiently, the fundamentals of classical story structure and the screenwriting process have already been adapted to your PowerPoint needs and incorporated into the story template.

In addition to a classical story structure, your story template also incorporates persuasive techniques that are useful for many types of presentations in different contexts. These techniques include using Aristotle's classical concept that to persuade, you must appeal to emotion, reason, and personal credibility. Even if your intent is to simply *inform* an audience about something, you still have to *persuade* them to pay attention. Why should they listen? What's in it for them? Act I of your story template will make sure that you persuade your audience to focus on your message, and Act II will make sure that you provide the logical reasoning they need to make a decision. You will infuse the entire presentation with personal credibility in terms of verbal clarity and conciseness and add visual credibility by matching your graphics and aesthetics with your audience.

## Theory Becomes Practical

The innovation of the story template is that it brings together theory and a process into a practical tool you open up and use to structure and start every presentation. Everything you do here in the story template shapes the visuals and narration to come and sets up your ideas in a way that preconfigures and aligns information to best prepare it for its passage through the working memory of your audience. The story template ensures that every presentation accomplishes what you intend—understanding your audience members, tailoring your material to them, getting to the point, and establishing a priority and sequence for your ideas.

You don't have to be an expert storyteller or an expert in cognitive theory; the template makes structuring your story as easy as filling in the blanks. In the cells of the story template, you'll write out a complete sentence that describes what is happening at each point in your story, similar to writing a newspaper headline. As you fill in the blanks, you will be writing the actual story that you will present. When you've finished, you'll have a completed one-page or two-page script. This process ensures that you stay focused on your ideas and include all the elements that make up a good story.

When you write your PowerPoint script using the story template, you focus on your ideas first rather than your graphics. After you complete the template in Word 2007, you'll import the headlines into PowerPoint 2007, where each complete sentence you wrote will become the headline of a slide, as shown in Figure 3-5. This ensures that before you start working in PowerPoint 2007, you already know the key point you intend to make on each slide. Next you'll take care of narration and sketch a graphic that you'll soon replace with a finalized graphic.

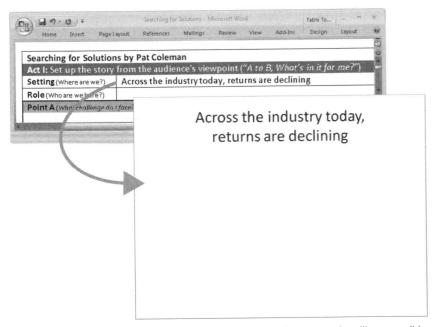

**FIGURE 3-5** Each headline you write in the story template becomes a headline on a slide.

This pivotal technique of turning your story template into a set of PowerPoint slides will help you to transform your written words into the foundation of a visual story. This will make your job of finding visuals easier by establishing exactly what you need to illustrate on every slide, and it will help your audience to understand your new information much faster by indicating clearly in the title area the meaning of every slide.

You'll begin applying BBP step by step in Chapter 4; the following is a visual tour of how the three steps of BBP will unfold as you apply BBP to the specific presentation example in this book. Here you can see how each slide finds its context in the bigger presentation picture by following the three steps of BBP that help you, and your audience, sew up understanding.

# Step 1: Choose a Story Thread and a Pattern to Follow

You need to quickly make an emotional connection with an audience in order to motivate them, and you can see the specific words that do that in Act I, where you write out the classical elements of a strong story beginning. The first five headlines you write in Act I of the story template will connect emotionally with an audience, define a problem they face, and explain how they can solve it. This forms the story thread that will carry attention through the entire presentation. You will reinforce the strength of the thread to carry new information through the working memory of your audience by applying a familiar pattern in the form of a verbal and visual *motif*, or recurring theme. After you complete Act I and the rest of the story template, you will import these five headlines into your PowerPoint presentation, where each statement becomes the headline of a PowerPoint slide, as shown in Figure 3-6.

**FIGURE 3-6** The five sentences you write in the story template become the headlines of your first five slides.

When you view the first five slides in Slide Sorter view, you can see by reading the headlines of the slides the story thread that will carry your specific sequence of ideas through the eye of the needle of working memory of your audience, as shown in Figure 3-7; this sequence will also provide the framework for your visuals and narration.

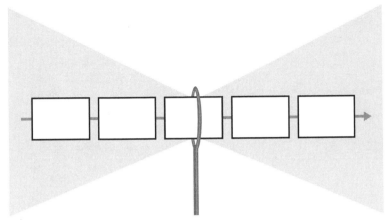

**FIGURE 3-7** Act I defines what you will show to working memory in the first five slides.

## Step 2: Pull Through What's Most Important First

You set in motion a number of powerful processes in Act I of the story template that continue to play out as you create the rest of the slides in your presentation. Just as in Act I, you will break up your ideas in Act II into digestible pieces by writing out complete sentence headlines in the story template. Later each sentence will become the headline of a slide, as shown in Figure 3-8.

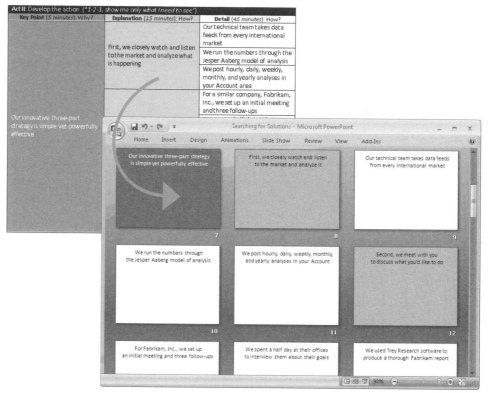

**FIGURE 3-8** The headlines you write in Act II of the story template become the headlines of the rest of your Act II slides.

The challenge of any presentation is not to show *all* the information you have but instead to select the *appropriate* information to present. The story template guides you through the important process of selecting only the ideas your audience needs to know and breaking them into digestible chunks that are easier for your audience to understand. A logic-tree structure is built into Act II of the story template, as shown in Figure 3-9; this structure helps you put the most important information at the top level of attention, to increase memorability and application. A presentation should have a few key points, and you literally can see them in Act II, where you clarify and identify these top-level points, create a logical and clear structure, and perhaps most important, leave out nonessential information.

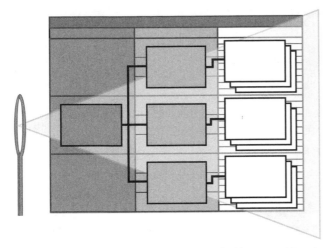

**FIGURE 3-9** A built-in logic-tree structure prioritizes your ideas from most important to least.

Completing Act II of the story template can be the hardest thing you do in BBP if you're new to this way of thinking. But the investment in learning will sharpen your critical thinking skills and ensure that the new information in your presentation appears in the order and sequence needed to prevent overloading the working memory of your audience, as shown in Figure 3-10.

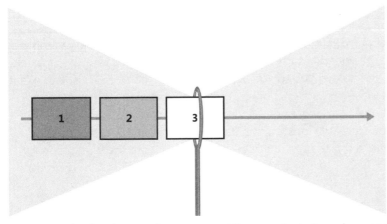

**FIGURE 3-10** Act II makes sure that you present the correct priority and sequence of slides to working memory.

# Step 3: Guide the Visual and Verbal Strands with Your Storyboard

With a completed script in hand, a filmmaker usually turns to a storyboard artist to sketch selected scenes from the story to show how things will look on screen. Story-boards help teams collaborate effectively—the sketches help everyone see how the story will look so that they can plan various aspects of production.

Your BBP storyboard will solve many of the problems found in the conventional Pow-erPoint approach because you start designing visuals and narration with a strong and coherent foundation in the form of a story structure that shapes the entire presentation. This story thread ties everything in the storyboard together and keeps one idea flowing to the next. No idea—or slide—is without specific meaning, context, and sequence.

Even before graphics and narration have been added to this presentation, you have already accomplished a significant task while completing the story template. You've broken up complicated ideas into digestible chunks to aid their passage through work-ing memory. You will be able to work with your story in Slide Sorter view from now on to review your story structure and sequence, check your pacing and flow, and use visuals to tie together the various parts of your story. This planning ensures that you continually build on and improve your strong story foundation with a single unified set of visuals and words.

Next you will quickly apply layouts with slide backgrounds that indicate the three hierarchical levels of Act II slides, as shown in Figure 3-11, to set up preliminary visual cues that designate which slides are more important than others and how those slides fit into a sequence. After you do this, you will be able to easily see the three most important slides in your presentation—the dark gray ones. You'll also be able to see your second-most important slides—the light gray ones—and your third-most important slides—the white ones—so that you can easily locate and hide them if you need to quickly scale down the presentation to a shorter amount of time. These slides are the foundation for the fully designed layouts and backgrounds you use to cue working memory when you add graphics in Chapter 8.

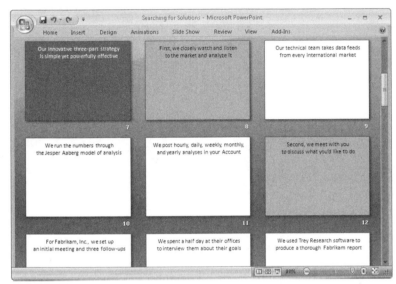

**FIGURE 3-11** Next you'll cue working memory by applying layouts with preliminary slide backgrounds to the three hierarchical levels of Act II slides.

Next you will plan the narrated soundtrack of the presentation by writing out the verbal explanation for each headline in the off-screen text box in Notes Page view, as shown in Figure 3-12. In line with the dual-channels theory described in Chapter 2, this helps you seamlessly integrate each visual with its verbal explanation. By capturing in the notes area a record of the rich verbal explanation that will accompany the slide, you then will choose the simplest possible visual to illustrate the headline of each slide.

**FIGURE 3-12** First you write out what you will say for each headline in the off-screen notes area (bottom). After you have recorded the information that you will convey with your voice, you will next add a simple graphic to the on-screen slide area (top).

## Sketching the First Five Slides

With your clear and concise story line in place in your slide headlines and with your narration written out in the off-screen notes area, your next step will be to tap into your team's visual thinking skills by brainstorming an illustration for each headline of each of the Act I slides of your storyboard. You'll do that by sketching a visual idea on each of the five slides, which you'll learn about in Chapter 7, either using a Tablet PC, as shown on the slides in Figure 3-13, or using printouts of the slides.

When you do this, your focus is on making full use of the powerful visual channel of your audience members by sketching out a crisp and compelling visual story that comple-ments your clear and concise headlines. Just as your headlines tell a story with only words, your sketches now should complement, enhance, and intensify that story on individual slides, as well as across slides. Here you'll also plan for both on-screen and off-screen media such as physical props, demonstrations, video, dialog, or other types of media or interactive techniques.

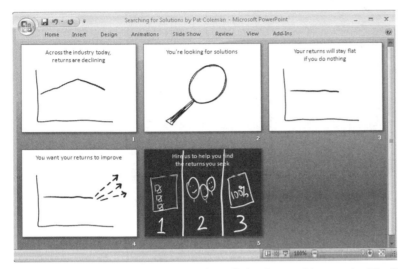

**FIGURE 3-13** Once you have a storyboard, you'll sketch a graphic on each of the five slides.

## Sketching the Rest of the Slides

As with Act I, completing the story template for Act II creates a solid foundation that will help you choose exactly what you will show and say as you present the working memory of your audience with new information. With this infrastructure in place, you'll have endless creative options to make the crisp and clear underlying story even more powerful. Here on the Act II slides, as shown in Figure 3-14, you will visually carry through the motif you establish in Act I to help working memory better select and organize the large amount of new information.

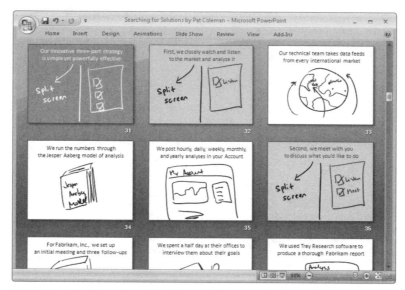

**FIGURE 3-14** You'll continue sketching graphics on each of the rest of the slides.

## Applying Custom Layouts

After your team has agreed and signed off on the sketches, the last step is to find and add a specific photograph, chart, or other graphic to each of the slides. But before you do that, you will apply custom layouts to each of the different sections of your storyboard, according to the way you sketched the layout of each slide. As shown in Figure 3-15, this creates a visual foundation for the slides based on the hierarchy from the story template.

By applying layouts and backgrounds, you use graphical indicators that cue working memory to the relative importance of each slide, as shown in Figure 3-16. In this example, the striking black-and-white, split-screen layout indicates the most important slides. The dark gray slides are the second-most important, and the white slides are the third-most important.

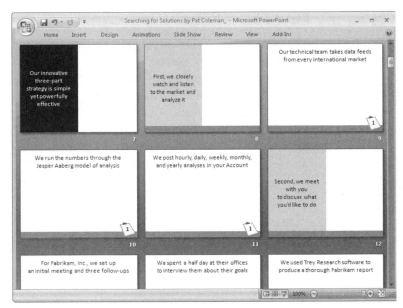

**FIGURE 3-15** Storyboard with custom layouts applied.

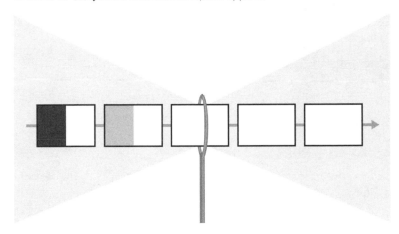

**FIGURE 3-16** The slide layouts and backgrounds cue working memory to each slide's relative importance within the big picture.

## Adding Graphics to the First Five Slides

The last step is to find and add graphics to each of the slides using your sketches as a guide. Here is where you savor the fruits of the labor of writing Act I in the story template, because you know you've got the specific PowerPoint slides that will ensure that you start strong in your presentation, as shown in Figure 3-17. The visual and verbal clarity you achieve is possible through using the story template, which has established the foundation for everything you have done.

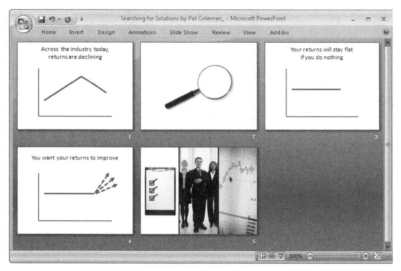

**FIGURE 3-17** Adding graphics to the first five slides of Act I.

## Adding Graphics to the Rest of the Slides

After you add graphics to the Act I slides, you continue by adding graphics to the rest of your slides, as shown in Figure 3-18. Here you might use photographs, screen captures, logos, charts, and other illustrations.

**FIGURE 3-18** Adding graphics to the rest of the slides.

## Stepping into the Screen

Using the approach described in this book, you'll be well-equipped to produce a media experience that will get you the results you want anytime you give a presentation. Focusing and distilling your ideas using a story template and clarifying them using a storyboard blends your message with your media and significantly expands your ability to enhance your presentation with sophisticated media tools and techniques. The large screen directly behind you, as shown in Figure 3-19, completely integrates your voice and body into a media experience greater than the sum of its parts. This approach brings together a range of media techniques—including those from stage, screen, theater, and television—and blends them together with your body and your clear message into a seamless presentation experience.

**FIGURE 3-19** BBP immerses the audience in the experience and ensures that the attention of the audience is not split between screen and speaker.

When you project your slides on a large screen, they work as visual triggers that increase your confidence as a speaker. You're no longer tied to the uncomfortable task of reading text off the screen and unintentionally ignoring your audience. Instead the clear headline and graphic quickly prompt you to use your natural voice and authority as you explain them. While the slide is displayed, you are free to look at your audience instead of at the slide. And even if you had a fear of public speaking in the past, you'll breathe much easier with your new PowerPoint approach. These powerful tools increase your confidence and improve the quality of everything you communicate with your spoken words and projected images. Because you're more relaxed as a speaker, you'll become more confident in improvising during your live presentation.

## Presenting in Multiple Views

Making use of Notes Page view to write out your narration in advance increases your ability to present confidently during a live PowerPoint presentation. While your audience sees the simple slide on the screen shown on the upper left in Figure 3-20, your Presenter view in PowerPoint on your own computer displays a speaker notes pane on the right that shows what you wrote in the off-screen text box in Notes Page view. You can easily zoom in on the notes to enlarge the size of the font so that the text is easy to see.

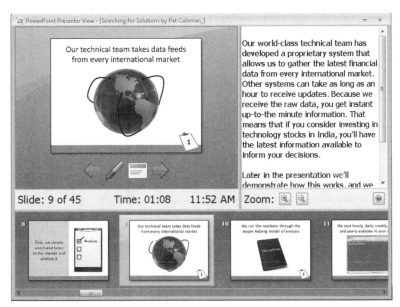

**FIGURE 3-20** Presenter view allows you to see the clear and focused on-screen slide that the audience sees, alongside the text you wrote in the off-screen notes area in Notes Page view.

BBP transforms the social space and opens a wide range of new possibilities for treating your PowerPoint screen as a canvas to promote dialog and collaboration. The clear story structure and innovative techniques engage your audience, but there are many more things you can do to help them feel more involved, such as using other media and physical props. When you sketch your storyboard in Chapter 7, you choose the specific tools and techniques you will use during each slide to highlight and reinforce your most important ideas.

## Presenting with a Tablet PC

With BBP, you can make maximum use of a Tablet PC by writing directly on the screen to increase engagement and dialog, as shown in Figure 3-21. Chapters 7, 8, and 9 will show you a range of ways to sketch and use graphics to prompt interaction using a Tablet PC.

**FIGURE 3-21** Presenting a BBP slide using a Tablet PC.

## Presenting Online

Your visually engaging BBP slides are a great fit with online meeting tools such as Microsoft Office Live Meeting, as shown in Figure 3-22. Because the slides are designed to be visually simple, they increase the need for people to pay attention to your voice on the other end of the telephone or computer speakers.

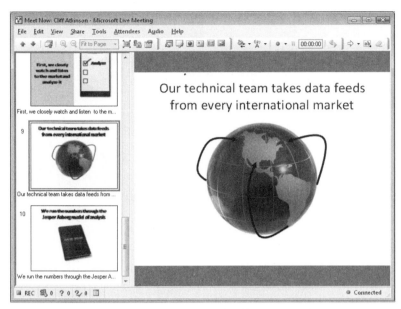

**FIGURE 3-22** Presenting online using Microsoft Office Live Meeting.

# Documenting the Experience

BBP helps you use PowerPoint in a way that gives you more than just an effective in-person presentation. As described in Chapter 2, using the conventional approach can torpedo interpersonal dynamics and produce PowerPoint files that neither work well for in-person presentations nor work well as stand-alone documents. Instead, aligning with the dual-channels theory allows you to use PowerPoint in a way that produces both an effective presentation and an effective printed handout, as shown in Figure 3-23. Looking at Notes Page view on the left, the on-screen slide area contains a headline and a simple graphic, while the off-screen notes area captures what is spoken aloud by the presenter. Keeping the narration off the screen creates effective slides (upper right), along with effective handouts (lower right).

When you distribute the PowerPoint file to people who were not present for the live presentation of visuals and narration, you send the notes pages, not the slides. You can print out the notes pages to create a physical copy or create a PDF version that you can distribute electronically.

Using Notes Page view taps into the unique value PowerPoint offers you as a communications tool, because no other tool can produce a single file that works effectively like this on a screen, on a piece of paper, and even online.

**FIGURE 3-23** Notes Page view, showing a well-designed slide and a well-designed handout with the complete verbal explanation of the slide.

## The Relative Importance of the Three Steps

You'll cover the three steps of BBP through the chapters of the book as follows:

- **Step 1: Choose a story thread and a pattern to follow.** Chapter 4 walks you through planning the first five slides of the presentation by completing Act I of the story template.

- **Step 2: Pull through what's most important first.** Chapter 5 walks you through planning the priority and sequence of the rest of the slides in the presentation.

- **Step 3: Guide the visual and verbal strands with your storyboard.** Chapters 6, 7, 8, and 10 walk you through setting up your storyboard and narration, sketching your storyboard, adding graphics to the storyboard, and then delivering the presentation.

Although step 3 takes more time and more chapters than steps 1 and 2, the three steps are relatively equal in importance because of the role each one plays in guiding the working memory of your audience. Step 1 is critical because here you make the fundamental decisions about how to focus the presentation based on how well you know the audience and what they will hear and see. If you don't get these first five slides of your presentation right, the rest of the presentation will be off base. Step 2 is important because it takes time to prioritize your ideas. If you don't distill your ideas to their essence and identify your key points, there's no way to highlight the most important information to your audience. Step 3 consists of the visual and verbal expressions of your idea built on the previous two steps. If you don't match your visuals to the audience, set the verbal context for the visuals, and tie the experience together with your physical presence, the two preceding steps could fall short.

Together these three steps create a powerful synergy that works together to ensure that you create a powerful and meaningful experience for your audience.

# Getting Started with the BBP Story Template

To use the story template, copy BBP Story Template 2007.dotx from the companion CD, and save it on your local computer. Locate the BBP Story Template on your local computer, and double-click it. Because the file is a Word 2007 template, indicated by the .dotx file extension, double-clicking the file will open a new presentation based on the template's formatting. Save the new presentation, and then review the story template.

## THE BBP GROUND RULES AND CHECKLISTS

As you follow the steps in upcoming chapters, you'll find sets of BBP Ground Rules for writing your story template, sketching your storyboard, adding graphics, and producing the presentation experience. You'll also find at the end of key chapters a checklist of items to make sure that you've covered them. Refer to Appendix A on the companion CD for a complete list of the ground rules and checklists that you can print and keep handy as you work with BBP.

# Writing Headlines Using Three Ground Rules

Because the text in your story template will fill the title area in your PowerPoint slides, your sentences will require a certain format. You achieve this format by following three important ground rules that apply to every statement in your story template.

## Rule 1: Write Concise, Complete Sentences with a Subject and a Verb in Active Voice

Everything you do in your presentation from this point forward will build on the headlines you write in your story template. To effectively communicate your message consistently and clearly through your entire story, your headlines must be complete sentences with a subject and a verb. The verbs should be in active voice to keep your language dynamic and direct; the same principles, techniques, and rules that define good writing also define good headlines in your template.

**See Also** For an excellent reference guide to writing the headlines of your story template clearly and concisely, see William Strunk Jr. and E. B. White's, *The Elements of Style* (Longman, 2000).

Writing headlines in the form of complete sentences imposes a discipline on your ideas by forcing you to turn them into coherent thoughts and remove any ambiguity. Later, when you import your headlines into the title area of your PowerPoint slides, your audience will have no doubt about what you want to communicate because they can read it for themselves at the top of each slide. Write your headlines using sentence case, with the initial word capitalized and the rest in lowercase.

When you write your headlines for Act I, constrain them to only one line that fills the width of the cell without extending to a second line. The columns in your template for Act II are narrower, so you can extend those headlines to a maximum of about two and a half lines. Constraining your headlines to these limits keeps you from being wordy and ensures that your headlines will fill a maximum of two lines when you send them to the title area of your PowerPoint slides.

**TIP** ✓ If you're looking for practical examples of how to write concisely, look no further than the headlines of a newspaper. When writing a headline, an editor has limited space to communicate an idea clearly, so the language ds to be clear, direct, and engaging.

It might be a challenge to keep your headlines brief, but that's part of the process of boiling down your complicated ideas to their essence. This distillation will help you to get right to the point in your presentations.

## Rule 2: Be Clear, Direct, Specific, and Conversational

Each statement in your story template will speak directly to your audience when it fills the title area of a slide, so use a conversational tone that is simple, clear, and direct. Say what you mean in plain language. When you make your point, include the details that give it specificity, color, and impact. You should tailor your words to the level of understanding of everyone in the audience and place nothing in the headline that is not in the audience's vocabulary. The point of the headline is to help your audience understand your point as efficiently as possible—if you use words unfamiliar to them, you create obstacles to understanding, and they will wonder what the individual words mean instead of attending to the overall message. The exception to using simple words is if everyone in the audience has prior understanding of the technical language you are using.

When you write your headlines, imagine that you are addressing a few members of your audience sitting in chairs next to your desk. Because you're simply having a conversation, your voice should be relaxed and casual—not tense and formal. This conversational tone will help you keep your headlines from getting wordy. Later, when your audience reads your headlines in the title area of your slides, the conversational tone will help them to feel more relaxed and open to your ideas. Although presenters might assume formal language gives them more authority, research shows people learn better when information is presented in a conversational style rather than a formal style.

### THREE GROUND RULES FOR WRITING HEADLINES

Your story template depends on a special writing style that boils down your story to its essence. Follow these three ground rules to keep your writing concise:

**Rule 1:** Write concise, complete sentences with a subject and a verb in active voice.

**Rule 2:** Be clear, direct, specific, and conversational.

**Rule 3:** Link your ideas across cells.

## Rule 3: Link Your Ideas Across Cells

As you'll see in Chapters 4 and 5, you'll be breaking up your ideas into smaller pieces as you write your thoughts in the cells of the story template. As you do that, you want to make sure that you link your ideas so that they flow to one another as you read them across the cells. You can make sure you do this by choosing a consistent tense across all headlines—you'll generally create a more dynamic story if you use the present tense. You should also link your ideas by using a parallel sentence structure across cells, which keeps everything sounding clear and coherent. Linking your cells verbally in the story template becomes important when you sketch and add graphics to your storyboard visually, as you'll see in Chapters 6, 7, 8, and 9.

### THE WRITING ON THE WALL

Although writing is usually considered a solitary experience, don't write your PowerPoint script alone. Invite the members of your team to join you in a conference room. To get started, attach a projector to your laptop computer and display your story template as a Word document on the screen. When the story template is projected onto a wall, it becomes a tool for a group of people to see, create, discuss, debate, and agree on the structure of any presentation. Organizations have found the story template tool to be a breakthrough innovation because it guides a collaborative process, gives people ownership, taps into collective brainpower, and literally gets everyone on the same sheet of paper.

Now that you've prepared your story template and reviewed the ground rules, it's time to get specific and start with the beginning—the first five slides of your PowerPoint presentation.

CHAPTER 4

# Planning Your First Five Slides

**IN THIS CHAPTER, YOU WILL:**

- Write the headlines for the first five slides of your presentation.

- Use a story sequence to orient, interest, engage, motivate, and focus your audience.

- Use a story theme to make new information easier to digest.

**WHEN YOU** stand up to make a presentation, your audience has many other things on their minds that compete with their attention to you and your information. You have to break through the clutter quickly, or you lose your chance to focus their working memory on the new information you will present. In addition to the limited capacity of working memory, you also have only a limited amount of time to make a first impression. In the first minutes of a presentation, an audience forms an opinion about you and determines your credibility to talk about the topic in the first place. This puts you in a critical situation where you really need to get it right the first time.

A Microsoft® Office PowerPoint® 2007 presentation—like a story—is a sequence of ideas over a finite period of time. People naturally follow this linear structure when they tell one another stories, whether in person or in novels and films. The beginning of a story defines your specific opportunity to lay down the sequence of ideas that will make the most efficient use of your audiences' limited capacity for new information and your limited time to make a first impression. If this sequence is put together well, it can quickly and efficiently engage your audience.

# What Will You Show, Say, and Do in the First Five Slides?

Although there are many abstract theories about what it takes to focus your audience and make an impact in the first few minutes of a presentation, the nice thing about PowerPoint is that it forces you to make abstract ideas practical. After all, next week or whenever you present, you will be the specific person standing at the front of a specific room, with a specific presentation on your computer. The Microsoft Office Word 2007 document that holds your story template is the specific place where you will get ready for that day.

With your story template document open, locate the Zoom toolbar on the lower right of the screen, and click and drag the Zoom toolbar so that Act I fills the screen, as shown in Figure 4-1. Here you see the five cells where you will write the five headlines of Act I following the three ground rules described in the "Writing Headlines Using Three Ground Rules" section in Chapter 3.

**FIGURE 4-1**   The five cells where you will write the five headlines in Act I of the story template.

Although you will be working in a Word document for now, it's helpful to keep in mind that the specific words you write here will become the headlines of the first five slides of your PowerPoint presentation, as shown in Figure 4-2. These five slides will determine everything you say, show, and do in the critical first few minutes of your presentation, and they also represent your opportunity to start strong and clear and to guide working memory through the entire presentation.

**FIGURE 4-2** The five headlines you write in Act I of the story template will become the headlines of the first five slides of your presentation that determine what you will show, say, and do during the critical first few minutes.

Inspired by the basics of classical story structure, Act I of the story template includes the specific elements that make up the beginning of a well-crafted story, ensuring that you always have the essential pieces to begin your presentation properly. Once you have a solid foundation established in Act I, you'll have limitless creative options for what you actually do visually and verbally in the presentation. Later you'll look at a range of ideas for creating the words and images for these first five slides. But first you'll write a specific example to see exactly how all the pieces of Act I fit together in a tight and smooth sequence.

# Starting with the Title and Byline

The scenario for this example presentation is that you're the CEO of a financial services company. You have developed with your team a new line of investment services that you plan to present to executives who might hire your firm to provide the services. Your audience of savvy and experienced businesspeople don't have time to waste, so they expect you to get right to the point. So with that, you start at the top of the story template.

In the top cell above Act I, replace the text *Title and byline* with the title of your presentation—in this example, **Searching for Solutions.** Type a byline for the script following the title—in this example, **by Pat Coleman,** as shown in Figure 4-3.

| Searching for Solutions by Pat Coleman | | |
|---|---|---|
| **Act I:** Set up the story from the audience's viewpoint (*"A to B, what's in it for me?"*) | | |
| **Setting** *(Where am I?)* | | |
| **Role** *(Who am I here?)* | | |
| **Point A** *(What challenge do I face?)* | **Call to Action** *(How do I get from A → B?)* | **Point B** *(Where do I want to be?)* |
|  |  |  |

**FIGURE 4-3** Type the title and byline in the top cell of the story template.

Now that you've added a title and byline, the story template is ready for you to start writing Act I.

## WHY A BYLINE IS IMPORTANT

The byline of the story template is important because it names the person who is responsible for the story's successful delivery: the presenter. In many organizations, PowerPoint files will pass through many hands as they're being developed, and ownership can easily become lost or unclear. The impact of these presentations diminishes because they are disconnected from the real names and faces of the people who will stand at the podium. Many people can contribute to a presentation, but only one person will ultimately make the presentation. The byline at the top of the story template makes it clear at all times who is behind the slides and whose reputation and credibility are on the line.

# Choosing a Story Thread

Act I of the story template lays down the pattern for the headlines of the first five slides in a sequence that will orient the audience, interest them, engage them, motivate them, and then focus them on a path forward. These five headlines will answer the clarifying questions that every audience silently asks every presenter: *where* and *when*, *who*, *why*, *what*, and *how*.

In Act I, you shape the answers to these questions in a creative way that awakens the imagination of your audience, connects with their emotions, and persuades them that they want to participate in your story.

## Orienting the Audience with the Setting Headline

The headline of your first slide establishes the context for your entire presentation. In a film or television show, if a scene takes place in the living room of a house in the day-time, you might first see a shot of the exterior of the house in daylight that then fades into a shot of the living room where the action will take place. This film technique is called an *establishing shot* and quickly shows the audience the *where* and *when* of a story.

To begin writing the first headline of Act I, type a headline in the row in the template labeled *Setting* that describes the establishing shot and answers the questions your audi-ence members are silently asking: *"Where* am I, and *when* is it?" *Where* is not necessarily a literal geographic location but could be an abstract setting such as a profession or a general topic of discussion that establishes the context for the presentation. *When* could be an implied time, such as today, if that's obvious to the audience. For the Setting head-line of Act I of this story, enter **Across the industry today, returns are declining**, as shown in Figure 4-4.

| Searching for Solutions by Pat Coleman | | |
|---|---|---|
| **Act I:** Set up the story from the audience's viewpoint (*"A to B, what's in it for me?"*) | | |
| **Setting** *(Where am I?)* | Across the industry today, returns are declining | |
| **Role** *(Who am I here?)* | | |
| **Point A** *(What challenge do I face?)* | **Call to Action** *(How do I get from A → B?)* | **Point B** *(Where do I want to be?)* |
| | | |

**FIGURE 4-4** Write your first headline of Act I to describe the setting.

The beginning of this headline, "across the industry," establishes the location for this presentation in this specific field of business, and "today" indicates the time frame. Now that the *where* and *when* have been established, the rest of the headline can say some-thing about the setting that everyone in the room agrees is true—in this example, that "returns are declining." At this early stage in the presentation, the headline should not say something controversial or unclear, or else you'll quickly derail your presentation before you even get started.

The reference to "returns are declining" is an example of establishing the setting at a macro level—presenting the big picture of the situation, to which you will zoom in with laser-like focus shortly. This makes sense for this audience of executives because they all would know about trends in the industry, and this headline affirms what they know to be true—perhaps more succinctly than normally would be said in a presentation.

This first slide is important because when your presentation begins, audiences might have different expectations than you do. The Setting headline invites them to join you at the same location, establishes a common ground, and leaves no doubt about the context for what you are about to say.

## THE SETTING HEADLINE

The Setting headline answers the question the audience members are silently wondering: *"Where* am I, and *when* is it?"

When you have written the Setting headline, you have made sure that you will orient the audience by establishing the where and when of the story in the first slide of your presentation, as shown in Figure 4-5.

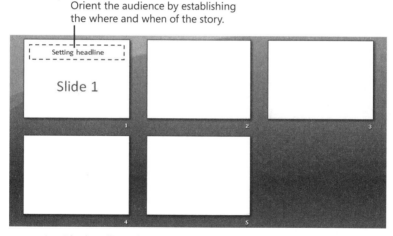

**FIGURE 4-5** The headline of the Setting slide orients the audience to where they are and when it is.

After you write a headline for the Setting slide, it's time to add some character to the presentation.

## Interesting the Audience with the Role Headline

The headline of your second slide names the role of the main character of the story. Every story is about somebody, and that includes your PowerPoint story. The *main character* of your story is the person who will make a decision to do something or come to believe something by the end of the experience. According to this definition, the main character of every nonfiction presentation is *your audience.*

Establishing your audience as the main character in your second slide makes your presentation personal to them. Because the audience members have a direct involvement and stake in the outcome, they will pay attention. Making your audience the main character also helps you to stay focused on your audience and makes sure that you tailor your presentation to their needs. Many PowerPoint presentations tend to be "all about me," with little if any consideration of the audience. With this single slide, you remind your audience that this is "all about you."

■ **REMEMBER  The main character of every presentation is your audience, and you are a supporting character. This is the crucial spin on crafting stories for live presentations.**

The main character of a presentation could be a single person, such as a customer or client, or it could be a group, such as a committee, a team, a jury, a board, or an organization. In this presentation, the executives are the main character because they collectively will decide whether they invite you to help them.

Now that you have a star for the leading role in your presentation, write a headline that acknowledges your audience's role in the setting you described. In the row labeled *Role*, type a headline that answers the question your audience is wondering: "*Who* am I here in this setting?" In this example, enter **You're looking for solutions**, as shown in Figure 4-6.

| Searching for Solutions by Pat Coleman | | |
|---|---|---|
| **Act I:** Set up the story from the audience's viewpoint ("*A to B, what's in it for me?*") | | |
| **Setting** *(Where am I?)* | Across the industry today, returns are declining | |
| **Role** *(Who am I here?)* | You're looking for solutions | |
| **Point A** *(What challenge do I face?)* | **Call to Action** *(How do I get from A → B?)* | **Point B** *(Where do I want to be?)* |
| | | |

**FIGURE 4-6** Write your second headline of Act I to describe the audience role.

In any particular context, a person could have a number of different roles—for example, the same individual could be the supervisor of one person, the peer of another person, and the subordinate of yet another person. Here you choose the specific role your audience members play in the context of the setting you just established. The subject of this headline, "you," establishes the audience, the executives, as the main character of this story. Now that the *who* of the story is clear, the rest of the headline can simply affirm something about the audience's situation that everyone in the room can agree on. In this case, the executives would concur that they are "looking for solutions."

## THE ROLE HEADLINE

The Role headline answers the question the audience is silently wondering: "*Who* am I here in this setting?"

When you have written the Role headline, you have made sure that you will interest the audience by acknowledging their role in the second slide of your presentation, as shown in Figure 4-7.

**FIGURE 4-7** The headline of the Role slide interests the audience by making them the main character of the story.

In the next slide headline, it's time to stir things up for the main character.

## Engaging the Audience with the Point A Headline

The headline of your third slide begins the action and presents an important opportunity to quickly engage your audience. Because you should make an emotional connection within the first few minutes of a presentation, this is the specific slide where you make that abstract concept a reality.

Stories are about how people respond to something that has changed in their environment. People like stories of how other people handle changes in circumstances and what their choices reveal about their characters. When a main character experiences a change, an imbalance is created because things are no longer as they used to be. This creates a challenge that sets the story in motion. In your story template, you will define this challenge with the Point A headline. This headline is called Point A because it defines the specific point where your audience begins the action of this story. Later you will define the specific point where your audience wants to be in light of this challenge—Point B.

The Point A challenge that has brought everyone to the presentation today could be a crisis brought on by an external force that has changed your organization's environment, such as a sudden economic shift or the action of a competitor. It could be the result of an internal change, such as a revised opinion or mindset, a new piece of information, a new research report, or an anecdote from the field.

■ **REMEMBER  The Point A headline sets your story in motion by defining a specific challenge your audience faces.**

On the upside, a change could be brought on by an inspiration, a new idea, a discovery, or the appearance of a new opportunity that the main character hadn't seen before. On the downside, the challenge could be the realization that a mistake was made, a fall from grace, the loss of market share, declining profits, or a sudden drop in status. Whether positive or negative, all of these challenges are the core reasons why people gather for presentations.

Your Point A headline should establish the challenge that the specific audience faces in this story. Do this by answering the question your audience is wondering: "*What* specific challenge do I face in this setting?" in the cell labeled *Point A*. In this example, enter the headline **Your returns will stay flat if you do nothing**, as shown in Figure 4-8.

**See Also**  For more inspiration in writing your Act I headlines, see "Tip 2: 10 Story Variations," later in this chapter.

| Searching for Solutions by Pat Coleman | | |
|---|---|---|
| **Act I:** Set up the story from the audience's viewpoint ("*A to B, what's in it for me?*") | | |
| **Setting** *(Where am I?)* | Across the industry today, returns are declining | |
| **Role** *(Who am I here?)* | You're looking for solutions | |
| **Point A** *(What challenge do I face?)* | **Call to Action** *(How do I get from A → B?)* | **Point B** *(Where do I want to be?)* |
| Your returns will stay flat if you do nothing | | |

**FIGURE 4-8** Write your third headline of Act I to describe Point A—a specific challenge that your audience faces in this setting.

The first part of the headline, "Your returns will stay flat," gets right to the point by describing the challenge that starts the emotional engine of your presentation. Although you might be talking about numbers here, you can be sure that numbers can strike an emotional chord, especially when they are not what the audience wants them to be. In the rest of the statement, "if you do nothing" rounds out the challenge, making it clear that even though the executives might prefer things to stay as they are, doing nothing is no longer an option.

Here you've moved from the macro view of the Setting headline that presented the overall state of the industry and have now gone to the micro level, where you describe specifically how the big picture is playing out in the audience's lives. In other words, the earlier Setting headline was the big, general problem, and now with Point A, you've made the situation personal and identified the specific challenge the audience faces in the context of the setting. There are many other ways to write your Point A headlines—see Appendix C on the companion CD for a list of many other possibilities.

The point of the Point A headline is to arrive at an emotional touchstone that makes it crystal clear why your audience would want to engage with your presentation. As you're thinking of what to write, answer this question from the audience's viewpoint: "What is it that I would stand to lose if I missed your presentation today?" Or put another way, "What makes me lose sleep at night?" It might be related to sales, an insight, or the opportunity to find clarity or direction. By focusing on what the audience might feel they would lose, or what causes them to lose sleep, you will find the challenge they really care about that you should address in your Point A headline.

The challenge of the Point A headline defines your story and helps you to focus. You could tell a dozen stories about any particular topic; focusing on a single challenge helps you to narrow your scope to a single story presented to a specific group of people at a particular moment in time. Selecting one and only one challenge is often a difficult process, but because the capacity of working memory to process new information is so limited, you have to go through a difficult decision-making process and choose the one story thread that is the best fit. In order to write the best Point A headline, you have to know your audience as well as possible and make your decision based on the best of your and your team's experience, research, competitive intelligence, analysis, and intuition.

## THE POINT A HEADLINE

The Point A headline answers the question your audience is silently wondering: "*What challenge do I face?*"

When you have written the Point A headline, you have made sure that you will engage the audience by describing a challenge they face in the third slide of your presentation, as shown in Figure 4-9.

FIGURE 4-9 The headline of the Point A slide engages your audience by describing a challenge they face.

But despite the challenge in front of the audience in the Point A headline, a resolution will come into view in the next headline.

## Motivating the Audience with the Point B Headline

No one likes to remain in a state of discomfort. When you are challenged, you feel unsettled and emotionally uncomfortable until you bring the situation back into equilibrium. The same holds true for the main character in this story or in any presentation.

In the Point A headline, you described a challenge that faces your audience. Now, in the Point B headline, they naturally want to see how things will look when the situation is brought back into balance. To write the headline for this slide, in the cell labeled *Point B* in the template, type an answer to the question your audience is wondering: "*Where do I want to be?*" In this example, enter **You want your returns to improve**, as shown in Figure 4-10.

| Searching for Solutions by Pat Coleman | | |
|---|---|---|
| **Act I:** Set up the story from the audience's viewpoint ("*A to B, what's in it for me?*") | | |
| **Setting** *(Where am I?)* | Across the industry today, returns are declining | |
| **Role** *(Who am I here?)* | You're looking for solutions | |
| **Point A** *(What challenge do I face?)* | **Call to Action** *(How do I get from A → B?)* | **Point B** *(Where do I want to be?)* |
| Your returns will stay flat if you do nothing | | You want your returns to improve |

FIGURE 4-10 Write your fourth headline of Act I to describe Point B, where your audience wants to be when facing the Point A challenge.

This headline concisely affirms what the executives want—namely, that their returns improve. This establishes the desired outcome that will bring the main character's situation back into balance.

The Point A headline describes the challenge facing the audience, and the Point B headline shows them a vision of where they want to be in this context. When they see where they want to go, they'll be fueled by their desire to get there with your help.

## THE POINT B HEADLINE

The Point B headline of the fourth slide answers the question the audience is asking themselves: *"Where* do I want to be?"

When you have written the Point B headline, you have made sure that you will motivate the audience by affirming what they want in the fourth slide of your presentation, as shown in Figure 4-11.

**FIGURE 4-11** The Point B headline motivates your audience by defining where they want to be.

# Creating Dramatic Tension Between the Point A and Point B Headlines

In the story template, the two cells that hold the Point A and Point B headlines are separated from one another physically, as shown in Figure 4-12, while the cell between them is shaded a dark gray.

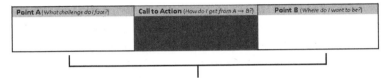

The gap between the Point A and Point B headlines creates the dramatic tension that energizes the story

**FIGURE 4-12** The gap between the Point A and Point B headlines is the emotional engine of the entire presentation.

Remember, the Point A headline puts your audience in an emotionally uncomfortable state of imbalance, and the Point B headline describes the state of balance that they want to achieve. These two headlines spark off one another to generate the energy that drives your story forward and makes your audience eager to hear your proposed solution. The gap between A and B engages your audience immediately with the unresolved tension of a story. This timeless storytelling technique of creating dramatic tension helps you quickly engage, motivate, and to further an emotional connection, and it answers another important question the audience is wondering: "*Why* am I here?

**TIP** An easy way to remember the essence of Act I is to think of the central question the audience is asking at the beginning of any presentation: "A to B, what's in it for me?"

The problem described by the Point A and Point B headlines not only helps your audience engage with your presentation, but later it also helps you to select and prioritize information. Of all the information available to you, how do you know which information to include? The answer is to select only information that specifically helps your audience close the gap between Points A and B. Any other information is unnecessary for this presentation and can be set aside for another story on another day.

## CAN I APPLY A STORY STRUCTURE TO AN "INFORMATIONAL" PRESENTATION?

One objection to using Beyond Bullet Points (BBP) is the misconception that a story structure is not appropriate for informational presentations. The thought that people don't need to be engaged or motivated when faced with new information is based on the mythology described in Chapter 3 that assumes that you can pour facts into the passive minds of your audience and they will automatically "get it." The research reality is that people need to actively engage new information, so offering them tools and techniques to do so will help them learn better. Why pass up the opportunity to engage your audience, when doing so can increase focus, and involvement? The Act I technique of creating dramatic tension by creating a gap between the Point A and Point B headlines is thousands of years old and offers a dynamism that still works today when it is applied to any type of presentation.

The problem created by the gap between the Point A and Point B headlines also forms the *purpose* of your presentation, so when you make the problem clear, you make your purpose clear. This problem is central to your entire presentation and forms the singular question that your presentation will try to answer. It creates an emotional center of gravity that focuses your story and makes it cohere across all of its separate parts. The gap between Points A and B defines the problem that you are there to help your audience to solve and also answers for the audience another important question: "What's in this for me?"

Whatever way you frame the gap between Points A and B is how you frame the entire presentation going forward. If you get this framing right, your presentation will create a connection with your audience; if you get it wrong, you will create a disconnect. Defining the problem for your audience is probably the hardest thing you'll do in your presentation. You and your team might go through several rounds of drafts and revisions to get the Point A and Point B headlines right, but when you do, the rest of your presentation will fall into place. There are many ways to write the Point B headline—see Appendix C on the companion CD for a list of some of the possibilities.

When you have a clear problem established with the Point A and Point B headlines, it's time to let your audience know how you propose to solve it.

## Focusing the Audience with the Call to Action Headline

Remember, the Point A headline defines a challenge, and the Point B headline shows your audience where they want to be in light of that challenge. Now you will literally fill the gap between A and B with your Call to Action headline.

The Call to Action headline defines the reason you're the presenter—you've taken the time to figure out how the main character can solve the problem at hand. To complete the fifth slide, in the dark gray cell labeled *Call to Action*, type an answer to the question your audience is wondering: "*How* do I get from A to B?" In this case, enter **Hire us to help you find the returns you seek**, as shown in Figure 4-13.

| Searching for Solutions by Pat Coleman | | |
|---|---|---|
| **Act I:** Set up the story from the audience's viewpoint ("*A to B, what's in it for me?*") | | |
| **Setting** *(Where am I?)* | Across the industry today, returns are declining | |
| **Role** *(Who am I here?)* | You're looking for solutions | |
| **Point A** *(What challenge do I face?)* | **Call to Action** *(How do I get from A → B?)* | **Point B** *(Where do I want to be?)* |
| Your returns will stay flat if you do nothing | Hire us to help you find the returns you seek | You want your returns to improve |

**FIGURE 4-13** Write your fifth headline of Act I to describe the call to action.

In this example, you ask the executives to "Hire us to help you find the returns you seek" to close the gap formed by the Point A and Point B headlines. In the context of the first five slides, the audience now affirms a problem they face, and they will be able to solve it if they let you help them in the story that will continue shortly.

Although the phrase "hire us" is more direct than you might want to use with this particular audience, it does strip down to the essence what you want from them in clear and direct language. If less-direct phrasing is in order, modify the wording to meet your and your audience's needs. In this example, other options include: "Join us in exploring the possibilities," "Partner with us for better results," or "Let's explore whether we're a good match for your needs." Whatever wording you choose, it should be a good fit for both you and your audience. Refer to Appendix D on the companion CD for a range of phrases that you can use to start off your Call to Action headlines.

### THE CALL TO ACTION HEADLINE

The Call to Action headline answers the question your audience is wondering: "*How* do I get from A to B?"

The Call to Action headline should describe what your audience should do or believe to solve the problem created by the gap between the Point A and Point B headlines—it is literally the *point* of the presentation. Your final wording is important, because the Call to Action headline clearly defines what you and your audience want to accomplish and offers a clear direction and road map that they will be able to use and follow through the rest of the presentation. As you go through the process of writing Act II in Chapter 5, you will thoroughly develop and test your Call to Action headline and will likely revise its wording.

The Call to Action headline also puts your ideas in a decision-making format that's important to people who want to accomplish something. In a single sentence, the wording of the Call to Action headline defines how you know if you were successful in your presentation, whether that success is a next meeting, a sale, an agreement, or a good grade. If your audience accepts your Call to Action headline by the end of your story, you'll know you succeeded.

## I'M STUCK!

What do you do if you get stuck somewhere in the process of writing the headlines for your first five slides? Visit Appendixes C and D on the companion CD for inspiration. Or when you're stuck in Act I, skip ahead to Act II and return to Act I later. Often the process of working through the structure in Act II will help you define and refine Act I.

When you have written the Call to Action headline in Act I of the story template, you have made sure that you will focus the audience by offering them a way to get from Point A to Point B in the fifth slide of your presentation, as shown in Figure 4-14. The Call to Action slide in this illustration now has a dark gray background like the corresponding cell in the story template, making it stand out from the others because it is in fact the most important slide in a presentation.  If you had only one slide to show, it would be the Call to Action slide—by the time you have finished with this slide in Chapter 8, it will distill your entire presentation into a single visual accompanied by your verbal narration.

FIGURE 4-14 The Call to Action headline focuses Act I and the rest of the story to come.

# Choosing a Pattern to Follow

Now that you have chosen a story thread to help new information pass through the eye of the needle, you can increase the efficiency of working memory by introducing a pattern for the story to follow. You can do this by adding a *motif*, or recurring theme, to the first five slides. A motif is one of the most powerful techniques you can apply to your presentations. It carries your ideas all the way through your story in a coherent way and adds color and interest to your language. It also makes the job of searching for graphics to add to your slides significantly easier because you can map the motif to your visuals.

A motif might seem like a "nice-to-have" addition to make the presentation colorful and interesting, but research shows that it can provide much more than just a pretty face to your presentation. Working memory cannot possibly process all of the new information it experiences, and without a clear structure to organize the new information, it has to create a structure from scratch—a very inefficient process. But with a structure that works, you can help working memory select, organize, and integrate the new information much more effectively. The structures that happen to work best are ones the audience already holds in long-term memory—they might take the form of a familiar metaphor, an organizing system like 1-2-3, or any number of familiar story themes.

**See Also** For more information about metaphor and its impact on the way people think, see George Lakoff's work, including *Metaphors We Live By*, 2nd ed. (with Mark Johnson; University of Chicago Press, 2002).

For example, most people are familiar with the process of putting together a puzzle, so a puzzle-making structure already exists in their long-term memory. When you apply a puzzle motif to the structure of your story, as shown in Figure 4-15, you increase the efficiency of working memory of your audience so they can much more quickly make sense of the new information. Introducing a preexisting structure reduces cognitive load because working memory doesn't need to exert as much energy to create a structure from scratch.

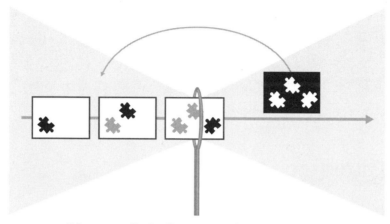

**FIGURE 4-15** When you pull a familiar structure from long-term memory and use it to structure a presentation, you make working memory more efficient.

There are many different motifs that you can apply to your presentation, which are incorporated into some of the example phrases in Appendix D on the companion CD that you can use to write your Call to Action headlines. To apply a motif to your presentation, integrate it through your headlines as in the following variations of the Act I example in this chapter. Keep the following general principles in mind when you search for a motif for Act I:

- **The motif should exist already in your audience's long-term memory.** You need to get into the minds of your audience to find the right motif, because the structure has to exist already in their long-term memories. You need to figure out what they think, and what they know, through your research, interviews, and analysis. In jury trials, lawyers will sometimes create juror questionnaires designed to find out what potential themes might resonate in a legal presentation. You might need to do similar in-depth research if your presentation is particularly important. If you don't know your audience or can't find enough information about them, choose a general metaphor like the checklist motif shown in Figure 4-16.

| A Checklist for Better Returns by Pat Coleman | | |
|---|---|---|
| **Act I:** Set up the story from the audience's viewpoint (*"A to B, what's in it for me?"*) | | |
| **Setting** (*Where am I?*) | You've seen revenue decline across the industry | |
| **Role** (*Who am I here?*) | Solving the problem at your company is at the top of your list | |
| **Point A** (*What challenge do I face?*) | **Call to Action** (*How do I get from A → B?*) | **Point B** (*Where do I want to be?*) |
| You're not sure what you should do | Check off 3 items to find the returns you seek | You'd like to make sure you do the right thing |

**FIGURE 4-16** The checklist motif is familiar to most audiences

- **The motif should resonate with your audience.** Your motif needs to be a good match with your audience, and they should be able to easily relate to it. A motif can work against you if the structure is a mismatch, because it distracts your audience or misleads them into thinking you're not serious. The motif should also resonate with you as the presenter—choose one that you personally can relate to so that it draws out your personality and warmth and brings your ideas to life with your natural enthusiasm. You can use a complex or special motif if everyone in your audience shares knowledge of it, as in the formula example shown in Figure 4-17.

| A Formula for Better Returns by Pat Coleman | | |
|---|---|---|
| **Act I:** Set up the story from the audience's viewpoint (*"A to B, what's in it for me?"*) | | |
| **Setting** (*Where am I?*) | Returns are declining across the industry today | |
| **Role** (*Who am I here?*) | You're looking for a way to solve the problem | |
| **Point A** (*What challenge do I face?*) | **Call to Action** (*How do I get from A → B?*) | **Point B** (*Where do I want to be?*) |
| Some companies are adopting a complex new strategy called Initiative Z | Follow a simple formula to understand how to make Initiative Z work for you | You'd like to know if Initiative Z will work for you |

**FIGURE 4-17** The formula motif can resonate with those who deal with numbers.

- **The motif has to be simple.** When you find a motif, it needs to be simplified and broken up into its essential elements so that you can apply it to your first five slides. For example, you need a more specific motif than just the general topic of puzzles, so focus the motif by using the phrase "put together the three key pieces of the puzzle," as in the example shown in Figure 4-18. The motif should be clear and easy to understand, and it should couch and complement your ideas without becoming convoluted or clichéd or making things confusing.

| Solving the Puzzle by Pat Coleman | | |
|---|---|---|
| **Act I:** Set up the story from the audience's viewpoint (*"A to B, what's in it for me?"*) | | |
| **Setting** (*Where am I?*) | Returns are declining across the industry today | |
| **Role** (*Who am I here?*) | Your returns are flat and you'd like to do something about it | |
| **Point A** (*What challenge do I face?*) | **Call to Action** (*How do I get from A → B?*) | **Point B** (*Where do I want to be?*) |
| You're hearing conflicting pieces of advice that leave you uncertain about the next step | Put together the three key pieces of the puzzle to find the returns you seek | Seeing the big picture will help you decide what to do to improve your returns |

**FIGURE 4-18** The puzzle motif is simple yet effective.

- **A motif is more memorable if it is unexpected.** Introducing a surprising motif in Act I will also increase memorability. Choose a surprising insight, a different way of looking at things, or another unexpected way to introduce your idea, as shown in Figure 4-19. Creatively applying a motif by putting it in a surprising context can heighten interest and stimulate creative thinking and mental participation. The more surprising and interesting and engaging the motif is, the more memorable it will be. But as mentioned earlier, make sure that in every case the motif is a good match with your audience.

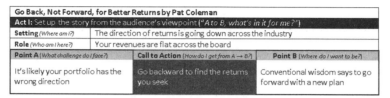

| Go Back, Not Forward, for Better Returns by Pat Coleman | | |
|---|---|---|
| **Act I:** Set up the story from the audience's viewpoint ("*A to B, what's in it for me?*") | | |
| **Setting** *(Where am I?)* | The direction of returns is going down across the industry | |
| **Role** *(Who am I here?)* | Your revenues are flat across the board | |
| **Point A** *(What challenge do I face?)* | **Call to Action** *(How do I get from A → B?)* | **Point B** *(Where do I want to be?)* |
| It's likely your portfolio has the wrong direction | Go backward to find the returns you seek | Conventional wisdom says to go forward with a new plan |

FIGURE 4-19 Telling someone to go backward instead of forward gives a twist to a journey motif.

## THE BLOCKBUSTER MOTIF

Some of the most powerful presentation motifs are drawn from popular culture, such as the opening statement of the jury trial described in Chapter 1 that used a *CSI* motif inspired by the popular television show. Finding a blockbuster motif that works well for your audience is a blend of science and art—the science of doing thorough research to know your audience and the art of applying an interesting theme in an innovative way to your information.

- **The best motifs are extendable.** Your motif will play out extensively through the rest of the presentation—structurally, verbally, and visually. The more elegantly a single motif can extend through all levels of the presentation, the more impact it will have. Sometimes a motif is straightforward, and other times it will be clever, humorous, or surprising. The deeper and more broadly your simple motif can be applied through the entire presentation, the more cohesive and elegant the communication.

You should invest a good amount of time considering your motif and trying on different ones for size, because if you find a good one, it can transform the fiber of your story thread into fiber optics as your new information travels through working memory.

# Closing the Curtain on Act I

Now that you have five headlines, you've completed the first draft of Act I. Review your headlines. They might seem simple, but they've helped you to accomplish many important tasks, such as tailoring your presentation to your audience and establishing criteria to narrow down the information you want to communicate. Consider these headlines a working draft as you complete the rest of the story template; you might need to return to them and revise them as you develop the rest of your presentation.

> **NOTE**  When a journalist puts the most important information somewhere else in the article rather than the front, it's called *burying the lead*. The structure of Act I ensures that you don't bury your lead by making sure that you always bring the most important information to the top level of attention at the start of every presentation.

If you haven't already done so, take the time now to review your five headlines with your team and anyone else who needs to approve your presentation. These headlines determine everything that will unfold next in your story, so it's important to get other people involved early in this writing process to make sure that you're on the right track.

Never rush through the process of writing your Act I headlines—the words that you write in Act I will make the difference between a strong start and a weak one. It's not uncommon for an individual or a team to completely revise Act I several times until the story is exactly right for the audience. An executive team might spend a great deal of time fine-tuning Act I because, in a bigger sense, these five headlines can define the way the organization understands and relates to its customers. These five simple headlines are in fact a communications strategy and are worthy of whatever resources you normally invest in developing strategic issues.

Review the tips at the end of this chapter to develop and refine your Act I headlines. Here are a couple of things you can do to test and review the headlines now.

## Reviewing the Five Headlines

Read the five headlines aloud so that you can verify that you have the tone, flow, and clarity of language that you want. Check your headlines to make sure that you answer each of the clarifying questions that every audience wants to know: *where* and *when*, *who*, *what*, *why*, and *how*. Here are the questions in their respective headlines:

- **The Setting Headline** *Where* am I, and *when* is it?

- **The Role Headline** *Who* am I in this setting?

- **The Point A Headline** *What* challenge do I face in this setting?

- **The Point B Headline** *Where* do I want to be?

- **(The Gap Between A and B)** *Why* am I here?

- **The Call to Action Headline** *How* do I get from A to B?

**Tip** If you ever have to give an off-the-cuff speech, use the five headlines of Act I to start your talk. This is a sure-fire way to answer your audience's clarifying questions and leave them thoroughly impressed.

## Appealing to Your Audience's Emotions

The members of any audience, including these executives, are not purely rational beings—they are emotional too. You avoid a strictly rational approach by using your Act I headlines to make an emotional connection with your audience and persuade them that the information is important to them. You achieve this connection by including the most important elements of a strong story beginning, in the form of headlines for the Setting, Role, Point A, Point B, and Call to Action slides. By tailoring each of these elements to your audience and presenting them in Act I, you make your story personal to your audience and ensure that you are off to a strong start.

■ **REMEMBER Your Act I headlines make an emotional connection with your audience.**

# Focusing Your Ideas

As you saw in Chapter 2, if the volume of information overwhelms your audience, especially at the start of a presentation, their minds will shut down, and you won't achieve the results you want. Act I of the story template helps you to establish criteria to narrow down all the things you *could* say to only the most important things you *should* say to this audience during this presentation. When you begin writing the Act II headlines in Chapter 5, you'll find that these Act I headlines have set up your story in a way that will limit the quantity of information to only what is necessary and the quality of information to the high standards you expect.

## BBP CHECKLIST: PLANNING YOUR FIRST FIVE SLIDES

Do the first five slides of your presentation:

❑ Orient your audience to the setting of the presentation?

❑ Interest them by acknowledging their role in the setting?

❑ Engage them emotionally by describing a challenge they face (Point A)?

❑ Motivate them by affirming what they want (Point B)?

❑ Focus them by offering a way to get from Point A to Point B (Call to Action)?

The process of writing the five slide headlines described in this chapter covers the fundamentals that apply to any presentation story and helps you to appeal to emotion and focus your ideas. Once you learn the basics, you can apply a broad range of creative resources, tools, and techniques to help you adapt this structure to your own style and circumstances.

When you're satisfied with your Act I headlines, it's time to flesh out your story in Act II. Before you move on to Chapter 5, scan through the 10 tips in the following sections to find ideas that might inspire you to improve on Act I after you're comfortable with the fundamentals.

# 10 Tips for Enhancing Act I

The Act I structure in the story template isn't a strict formula—it's a basic platform with the potential for endless innovation and improvisation based on the specifics of your situation. Just as writers can create endless story variations using this pattern, you can likewise create endless presentation variations with this tool. After you learn the fundamentals, there's plenty of room to adapt and improvise to suit your personality, audience, and situation.

If you're ready to take your presentations to the next level, here are 10 advanced tips for building on the basic structure of Act I.

## Tip 1: Inspiration from the Screenwriters

Spark your creative energy by going back to the past to see the future of presentation stories. All you need to do is consult with the original expert on story structure. Start by picking up copies of Aristotle's classics *Poetics* and *Rhetoric*. For a more recent adaptation of Aristotle's ideas, a number of excellent books on screenwriting can help you with writing your Act I headlines, including Robert McKee's *Story: Substance, Structure, Style and the Principles of Screenwriting* (Regan Books, 1997); Syd Field's *Screenplay: The Foundations of Screenwriting* (Dell, 1984); and James Bonnet's *Stealing Fire from the Gods: The Complete Guide to Story for Writers and Filmmakers* (Michael Wiese Productions, 2006). Any of these titles can help you learn more about the key elements of the first act of every story, including settings, character development, inciting incidents, and plot points. As you read these books for inspiration, keep in mind that your PowerPoint presentation is a specific type of story in which your audience is the main character and you are in a supporting role. Maintaining this focus will ensure that all of your stories align with the specific needs of your PowerPoint presentations.

## Tip 2: 10 Story Variations

After you've mastered the basics of the five Act I headlines, try improvising in your stories. For example, your story structure might involve changing the order of headlines in Act I. You could place the Point A and B headlines first and define the Setting, Role, and Call to Action headlines later. You could begin with the Call to Action headline to grab people's attention and then continue with the other headlines. At times, you might be able to delete a slide if the audience is absolutely in agreement about a situation, although it rarely hurts to clearly restate information to bring everyone to the same starting point.

Although the classical story structure of Act I is the foundation for limitless story variations, there is a more limited set of story types that can help you to frame your own stories. In his book *Moving Mountains* (Crowell-Collier Press, 1989), Henry M. Boettinger describes a dozen story types, summarized below, that describe various situations that people in organizations might face. Many of these story types can help you to refine the Point A and Point B dynamic you set up in Act I.

- **Historical narrative** "We have a history that makes us proud, and we want to apply our high standards to the current situation."

- **Crisis** "We have to respond to the danger facing us."

- **Disappointment** "We made a decision based on the best information we had available, but now we know it wasn't the right decision, so we have to try something else."

- **Opportunity** "We know something now that we didn't know before, which presents us with a new possibility if we act."

- **Crossroads** "We've been doing fine on the path that we're on, but now we have a new choice and we have to decide which path to take."

- **Challenge** "Someone else has achieved something amazing—do we have it in us to do the same?"

- **Blowing the whistle** "Although it appears everything is going fine, we have a serious problem we need to fix."

- **Adventure** "We know that trying something new is a risk, but it's better to take a risk than to stay in a rut."

- **Response to an order** "We've been told we have to do this, so we're here to figure out how to make it happen."

- **Revolution** "We're on a path to disaster if we don't radically change what we're doing today."

- **Evolution** "If we don't keep up with the latest, we'll fall behind."

- **The Great Dream** "If we can only see our possibility, we can make it our reality."

No matter what type of story you have, read through these story types when you start writing your Act I headlines to see whether one of them can help you to find the words you're looking for.

## Tip 3: Your Act I Screen Test

In filmmaking, a *screen test* puts actors in front of a camera to test how they will do on screen. In a PowerPoint presentation, your first screen test is for your Act I headlines, and your first audience is the members of your team. It's important to include other people at this stage of your presentation so that you can get early feedback and fresh perspectives. If you're working on a small or an informal presentation, ask a colleague or your boss to look over your Act I headlines.

Once you get the hang of writing an Act I with your group, try applying these techniques to other communications scenarios beyond your PowerPoint presentations. Crafting Act I of a presentation is a problem-solving framework that can also help a group to clarify strategy, develop marketing messages, create project plans, and resolve other challenges. Sharing your Act I headlines with a team is also a great way to kick off a project or orient someone new to a team. By reviewing the five headlines of Act I and the clarifying questions, team members can learn the situation quickly and efficiently.

## Tip 4: Multiple Stories, Multiple Templates

When it comes to presentations, one size might not fit all.

The beauty of your Act I headlines is that they are finely tailored and tuned to solve the specific problem of a specific audience. But what if your audience has more than one problem? What if you give the same presentation to different audiences that have different problems to solve? For example, you might need to present a marketing plan to different audiences, including the board, your advertising agency, and your sales team. In each instance, the presentation will have a different focus and will need a different version of Act I. If you don't tailor your presentations to your audiences, you won't connect with them.

One way to plan for these different situations is to create several versions of Act I, each of which is tailored to a specific audience. Create a copy of the Microsoft Office Word document that contains the five Act I headlines from your current story template. In the new document, revise the Point A and Point B headlines, which describe the central problem that your new audience faces. When you change these headlines to reflect a new problem, you might find that you need to revise the Setting and Role headlines if a different set of circumstances led to this problem. And you most likely will also need to revise the Call to Action headline because the solution for the new problem will probably be different from the solution to the previous problem. By creating separate versions of Act I, you can choose the most appropriate version for your next audience.

This multiple-version approach can also be used if you find that you have more stories to tell in addition to the one you're working on. If you sense another story emerging, open up a new story template, and keep it open while you're working on your current presentation, adding headlines to your second story as you go. As you develop your second presentation in parallel to the first, you might find that you're able to refine both versions at the same time.

## Tip 5: Visualize Your Audience

The more clearly you know your audience, the clearer your communications will become.

When you start writing your Act I headlines, take some time with your team to visualize everything that you know about your specific audience. To do this, open a blank PowerPoint presentation, create a blank slide, and insert a picture of a specific audience member or just type a specific name on the screen. If you're speaking to a large audience, consider the slide a composite of the average audience member.

Ask your group questions like these:

- What do we know about this person?
- What have we heard about his personality type?
- How does she make decisions?
- What can we learn from a Web search about his thinking process?
- What can we learn from our social network about how she works with other people?
- How do we effectively fashion an experience that aligns with his interests and personality type?

Type the information on the slide as your group gives feedback so that everyone has all the information captured on a PowerPoint slide. When you do this, you tap into the collective thinking of your group to better understand your audience. And you think more deeply about your audience and your purpose, which will significantly improve the quality of your headlines.

## Tip 6: What Problem Is Your Audience Facing?

To accurately define the problem your audience is facing, try putting yourself in the place of the audience.

Your Act I headlines identify a problem that your audience faces and a solution that you propose. But it's not always easy to figure out the problem so that you can be sure you have the right solution. The visualization exercise described in Tip 5 can help you to see into the mindset of your audience so that you'll be in a better position to write the appropriate headlines for them.

Another technique is role playing. When you review the rough draft of your Act I headlines, ask a member of the group to play the role of a decision maker or representative member of your audience. She can review the material you gathered from the preceding profiling exercise to help her to get into character.

Request that this person be a devil's advocate during your review session, continually asking questions such as these:

- What's in this for me?

- Why do you think this is important to me?

- Why should I care?

When you hear this critical voice during your review, you'll be able to test your headlines to make sure that you're hitting the mark. It's better to hear the questions from a fictional audience than to have them pop up unexpectedly during your actual presentation.

Once you've identified your audience's problem, don't be surprised if your presentation holds tightly together and your ideas start to emerge into clear meaning.

## Tip 7: Strategic Collage

If you have a high-stakes presentation to make, you might need to invest extra effort to get to know your audience in advance. One way to get to know them is to spend a day in their shoes—at least symbolically. Open up a new PowerPoint file, and then create six blank slides. On each of these slides, type one of the clarifying questions: **Where? When? Who? What? Why?** and **How?**

Use a digital camera to take pictures of the objects your audience uses every day or of the environments where they live and work and the people they might see. Your visuals should represent whatever data you have about your audience, whether it's market research, demographics, or focus group information. Go to the Microsoft Office Online Clip Art and Media site to download free images. Or go through your organization's photo libraries to find licensed photographs and clip art that you can use to show the buildings in which these people work, the products they use, and the places they visit. Use a digital scanner to insert pictures of documents, a pen tablet to make sketches, a video camera to insert video clips, and a microphone to collect sound.

When you've collected these multimedia elements, arrange them on each of the six PowerPoint slides to create six collages. Size the different elements according to how important you think each is to your audience—for example, if mobility is most important, make the picture of a car larger than less important elements.

Present the file to your team as you discuss what it's like to spend a day in your audience's shoes in the context of these six slides. Then open your story template and start working on Act I. Discuss with your team how well the headlines match the collages, and then edit the headlines to provide a good fit. The better your Act I story matches the reality of your audience's lives, the better your presentation.

## Tip 8: The Story of Advertising

Some of the most powerful examples of Act I story structure pass right before your eyes every day. If you look for them, you'll find an endless stream of ideas for your presentations. These stories are all around us—in the form of advertising.

Advertisers are well aware of Aristotle's ideas and techniques of storytelling and persuasion, because at its essence, every advertisement is a persuasive story. Whether you look up at a billboard, open a magazine, or watch television, you're seeing a mini-story built on the fundamentals of persuasion. Each advertisement has a singular goal in mind: to persuade you to do something—usually, to buy a product.

To persuade you, an advertiser will use the most current and sophisticated blend of multimedia possible. But beneath the media mix are the same classical story elements you've been working with in Act I of the story template: the clarifying questions *where* and *when*, *who*, *why*, *what*, and *how*. As in a PowerPoint presentation, the main character of an advertisement is usually the audience—in this case, you—because the advertiser's goal is to persuade you to buy or think something new.

So if you're watching a commercial for a laundry detergent, you can compare the questions your audience silently asks of your five Act I headlines with what you see on TV, something like this:

- **Where am I, and when is it?** I'm at home, and it's the afternoon.

- **Who am I here in this setting?** I'm a person getting ready to go out for the evening.

- *What* **challenge do I face?**  I dropped spaghetti on my favorite shirt.

- *Where* **do I want to be?**  I want to impress my date tonight by looking my best.

- *How* **do I get from here to there?**  If I buy Product X laundry detergent, my shirt will be clean in time for my date.

There's usually a one-to-one correspondence between your Act I questions and most advertisements because both have the same intent: to make an emotional connection and to persuade. And both creatively interpret the fundamentals of story structure to get the job done. The next time you notice an advertisement, observe the structure that gives it form. Sometimes the story elements might be implied or communicated using a photo, sound, or movement instead of words, but they will usually all be there.

As you begin to see this common persuasive story structure in advertising, you'll be more aware of the range of storytelling approaches, and you'll be able to apply these techniques to your own Act I headlines.

## Tip 9: Persuasive Education

Educators and trainers are in the same boat as the rest of us when it comes to the challenges of communicating today. They also are affected by the expectations of audiences who now are fluent in the visual language around them and expect the same level of media sophistication in the classroom.

For example, a university professor who's struggling to find a way to make his architecture course more interesting and engaging is struck by the fact that every one of the architects he'll discuss also struggled with change—economic change, social change, demographic change, and technological change. So he decides to adopt a classical persuasive technique and chooses the singular topic of change as the key theme of his course. The persuasive story in Act I goes like this:

- *Where* **am I, and when is it?**  Architects stand at the epicenter of economic change, social change, and technological change.

- *Who* **am I in this setting?**  As a new graduate, you will be facing the reality of the situation soon.

- *What* **challenge do I face?**  In a new job, you are most in danger of instability due to the forces of change.

- ***What* do I want?**  You'd like to have the skills to handle the situation no matter what changes occur.

- ***How* do I get from here to there?**  Learn three crucial techniques to ensure that you keep a firm footing.

This persuasive Act I structure provides an elegant framework for the entire course. It gives students a way to understand the single theme and follow it through the various events in the complicated history of architecture. And the dramatic and persuasive elements give students a way to relate personally to the material.

Finding a defining structure like this is not always easy, but it can make the difference between a boring lecture and an engaging presentation. Try applying the persuasive model the next time you teach or inform, and see whether you can make things more interesting for both yourself and your audience.

## Tip 10: Get the Writing Right

Beyond the nuts and bolts of writing down the words, consider ways you can apply literary techniques to convey clear meaning across your headlines. Act I is so brief and elegant that you are actually telling a rich but concise story in only five sentences. Using a motif is one powerful technique; see whether you can pick up other techniques from professional writers whose work you admire.

Writers such as poets are extremely good at communicating a great deal of information in a limited number of words. Pick up a book of good poetry, and pay attention to how the author uses words, metaphor, and pacing. Scan through the text in a range of news-papers, and consider how the writers manage to tell a complicated story in only a brief article. Listen to people speak, and try adapting the direct and clear phrases you hear to the words of your Act I headlines. If you have good writers on your team, ask them to help write your Act I headlines, and if you have the resources, hire a professional writer to help. The success of your entire presentation rests on the language you use for Act I, and any amount of time and resources you can invest in improving that language will be well spent.

And you can put that in writing.

CHAPTER 5

# Planning the Rest of Your Slides

**IN THIS CHAPTER, YOU WILL:**

- Write the headlines for the rest of the slides of your presentation.

- Distill your ideas to their essence.

- Establish a priority and a sequence for your slides.

**THE HEADLINES** you wrote for Act I will prepare the working memory of your audience for the crucial first few minutes of a presentation by orienting, interesting, engaging, motivating, and focusing them. Although you might have made quick work of planning these first five slides, things get much more challenging as you plan the rest of the slides in the presentation.

## The Problems of Sequence and Priority

Now, with a much larger number of slides than you'll need for a 45-minute or longer presentation, two new problems come into play. The first problem is how to handle the *sequence* of slides when you have many to manage. Chapter 4 described how the nature of a Microsoft® Office PowerPoint® 2007 presentation—like a story—is a sequence of slides over a finite period of time. In Act I, it will be easy for your audience to follow the linear sequence of only five headlines. However, in a much more extended sequence of slides, it will be hard for your audience to keep track of where they are—remember the limited capacity of working memory when it is faced with new information. Maybe your audience will still remember where they are in the story in the few slides after Act I, but what will your audience remember by the time they get to slide 17, 26, or 33?

The second new problem you face is how you determine the *priority* of your slides. In any presentation, you obviously have some points to make that are more important than others—if you're pressed for time and need to get right to the heart of the matter, these are the points that you want to make sure the audience members remember and apply. It's important that you make clear to their working memory exactly where these priority points are within the sequence of your slides.

The problems of sequence and priority present you with the issue of how to break up your ideas into a sequence of digestible pieces so that working memory can properly manage them, while at the same time making sure that your audience remembers the most important information you want to present, as illustrated in Figure 5-1.

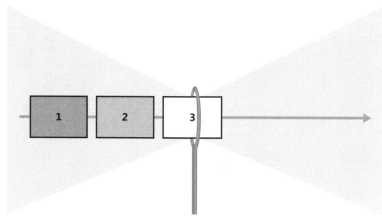

**FIGURE 5-1** A key challenge is to present new information to the working memory of your audience in a sensible sequence and priority.

Although you face difficult challenges and have hard choices to make, Beyond Bullet Points (BBP) is up to the job when you complete Act II of your story template. As in Act I, completing the story template for Act II creates a solid foundation that will help you choose exactly what you will show and say as you present the working memory of your audience with new information. With this infrastructure in place, you'll have endless creative options to make the crisp and clear underlying story even more powerful.

To begin, go to Act II of the BBP story template you've started to write, locate the Zoom toolbar in the lower right of the screen, and click and drag the Zoom toolbar so that Act II fills the screen, as shown in Figure 5-2. Here you see the empty cells where you will write the rest of the headlines of Act II following the three ground rules described in the section "Writing Headlines Using Three Ground Rules" in Chapter 3.

**Act II**: Develop the action  *("1-2-3, show me only what I need to see")*

| Key Point *(5 minutes)*: | Explanation *(15 minutes)*: | Detail *(45 minutes)*: |
| --- | --- | --- |
| | | |

FIGURE 5-2 The cells where you will write the rest of the headlines in Act II of the story template.

Although you are working in a Microsoft Office Word 2007 document for now, just as you did in Act I, the specific words you write in these cells in Act II will become the headlines of the rest of the slides of your PowerPoint presentation. But where the Act I headlines help you plan only five slides, your Act II headlines will help you plan most of the rest of the slides in your presentation. When you complete your Act II headlines, you also will have solved the problems of sequence and priority, because you will know the position of each slide in your sequence of slides, and you will also know which slides are most important, second-most important, and third-most important, as shown in Figure 5-3.

FIGURE 5-3 The headlines you write in Act II will determine the sequence and priority of the slides.

# Three Columns of Clarity

Act II in the story template contains three columns, labeled Key Point, Explanation, and Detail, as shown in Figure 5-4. Each column contains a deeper level of information about your Call to Action headline. In the Key Point column, you give the top three reasons your audience should accept your Call to Action headline. The Explanation column contains an additional level of information about the Key Point column headlines, and the Detail column contains the next level of information about the Explanation column headlines.

**FIGURE 5-4** The three column headings: Key Point, Explanation, and Detail.

One way to understand how Act II works is to see it as a *sentence outline* you might use to write a paper. In a sentence outline, beginning from a single thesis statement, you write out your topic sentences, explanations, and details and organize them by using numbers and letters along with indentation. For example, you write out your first topic sentence and then number it *1*. You then indent and number as *1.a.* the first explanation that follows the topic sentence and then indent and number as *1.a.i.*, *1.a.ii.*, and *1.a.iii.* the details that follow the explanation, as shown here:

**1. Topic sentence (Key Point)**

    a. Explanation

       i. Detail

       ii. Detail

       iii. Detail

    b. Explanation

You continue numbering and indenting your sentences in this fashion as you write the rest of the outline.

When you write your presentation outline using your story template, instead of indenting and numbering your headlines, you write them in the corresponding columns of Act II, which are colored according to the levels of indentation. For example, when you view Act II as a sentence outline, as shown in Figure 5-5, your thesis statement corresponds to the dark gray Call to Action cell in Act I (top). Your topic sentences in the first numbered level of your outline corresponds to the medium gray Key Point column in Act II (left). The next level of indentation corresponds to the light gray Explanation column (middle), and the next level of indentation corresponds to the white Detail column (right).

| | Call to Action (How do I get from A→B?) | |
|---|---|---|
| | **Thesis Statement** | |
| **Act II:** Develop the action ("1-2-3, show me only what I need to see") | | |
| **Key Point** (5 minutes): | **Explanation** (15 minutes): | **Detail** (45 minutes): |
| Topic Sentence 1 | 1.a. | 1.a.i. |
| | | 1.a.ii. |
| | | 1.a.iii. |
| | 1.b. | 1.b.i. |
| | | 1.b.ii. |
| | | 1.b.iii. |
| | 1.c. | 1.c.i. |
| | | 1.c.ii. |
| | | 1.c.iii. |
| Topic Sentence 2 | 2.a. | 2.a.i. |
| | | 2.a.ii. |
| | | 2.a.iii. |
| | 2.b. | 2.b.i. |
| | | 2.b.ii. |
| | | 2.b.iii. |
| | 2.c. | 2.c.i. |
| | | 2.c.ii. |
| | | 2.c.iii. |
| Topic Sentence 3 | 3.a. | 3.a.i. |
| | | 3.a.ii. |
| | | 3.a.iii. |
| | 3.b. | 3.b.i. |
| | | 3.b.ii. |
| | | 3.b.iii. |
| | 3.c. | 3.c.i. |
| | | 3.c.ii. |
| | | 3.c.iii. |

**FIGURE 5-5** The relationship between the three columns of Act II is similar to the indented levels of headings in a sentence outline.

## OTHER ACT II OPTIONS

Feel free to write Act II in a blank Word document using a traditional sentence outline if that works better for you—just be sure to write complete sentences as described in the section "Writing Headlines Using Three Ground Rules" in Chapter 3, and discipline yourself to keep your indented headings to three levels. Some BBP practitioners use tools other than Word to write their story templates, including Microsoft Office Excel® 2007, mind-mapping software, and even Post-it notes—visit *www.beyondbulletpoints.com* to learn more.

Once you complete the sentence outline that is built into Act II of the story template, the headlines will be used to create the rest of the slides of your presentation in a specific priority and sequence, as shown in Figure 5-6. The headline from the dark gray Call to Action cell from Act I will appear on the single most important slide in the presentation—the dark gray Call to Action slide (upper left). The headlines from the medium gray Key Point column will appear on each medium gray Key Point slide (upper right), the headlines you write in the light gray Explanation column will appear on each light gray Explanation slide (lower left), and the headlines you write in the white Detail column will appear on each white Detail slide (lower right).

**FIGURE 5-6** Following the Call to Action headline from Act I (upper left), the three types of headlines you write in Act II will appear on the Key Point, Explanation, and Detail slides.

You'll notice that the column headings in your story template also include time estimates: The Key Point column heading includes the phrase *5 minutes*, the Explanation column heading includes the phrase *15 minutes*, and the Detail column heading includes the phrase *45 minutes*. These time estimates indicate that for any presentation, you can choose to complete the columns that correspond to the level of information and length of presentation you want. The entire story template, including Act I and all three columns in Act II, contains 44 cells, each of which contains a single headline. If you spend an average of one minute per headline, you have enough material for a 45-minute presentation. If you skip the Detail column, you end up with a total of 17 headlines in your story template; if you spend an average of 50 seconds on each, you have enough material for a 15-minute presentation. If you skip the Explanation and Detail columns, you have 8 headlines; if you spend an average of 40 seconds each, you have a 5-minute presentation.

In this chapter, every cell in the example will eventually contain a headline so that you can see how the entire process works.

**See Also**  The headings in Act II of the story template describe the most common division of levels of information in a presentation. If you want to adapt the headings to align more closely with your profession, see "Tip 3: Tailor Your Act II Column Headings to Your Profession"—it might be worth taking a quick look at these now so that you can keep them in mind as you learn how to use Act II of the story template.

## Threading the Eye of the Needle Using a Hierarchy

Act II might look bland and unassuming with its various rows and cells in a Word document, and the idea that it is a form of a traditional sentence outline does not make it seem exceptional. But appearances are deceiving—it is, in fact, a powerful critical thinking tool that has helped many people in a range of professions to break through intellectual clutter and find a compelling story structure beneath mountains of data, charts, and bullet points. Built into the arrangement of these simple cells is a process that wields tremendous intellectual power to help you get right to the point.

When you use indentations in a sentence outline as described earlier, you are applying a *hierarchy* to your ideas by consciously specifying some ideas (your topic sentences) as more important than other ideas (your explanation), which are in turn more important than other ideas (your details). You can show the relationships between levels of ideas in a hierarchy with a *logic tree*, also called a *tree diagram*—a concept that dates back at least 1,700 years. The basic look of the logic tree diagram is recognizable today in the form of an organizational chart. When the logic tree that is built in to Act II of the story template is placed on its side, you can draw a triangle around the logic tree to show its shape, as shown in Figure 5-7. This triangle shape is the powerful tool you will use to distill your ideas to their essence, prioritize them, and arrange them in the sequence in which you will present them in the form of slides to the working memory of your audience.

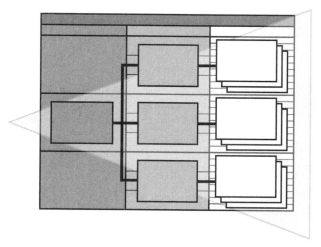

**FIGURE 5-7** Act II of the story template is built on the powerful foundation of a hierarchy.

The concept of a hierarchy illustrated by the triangle in Act II might not be popular these days, with trends moving more toward free-flowing, organic, free-association relationships among people and ideas. But you absolutely need an *idea hierarchy* to help you decide which of your slides are more important than others. You cannot present the working memory of your audience with an unprioritized and unstructured sequence of slides, because its limited capacity will be quickly overwhelmed. A hierarchy breaks up a complex body of information into smaller pieces that are easier for working memory to handle and then prioritizes those pieces and places them in a particular sequence.

A hierarchy is the natural way people routinely go through a reasoning process—if you are completely new to a topic, you might start with a large amount of unstructured information (bottom of a hierarchy) when you first assemble the many details of the information you want to present. You then apply your reasoning process to sort the information into smaller groups to explain what it means (middle of the hierarchy). Last you develop the key points or conclusion about what you analyzed (top of the hierarchy). You can also approach a reasoning process the other way around, as you'll do when you complete Act II in this chapter—if you've already completed the reasoning process by the time you're ready to prepare a presentation, you begin with the key points you want to make, follow those with your explanation, and then follow your explanation with the details. Either approach to Act II is perfectly valid.

| TIP ✓ | An easy way to remember the essence of Act II is to imagine the audience saying to you as you decide what to keep in your presentation, "1-2-3, show me only what I need to see." |
|---|---|

With the hierarchy concept firmly established as the foundation of Act II, it's time to make things practical and apply the hierarchy to the specific slides in the example presentation.

### THE POWER OF A PYRAMID

The design of Act II of the story template is inspired by Barbara Minto's book, *The Minto Pyramid Principle: Logic in Writing, Thinking, and Problem Solving* (Minto International, 1996). The book is a sophisticated, thorough, and comprehensive application of a logic tree technique that Minto developed 30 years ago to teach management consultants to write business documents more effectively, and she now teaches her approach as an independent consultant to senior executives around the world.

## Prioritizing Your Slides

To recap your story so far: Your Act I headlines define the Setting, Role, Point A, Point B, and Call to Action slides. You make your audience's problem clear with the gap between the challenge they face in the Point A headline and where they want to be in the Point B headline. The gap between these headlines forms the dramatic tension for the entire presentation, causing your audience to now pay close attention to find out how they can solve this problem. With this gap wide open, you focus the entire presentation with the Call to Action headline. This makes the headline of the Call to Action slide the top of the triangle, as shown in Figure 5-8, and Act II is the rest of the triangle that will pull your slides through the eye of the needle of your audience's working memory based on a sensible sequence and priority.

The Call to Action headline focuses all the slides in the hierarchy.

**FIGURE 5-8** The tip of the hierarchy is the headline of the Call to Action slide from Act I.

In the example presentation, your proposed Call to Action headline is to "Hire us to help you find the returns you seek," as shown in Figure 5-9.

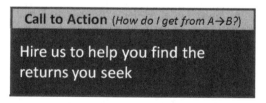

**FIGURE 5-9** The Call to Action cell from Act I with the headline completed.

Now that your audience knows your recommended Call to Action headline, they're eager to hear why and how it is a good idea, which is what you'll justify next. Focusing exclusively on explaining your Call to Action headline in Act II gives you the criteria you need to reduce the amount of information in your presentation. You'll include only information that supports your reasons for recommending the Call to Action headline and exclude everything else.

**See Also** As you work on Act II, refer to the completed story templates available at *www.beyondbulletpoints.com*. These templates include a range of Act II examples from different types of presentations.

## Justifying the Call to Action Headline with the Key Point Headlines

As you begin Act II, your first goal is to write the headlines for the most important slides you will present. If your audience will remember only three key points in your presentation, you need to know specifically where those corresponding slides are in your presentation and allow ample time to show and speak about them. In order to create these important slides, you will justify your Call to Action headline. You'll do this by boiling down to only three Key Point headlines the reasons why your audience should accept your recommended Call to Action or the main steps that describe how they should implement it. You will accomplish that by writing three headlines in the first column of Act II.

**See Also**  It's always a good idea to limit your ideas to groups of three, as described in "Tip 1: The Power of Three" later in this chapter. But if you need to expand your groupings to four, you can use the expanded template version that's described in "Tip 2: Make Room for Four."

To begin filling in Act II in the story template, position your cursor to the right of the Key Point column heading. If the Call to Action headline recommends your audience do something, they will want to know *why* they should do it. If your Call to Action headline recommends they follow a set of steps, they will want to know *how*. This is a critical decision-making point, because whether you choose *why* or *how* will shape every slide to follow in Act II. If you choose *why*, you are giving the entire presentation a persuasive orientation. If you choose *how*, you are giving the entire presentation an explanatory orientation. When the singular focus of the presentation is to persuade someone to do or think something, choose *why*. When the audience already has agreed to the idea and now your singular focus is to explain something, choose *how*. You can create a hybrid persuasive-explanatory presentation by choosing *how* for the first column and *why* for the others, or vice versa.

Choose the question that best describes what your audience will want to know next about your Call to Action headline, and type the question to the right of the Key Point column heading—in this case, **Why?**—as shown in Figure 5-10.

| **Act II:** Develop the action (*"1-2-3, show me only what I need to see"*) | | |
|---|---|---|
| **Key Point** (*5 minutes*): Why? | **Explanation** (*15 minutes*): | **Detail** (*45 minutes*): |

**FIGURE 5-10** The Key Point column indicates the question Why?

## THREE CRITICAL DECISION POINTS

The three critical decision points that have the biggest impact on your presentation are: identifying in Act I the gap between a challenge the audience faces in the Point A headline and where they want to be in the Point B headline, defining in Act I the Call to Action headline that focuses the entire presentation, and choosing in Act II *why* or *how* for your Key Point headlines, which determines whether the rest of your presentation will have a persuasive or an explanatory orientation.

Your Key Point column heading now indicates the question that your audience is wondering about your call to action—in this case, *"Why* should we hire you to help us find the returns we seek?"* You'll answer their question by explaining the three main reasons why they should approve the plan. Follow the three ground rules described in the section "Writing Headlines Using Three Ground Rules" in Chapter 3 to write out your headlines in each of the three medium gray cells of the Key Point column, prioritizing them in descending order of importance. Limit your headlines to a maximum of about two and a half lines, as shown in Figure 5-11.

**Act II**: Develop the action. *("1-2-3, show me only what I need to see")*

| Key Point (5 minutes): Why? | Explanation (15 minutes): | Detail (45 minutes): |
| --- | --- | --- |
| Our innovative three-part strategy is simple yet powerfully effective | | |
| Our experienced team will be like an extension of your staff | | |
| Our clients are so satisfied with their results, they never leave | | |

**FIGURE 5-11** Act II of the story template, with the Key Point column cells completed—note the parallel construction of the headlines across the cells.

Your first Key Point headline states that your "innovative three-part strategy is simple yet powerfully effective"; the second Key Point headline states that your "experienced team will be like an extension of your staff"; and your last Key Point headline states that your "clients are so satisfied with their results, they never leave." These three Key Point headlines are clear, concise, and literally to the point(s), giving your audience a sense of coherence and focus as you develop the details of the information to come. It will be relatively easy for working memory to hold on to these most meaningful visual and verbal pieces and integrate the information into long-term memory.

Your three Key Point headlines might come easily if you've been thinking about these issues for a long time and you can simply write them down. Or they might take some work because you're still figuring them out and you need to cluster together related ideas in a single main idea. If you're at a loss for words, try an interviewing technique by asking someone to read the Key Point column question out loud to you. Speak your answers out loud as you formulate them, and then type them in the Key Point column cells.

It is not always easy to boil down complexity to its essence, but it's critical that you do so to reduce the amount of information you present to the limited capacity of your audience's working memory. You simply cannot show and narrate 100 possibilities; rather the aim is to distill the information to the three most meaningful concepts. Finding the essence is about simplicity rather than simplification; it's about raising the cream of your critical thinking to the top, not the fluff. If you're still not sure of your answers, draft a placeholder set of Key Point headlines so that you have a place to start. You will want to spend ample time on writing the Key Point headlines because together with the Call to Action headline, they are the most important information you want your audience to remember and apply.

As you formulate your Key Point headlines, think of how they will read when you present them in their corresponding sequence of slides. After you create a slide from each of these headlines in Chapter 6, you will sketch initial ideas to illustrate each of these headlines, as shown in Figure 5-12. When you imagine your headlines visually as slides like this, you get a better sense of how they will relate to one another as you present them. The goal is to make these three Key Point headlines a neatly coordinated package that flows together from one idea to the next so that it will be easy to illustrate them when you get to your sketches later.

**FIGURE 5-12** Keep in mind how your Key Point headlines will become the foundation for a visual story you tell across the corresponding slides in the storyboard.

Tighten the relationship among these three Key Point headlines and increase their memorability by carrying your motif from Act I through their wording. Remember, a motif is about much more than being clever—it is about finding a familiar, long-term structure that will ease the introduction of new information to working memory. For example, if you use the puzzle motif in the Call to Action headline *Put the three pieces of the puzzle together to find the returns you seek*, place in front of each Key Point headline the corresponding phrase: *Puzzle Piece 1*, *Puzzle Piece 2*, and *Puzzle Piece 3*. You could use a puzzle motif in two different ways, with the puzzle pieces of the three points either revealing or concealing the final picture.

There are endless ways to lay out the top-level story thread across your Key Point headlines. Whatever you decide depends on what you carry through from the Call to Action headline in Act I. For example, extend a chronology across your Key Point headlines based on the Call to Action headline *Follow the story through the three crucial time periods*, or use a simple list format based on the Call to Action headline *Check off the three items* or *Follow the three parts*. Heighten engagement and suspense through the three Key Point headlines by withholding what will happen, as in *Uncover the three secrets* or *Follow the three clues*—allowing the audience to get involved and fill in the blanks for themselves. As described in Chapter 1, a trial lawyer might tap into a familiar story structure by following a formula such as *Motive + means = death* or one of its variations such as *Denial + deception = injury*. For inspiration on motifs, review the phrases you can use to begin your Call to Action headlines in Appendix D and consider how you could carry the same themes through the language of the Key Point headlines.

Whichever way you decide to go with your motif, make sure you integrate it through the wording of the Call to Action and the Key Point headlines because later you will apply a similar visual design related to the motif to the corresponding slides. Although it is suf-ficient to integrate a motif only through a set of Call to Action and Key Point headlines, if you can extend it later through the words of the rest of your Act II headlines, it will be that much more powerful. Don't stretch a motif beyond its sensible limits, though—

remember from Chapter 4 that a motif has to resonate with you audience, and if it starts to sound trite or overused, it will hurt your message rather than help it.

When you've entered your three headlines in the Key Point column, test them by filling in the blanks in this sentence:

> The three main reasons/ways *(insert audience from Act I)* should *(insert Call to Action headline)* are: *(insert Key Point headline 1)*; *(insert Key Point headline 2)*; and *(insert Key Point headline 3)*.

In this presentation example, the completed sentence reads:

> The three main reasons you (the executives) should hire us to help you find the returns you seek are: our innovative three-part strategy is simple yet powerfully effective, our experienced team will be like an extension of your staff, and our clients are so satisfied with their results, they never leave.

## THE KEY POINT HEADLINES TEST

Test the three Key Point headlines by filling in the blanks in this sentence:

The three main reasons/ways *(insert audience from Act I)* should *(insert Call to Action headline)* are: *(insert Key Point headline 1)*; *(insert Key Point headline 2)*; and *(insert Key Point headline 3)*.

For this sentence to sound right, each Key Point headline should be written in a similar form and should contain a similar type of information. Just as the Key Point headlines explain the Call to Action headline, the Call to Action headline should also summarize the Key Point headlines.

Your Call to Action and Key Point headlines should neatly distill to the essence what you want to communicate in your presentation and define your measure of success—if your audience can remember and apply these points, you've succeeded in your presentation mission. If your measure for success is not present in the wording of your Call to Action and Key Point headlines, you need to go back and change the wording so that the core of your message is clear and visible without a doubt.

As you test your three Key Point headlines, you might find that the Call to Action headline isn't exactly what you intended and you need to go back and revise it or entirely rework Act I. Or you might need to revise your three Key Point headlines to make sure that each supports the Call to Action headline in a way that makes your test sentence sound right. You'll probably need to do a couple of rounds of testing and revising before you're satisfied with your results and are ready to move on to the next step.

When you have written your three Key Point headlines, you have made sure that you will justify the Call to Action slide with the Key Point slides that follow it. Your Call to Action and Key Point headlines form the most important information at the top level of the hierarchy, as shown in Figure 5-13, which defines the most important and meaningful information that you want your audience's working memory to engage and integrate into long-term memory.

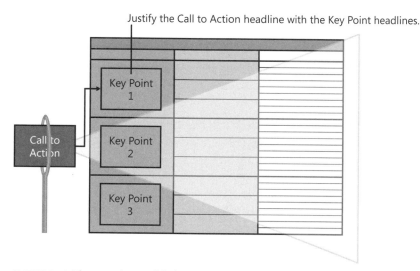

**FIGURE 5-13** The top of your slide hierarchy consists of your most important slides—the Call to Action slide and the three Key Point slides. In a sentence outline, the Call to Action slide corresponds to the thesis statement and the Key Point slides correspond to outline items 1, 2, and 3.

## Clarifying Each Key Point Headline with Its Explanation Headlines

Now that you've written the headlines for the Key Point slides, the next step is to write the headlines for the second-most important slides—the Explanation slides. Each Act II *scene* in your story template is represented by a horizontal row of cells that begins with each Key Point cell and extends to the right to include all of the adjacent cells in the Explanation and Detail columns, as shown in Figure 5-14.

**FIGURE 5-14** Act II, Scene 1, extends horizontally from left to right in the story template.

As in this example, the headline in the single Key Point cell anchors each Act II scene by maintaining a singular focus horizontally across all three columns. The Explanation and Detail columns will flesh out the main idea in increasing depth as you enter the headlines of your scene from left to right, top to bottom. This keeps all the pieces of information related to the single Key Point headline organized and coherent.

To start writing the rest of Act II, Scene 1, position your cursor to the right of the Explanation column heading and type the question (either *why* or *how*) that your audience will want to know next about your three Key Points headlines—in this case, **How?** Reread your Key Point headline, and ask yourself *how* this is true—in this case, "*How* is your innovative three-part strategy simple yet powerfully effective?" As you did in the Key Point column, type your three answers in descending order of importance in the three cells of the Explanation column. When you enter your first reason in the top cell of the Explanation column, your story template should look similar to Figure 5-15.

**FIGURE 5-15** Act II, Scene 1, with the top cell of the Explanation column completed.

Enter your second answer in the cell below, and enter the third answer in the cell below that, as shown in Figure 5-16. Your Explanation column answers should offer more detailed support for your Key Point headline and cite specific evidence such as findings from research, case studies, financial analysis, or anecdotes.

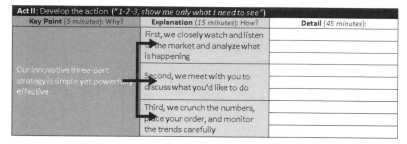

**FIGURE 5-16** Testing the three headlines in the Explanation column to make sure that they support the Key Point to the left.

Test the three answers in the Explanation column by filling in the blanks in this sentence:

> The three main reasons/ways *(insert Key Point headline)* are: *(insert Explanation column, answer 1)*; *(insert Explanation column, answer 2)*; and *(insert Explanation column, answer 3)*.

In this example, the test sentence reads:

> The three main ways our three-part strategy is simple yet powerfully effective are: first, we closely watch and listen to the market and analyze what is happening; second, we meet with you to discuss what you'd like to do; and third, we crunch the numbers, place your order, and monitor the trends carefully.

As in your earlier test sentence, for this sentence to sound right, each answer should be written in a similar way and should contain a similar type of information. You can apply this test visually by reading the test sentence from the left column to the right. You should also test the headlines the other way, from the right column to the left—after you read your three Explanation column headlines, you should find that the Key Point headline summarizes them.

Just as you thought of the Key Point headlines as a tightly related package of thoughts that you will show over a sequence of slides, think of the Explanation headlines the same way. The headlines from the three Explanation column cells in Figure 5-16 will form the headlines for the corresponding Explanation slides in the storyboard, and the sketches in Figure 5-17 show how the sequence of ideas in this example is the foundation for a three-part visual story.

**FIGURE 5-17** Keep in mind how your Explanation headlines will become the foundation for a visual story you tell across the corresponding slides in the storyboard.

Breaking up the explanation of each Key Point headline into smaller pieces that you will show and narrate reduces cognitive load across a sequence of slides. This aligns with the research-based *temporal contiguity principle*, which explains that people learn better when animation and narration are presented simultaneously. For example, if you were to show an entire diagram first and then the narration later, you would split the attention of your audience as their working memory struggles to coordinate what it sees and what it hears. The story template ensures that you break up every explanation into digestible pieces, so you end up tightly coordinating what you say and what you show, one idea at a time.

You can organize your ideas within the cells of the Explanation column in any number of ways, such as the "checklist" structure in the preceding example, a chronology, a list, a 1-2-3 sequence, or any other way you might explain an idea in three parts.

## THE EXPLANATION HEADLINES TEST

Test the three Explanation headlines by filling in the blanks in this sentence:

The three main reasons/ways *(insert Key Point headline)* are: *(insert Explanation column, answer 1)*; *(insert Explanation column, answer 2)*; and *(insert Explanation column, answer 3)*.

When you have written your Explanation headlines, you have made sure that you will clarify each Key Point slide with the Explanation slides that follow it. The Explanation slides form the middle of the slide hierarchy, as shown in Figure 5-18, which presents the second-most important informational pieces to working memory—the sub-parts of your Key Point headlines.

Clarify each Key Point headline with its Explanation headlines.

**FIGURE 5-18** The middle of your slide hierarchy consists of your second-most important slides—the Explanation slides. In an indented sentence outline, these slides correspond to outline items 1.a.,1.b., and 1.c.

## Backing Up Each Explanation Headline with Its Detail Headlines

Now that you've written the headlines for your Key Point and Explanation slides, the last step is to back up each Explanation headline by writing headlines for its Detail slides. Fill in the Detail column using the same techniques you used for the Explanation column. Position your cursor to the right of the Detail column heading, and type the question (*why* or *how*) your audience will want to know next about your Explanation headlines—in this case, **How?** The questions you choose for your column headings will vary according to your topic, and sometimes they might be all *why*, all *how*, or combinations of the two. Now read each headline in the Explanation column, and ask why or how that headline is true. In this example, you'll be asking the question *how*, as in: "*How* do you closely watch and listen to the market and analyze what is happening?"

As you did in the Key Point and Explanation columns, type your three answers in the three cells of the Detail column in descending order of importance—the cells will expand to hold your text. Keep your headlines limited to about two and a half lines, as you did in the other two columns. The answers you enter in the Detail column should offer more detailed support for the Explanation headline and cite specific evidence that backs it up, as shown in Figure 5-19. This is where you include quantitative information, case studies, charts, graphs, anecdotes, analysis, and any other details that support the Explanation headline in the column to the left.

| Act II: Develop the action *("1-2-3, show me only what I need to see")* | | |
| Key Point (*5 minutes*): Why? | Explanation (*15 minutes*): How? | Detail (*45 minutes*): How? |
| Our innovative three-part strategy is simple yet powerfully effective | First, we closely watch and listen to the market and analyze what is happening | Our technical team takes data feeds from every international market |
| | | We run the numbers through the Jesper Aaberg model of analysis |
| | | We post hourly, daily, weekly, monthly, and yearly analyses in your Account area |
| | Second, we meet with you to discuss what you'd like to do | |
| | Third, we crunch the numbers, place your order, and monitor the trends carefully | |

**FIGURE 5-19** Testing the three Detail headlines to make sure they back up the Explanation headline to the left.

As with the Key Point and Explanation headlines, think of the way you will end up presenting these headlines visually in a sequence of slides, as shown in Figure 5-20. As before, you are breaking up the previous column's headline into smaller pieces that you will present visually and verbally across slides. Whatever specific wording you choose for each Detail headline, you will back it up by the appropriate type of visual evidence, whether it is a screen capture, chart, graph, photograph, diagram, or other illustration. And just as you did in the previous columns, you can organize your headlines in a wide range of formats, including chronological, before-and-after results, 1-2-3 lists, and more.

**FIGURE 5-20** Keep in mind how your Detail headlines will become the foundation for a visual story you tell across the corresponding slides in the storyboard.

After you've entered three answers in the Detail column, test them by filling in the blanks in this sentence:

> The three main reasons/ways *(insert Explanation column headline)* are: *(insert Detail column, answer 1)*; *(insert Detail column, answer 2)*; and *(insert Detail column, answer 3)*.

In this example, the test headline would read:

> The three main ways we closely watch and listen to the market and analyze what is happening are: our technical team takes data feeds from every international market; we run the numbers through the Jesper Aaberg model of analysis; and we post hourly, weekly, monthly, and yearly analyses in your Account area.

After you test your Detail column answers, go to the second Explanation headline and repeat this process for its corresponding Detail headlines. Then go to the third Explanation headline and repeat the process for its Detail headlines. When you've finished, you will have completed Act II, Scene 1, of your story template, as shown in Figure 5-21.

| **Act II:** Develop the action *("1-2-3, show me only what I need to see")* | | |
|---|---|---|
| **Key Point** *(5 minutes):* Why? | **Explanation** *(15 minutes):* How? | **Detail** *(45 minutes):* How? |
| Our innovative three-part strategy is simple yet powerfully effective | First, we closely watch and listen to the market and analyze what is happening | Our technical team takes data feeds from every international market |
| | | We run the numbers through the Jesper Aaberg model of analysis |
| | | We post hourly, daily, weekly, monthly, and yearly analyses in your Account area |
| | Second, we meet with you to discuss what you'd like to do | For a similar company, Fabrikam, Inc., we set up an initial meeting and three follow-ups |
| | | We spent a half day at their offices to interview them and their staff about their goals |
| | | We used Trey Research software to produce a thorough report of Fabrikam's goals |
| | Third, we crunch the numbers, place your order, and monitor the trends carefully | We allocated Fabrikam's investment according to careful analysis |
| | | We post returns instantly in their secure online Account area |
| | | We constantly monitor the trends and fine-tune the investment as needed |

**FIGURE 5-21** Act II, Scene 1, of the sample story template, with all cells completed.

## THE DETAIL HEADLINES TEST

Test the three Detail headlines by filling in the blanks in this sentence:

> The three main reasons/ways *(insert Explanation headline)* are: *(insert Detail column, answer 1)*; *(insert Detail column, answer 2)*; and *(insert Detail column, answer 3)*.

As always, it is helpful to think of how your headlines will play out across the slides of your storyboard. In Figure 5-22, the Detail headlines tell the story of the second Explanation headline in the form of an anecdote told chronologically across the three slides.

**FIGURE 5-22** Sketches showing how the Detail headlines tell a chronological story.

In Figure 5-23, the Detail headlines play out differently, as sketches of charts and screen captures explain the third Explanation headline with a step-by-step sequence of details across the slides.

**FIGURE 5-23** Sketches showing how the Detail headlines relate quantitative information across slides.

When you have written your Detail headlines, you have made sure that you will back up each Explanation slide with the Detail slides that follow it. This is the bottom of the hierarchy, as shown in Figure 5-24, which presents the third-most important informational pieces to working memory—the sub-parts of your Explanation headlines.

Now that you've finished writing the headlines for Act II, Scene 1, it's time to move on to Scenes 2 and 3.

Break up each Explanation headline with its Detail headlines.

**FIGURE 5-24** The bottom of your hierarchy consists of your third-most important slides—the Detail slides. In a classical indented outline, these slides correspond to outline items 1.a.i., 1.b.ii., 1.c.ii., and so on.

## Fleshing Out the Rest of Act II

With Act II, Scene 1, complete, your final job is to write the headlines for the rest of the slides in Act II. You'll do this by applying the same process to both Scene 2 and Scene 3. Continue to check your reasoning with test sentences at each level, and revise your story template headlines as needed to keep the test sentences clear and consistent.

Act II of the story template is structured using groups of three ideas to make your ideas easier for your audience to understand, but you might find that you don't have exactly three supporting headlines to write at any level in the template. If you want to use only two headlines, simply leave the third cell blank. If you need to add a fourth cell to the Explanation or Detail column, position the cursor in a cell, right-click, and select Insert Row—if the extra row creates extra cells in the Key Point and Explanation columns, merge the new cells into adjacent cells within the column. If you need to create four Key Point headlines, see "Tip 2: Make Room for Four," later in this chapter. If you have more than four Key Point headlines, you'll need to find a way to reduce that number, either by reworking your ideas or by merging several ideas into one main headline.

If you are having difficulty completing any point of the story template, try tackling it from a different direction. This chapter followed a process of completing Act II working from the top of the hierarchy to the bottom, which you may choose to do if you know your topic well. If you're not completely sure of your message or your Key Point headlines, by all means start first from the Detail column on the right, and work left through the Explanation column and finally the Key Point column.

When you complete the three scenes of Act II, your story template will likely extend across more than one page. In the completed Act II section of this story template, shown in Figure 5-25, the Detail column headlines have been abbreviated so that you can see the three scenes on a single page.

| **Act II:** Develop the action  ("*1-2-3, show me only what I need to see*") | | |
|---|---|---|
| **Key Point** (*5 minutes*): Why? | **Explanation** (*15 minutes*): How? | **Detail** (*45 minutes*): How? |
| Our innovative three-part strategy is simple yet powerfully effective | First, we closely watch and listen to the market and analyze what is happening | Our technical team takes data... |
| | | We run the numbers through... |
| | | We post hourly, daily, weekly... |
| | Second, we meet with you to discuss what you'd like to do | For a similar company, Fabrikam. |
| | | We spent a half-day at their... |
| | | We used Trey Research software |
| | Third, we crunch the numbers, place your order, and monitor the trends carefully | We allocated Fabrikam's... |
| | | We post returns instantly in... |
| | | We constantly monitor the... |
| Our experienced team will be like an extension of your staff | Our senior team combined has experience in every major investment firm | Our CEO Nancy Anderson leads... |
| | | Michael Allen is one of several... |
| | | You may know Ezio Albani from... |
| | Your account team, led by Chris Gray, is always on call and only a text message away | Chris has a background in... |
| | | His quick response team will... |
| | | Our average response time is.... |
| | We tailor our communications according to your style – from daily updates to annual reviews | We find executives vary in their... |
| | | When we discuss your style, we.. |
| | | Our capabilities range from.... |
| Our clients are so satisfied with their results, they never leave | We've taken on 125 clients since we opened five years ago, and no one has left | We started out with five clients... |
| | | Today we have 150, including... |
| | | No one has left for another..... |
| | Our customer satisfaction rating has never dropped below 100% | We ask our clients to complete... |
| | | Our response rate is 100%, and... |
| | | Our ratings have never dropped.. |
| | Every one of our clients has agreed to take your call if you would like to talk with them | All of our clients have agreed to.. |
| | | We can set up a call or a.... |
| | | You can choose a private venue... |

**FIGURE 5-25** Act II of the sample story template, with all three scenes completed.

Each idea you introduce in the presentation will prompt your audience to wonder, "*Why* or *how* is this true?" Because each column in your story template is set up to answer the question *why* or *how*, you can provide immediate answers. In story terms, this creates a steady dynamic of action/reaction—one column is an "action," and the next column is a "reaction" to it. This dynamic structure in Act II helps you to examine all of the possible directions for your story. It also helps you to align your information with the way people naturally think and reason, making your story more interesting and engaging.

## AN INTELLECTUAL MACHETE

Just as much as you need to identify what you want to include in a presentation, the hierarchy in Act II is equally important for the *potential* slides it leaves out of a presentation. With the limited capacity of your audience's working memory, you cannot present everything you know—instead, you present only the information your audience needs to know. The built-in hierarchy of Act II guides you through a sometimes difficult but disciplined critical-thinking process that forces you to decide what to include in a presentation and what to leave out. The process of completing Act II acts like an intellectual machete that chops away unneeded data so that clarity shines through. It also helps you create and arrange your slides in both sequence and priority to ensure that you properly manage your ideas as they pass through the eye of the needle of the working memory of your audience.

You will find that there is a great deal of information that did not make it into your presentation. If you're missing something important, go back and include it in your headlines. What does not make it into the hierarchy, such as detailed quantitative analysis, can be captured and documented and can then be handed out at the start of the presentation.

When you have written the rest of your Act II headlines, you have made sure that you have fleshed out the rest of the slides of your presentation. Now every slide in your presentation will be prioritized in your slide hierarchy, as shown in Figure 5-26.

Flesh out the rest of the headlines in Act II.

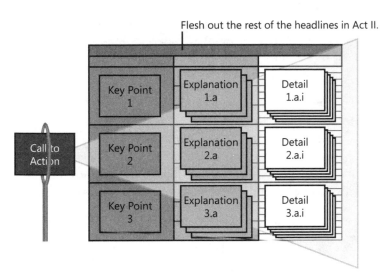

**FIGURE 5-26** You determine the rest of your slide hierarchy when you flesh out the rest of your slides in Act II, and in the process you have prioritized every slide.

Don't worry about Act III of your story template at this point—you'll quickly take care of that soon when you add graphics to the storyboard in Chapter 8.

## BBP CHECKLIST: PLANNING THE REST OF YOUR SLIDES

Do the rest of your headlines in Act II:

❏ Justify your Call to Action headline with your key points?

❏ Clarify your Key Point headlines with further explanation?

❏ Back up your Explanation headlines with the appropriate detail?

❏ Put your ideas in a logical sequence and priority?

❏ Integrate your motif verbally through your headlines?

# Pulling Through What's Most Important First

Now that you've completed the story template, you have accomplished what you set out to do at the start of the chapter—that is, prioritizing your ideas and finding the right sequence in which to present them. The three columns of Act II established the priority of your ideas from Key Point headlines at the top of the informational hierarchy, to

Explanation headlines in the middle, to Detail headlines at the bottom. The process of creating Act II helps you write out information in complete thoughts, rather than lists and fragments that the audience has to sort through. Now there is a clear flow that connects each idea to the next in a logical way.

When you import your headlines into PowerPoint to become your storyboard next in Chapter 6, your slides will automatically appear in the same order you wrote them in Act II, as shown in Figure 5-27. In your storyboard, you will cue the audience to the levels of the hierarchy with the slide layouts and backgrounds as you present each idea in the sequence you wrote them. This is an important innovation of the BBP approach that has both prioritized your ideas with a hierarchy and prepared them for a logical sequence in your storyboard.

**FIGURE 5-27** The hierarchy provides both a priority for your slides and a proper sequence in which to show them.

Writing your slide headlines using the Act II columns has now given your presentation an important scalability that will play out when you work in PowerPoint. When you create a presentation with three columns, you are prioritizing your ideas in order of importance, from left to right. If you have a 45-minute presentation, you'll present all of your slides in Act II. If your time is unexpectedly cut to 15 minutes, you'll skip the Detail slides, and if your time is cut to 5 minutes, you'll also skip the Explanation slides. Because you have applied the power of a hierarchy to prioritize your ideas, you can scale up or down to the level of information appropriate to the time you have, without sacrificing the integrity or the clarity of your thinking at any level.

But perhaps most important, what you've done in Act II reduces cognitive load by easing working memory into new information by presenting what is most significant first. Typical PowerPoint presentation outlines present the details first, then the explanation of the details, and finally the key points—the recommendations or conclusions—at the end. Or other presentations simply display lists of detail without any explanation or key points at all to provide context or a framework for understanding the detail. Either way, this approach tries to jam the wide bottom of the hierarchy through the eye of the needle, as shown in Figure 5-28. If you present all the details first, the working memory of your audience has to struggle to retain that information until it knows where your presentation is going.

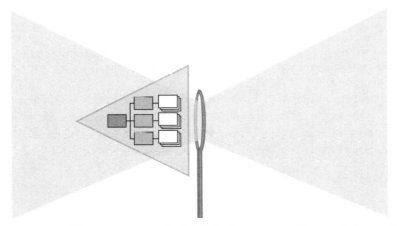

**FIGURE 5-28** When you present the details first, you can quickly overwhelm working memory.

Act II of your story template flips the typical outline around, presenting the most important information first and the supporting information after. You set up the focus with the Call to Action slide and follow it with the Key Point slides. The same technique works within the Act II scenes: you present a Key Point slide before presenting the supporting Explanation slides, and then for each Explanation slide, you present supporting Detail slides. This process ensures that the Detail slides are subordinate to the more important slides that come before them.

By presenting the tip, and the top, of the hierarchy first, you reduce the cognitive load on your audience by focusing first on what's essential and leaving out extraneous information that could clog the eye of the needle. When you summarize what you are going to say first, you make it easier for the working memory of your audience to understand what is coming, setting the context for all the details to follow. With BBP, you always pull through the eye of the needle what's most important first, as shown in Figure 5-29.

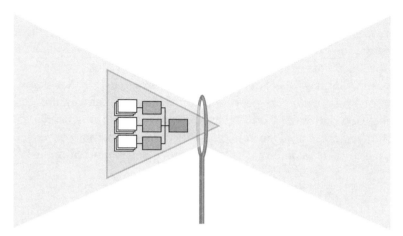

**FIGURE 5-29** When you present the most important information first, you properly manage working memory and provide a framework for the rest of the explanation and details to come.

When you use BBP to invert your usual way of thinking and present your conclusion first and supporting details later, people will more easily remember and understand what you say. Now, instead of the details and data driving the presentation, the proper management of the working memory of your audience is driving the presentation, which aligns with the three research realities described in Chapter 2.

## Lowering the Curtain on Your Story Template

The most obvious benefit of your story template is that you can now see all of your ideas in one place and quickly grasp how each idea relates to the others. A printout of your story template at this point will guide you through an initial reading of your story to make sure that everything sounds right.

Review your story template before you print it. If it extends over multiple pages, you might need to split Act II into separate scenes that each fit on a page. To do this, position the cursor in any cell in a Key Point column, and on the Table Tools tab, click Layout; and then in the Merge group, click Split Table to split that row from the row above. If you change your mind, click the Undo button on the Quick Access Toolbar.

As this book describes, the story template is the hard-working intellectual and structural engine that makes everything in your PowerPoint presentation work, or not. It is the battleground that determines whether your presentation is a success or failure. If you have an elegant infrastructure, the more time you spend on the presentation, the simpler it will get. If you don't have a solid structure, the more time you spend on it, the more confusing it will get. If you get the headlines right, they will clarify and expand understanding; but if you get them wrong, you will lead your audience in the wrong direction, in a fruitless, frustrating waste of time. That's why it's important to spend as much time as you can editing, tightening, and clarifying your words.

Just as you can use your story template to see and manage all of your headlines at a glance, other people can use it to review your story too. If you're working with only a few people, display the story template on your computer screen and make edits together. If you're working with a larger group and want to call a meeting to review your headlines, send a copy of the story template Word document through e-mail to all of the members of the team in advance.

> **IMPORTANT** Don't move forward from this stage of the process until you finalize your story template and get agreement from everyone who has a stake in your presentation.

Now it's absolutely essential that you get agreement on the story template from anyone who has a stake in the presentation. This includes the members of your team, people in other departments of your organization, and anyone who needs to give clearance and approval for what you'll say.

Using your story template as a review document, you can easily make quick adjustments to your wording or structure and invite others to contribute their expertise and take ownership in the success of your presentation. Getting approval for your story template allows everyone to focus on your ideas instead of on design issues, which would prove distracting right now. When you get final approval of the structure and sequence of your story up front, you'll reduce the likelihood that you'll need to spend unnecessary time and effort later, after you've invested time in the design process.

When you meet with others in person, either project the story template on the wall or print copies of your story template and bring them to the meeting. Talk through the ideas in the order in which you rehearsed them, and discuss the options you have to scale down the story if your presentation time is reduced from 45 minutes to 15 or 5.

You accomplish a number of sophisticated things with your completed story template. You find focus with a classical story structure. You appeal to emotion and reason. You create dramatic conflict, which will keep your audience interested. You select and organize your ideas in a priority and a sequence that helps people to pay attention to and remember the information you're providing.

Before you move on to the next major step in the BBP approach—storyboarding your script—read through the following 10 tips to find ideas that might improve your story template.

# 10 Tips for Enhancing Your Story Template

With your story template in hand, you can rest assured that you have a focused tale to tell at your next presentation. When you're comfortable with the basics of completing your template, try improvising on the concept using these 10 tips.

## Tip 1: The Power of Three

As much as you might want to load up your PowerPoint slides with data, the quantity of new information that people can understand is always constrained by the limitations of working memory. As mentioned in Chapter 2, you help your audience to understand information better by presenting new information to working memory in groups of three.

Your story template helps you to organize your ideas in groups of three in multiple ways. The essence of your story consists of your Call to Action headline and your three Key Point headlines. Each Key Point headline has three supporting headlines, listed in the Explanation column. Each Explanation headline has three supporting headlines as well, listed in the Detail column. It might be challenging to boil down your headlines to groups of three in this structure, but your hard work will pay off: your audience will more easily absorb, remember, and understand your ideas.

## Tip 2: Make Room for Four

Although three is a powerful number, you might find while working in Act II of your story template that you have four points to make in a column. As described earlier in this chapter, if you have fewer points to make in any section than you have cells, you can simply leave the cells blank; if you want to add another cell, you insert one. If you'd like to try other versions of story templates with four columns across, or four rows per Act II scene, visit *www.beyondbulletpoints.com*. The disadvantage of using a template with four levels of information is that the number of cells might significantly increase the size and complexity of your presentation. Keep in mind that the more headlines you have, the more time you need and the more information people need to process. To avoid long and complicated presentations, try to stick to three points rather than four.

## Tip 3: Tailor Your Act II Column Headings to Your Profession

The headings of the three columns of Act II are based on the most common categorization of information in a hierarchy. But there are many other ways to look at these columns—if one of the alternatives shown in the following list works better for you in your profession, simply type over the existing headings in your story template to replace them with new headings.

The most common categories for the three columns are Key Point, Explanation, and Detail:

**Act II:** Develop the action (*"1-2-3, show me only what I need to see"*)

| Key Point (*5 minutes*): | Explanation (*15 minutes*): | Detail (*45 minutes*): |
|---|---|---|

If you're a market researcher, your column headings might be Recommendation, Explanation, and Methodology/Data:

**Act II:** Develop the action (*"1-2-3, show me only what I need to see"*)

| Recommendation (*5 minutes*): | Explanation (*15 minutes*): | Methodology/Data(*45 minutes*): |
|---|---|---|

If you're a lawyer, your column headings might be Case Theme, Explanation, and Evidence:

**Act II:** Develop the action (*"1-2-3, show me only what I need to see"*)

| Case Theme (*5 minutes*): | Explanation (*15 minutes*): | Evidence (*45 minutes*): |
|---|---|---|

If you're an analyst, your column headings might be Conclusion, Analysis, and Fact:

**Act II:** Develop the action (*"1-2-3, show me only what I need to see"*)

| Conclusion (*5 minutes*): | Analysis (*15 minutes*): | Fact (*45 minutes*): |
|---|---|---|

If you're an executive, your column headings might be Summary, Breakdown, and Backup:

**Act II:** Develop the action (*"1-2-3, show me only what I need to see"*)

| Summary (*5 minutes*): | Breakdown (*15 minutes*): | Backup (*45 minutes*): |
|---|---|---|

If you're a salesperson, your column headings might be Benefit, Feature, and Demonstration:

**Act II:** Develop the action (*"1-2-3, show me only what I need to see"*)

| Benefit (*5 minutes*): | Feature (*15 minutes*): | Demonstration (*45 minutes*): |
|---|---|---|

If you're a writer, your column headings might be Act, Scene, and Action:

| **Act II**: Develop the action (*"1-2-3, show me only what I need to see"*) | | |
|---|---|---|
| **Act** (*5 minutes*): | **Scene** (*15 minutes*): | **Action** (*45 minutes*): |

If you're a journalist, your column headings might be Lead, Body, and Detail:

| **Act II**: Develop the action (*"1-2-3, show me only what I need to see"*) | | |
|---|---|---|
| **Lead** (*5 minutes*): | **Body** (*15 minutes*): | **Detail** (*45 minutes*): |

If you're a teacher or an instructor, your column headings might be Lesson, Explanation, and Detail:

| **Act II**: Develop the action (*"1-2-3, show me only what I need to see"*) | | |
|---|---|---|
| **Lesson** (*5 minutes*): | **Explanation** (*15 minutes*): | **Detail** (*45 minutes*): |

# Tip 4: Story Templates for Teams

Act II works well for teams and organizations that have multiple points they might have to make to different audiences. For example, most groups have a finite set of Key Point headlines they might want to write about a topic, so someone in the group can create additional Act II scenes to cover those. When you are ready to present, you present only the scenes you choose and hide the rest. This can also be done with Act I variations as you create a range of story template "shells" from frequently used story structures.

# Tip 5: The Story Nugget

A *story nugget* is a telling detail that encapsulates, distills, and frames the entire story—for example, the detail of a $6,000 shower curtain represented to most people the excess of company executives found guilty of taking money from a large, international corporation as reported in the news. You can place a story nugget in one of the headlines in Act I as an encapsulation of the whole story, or you can place it as a detail in a strategic place in the Detail column. Be careful with your story nuggets—if the information is truly important and you want to be sure it's remembered and applied, integrate it into the Key Point headlines. If your points are already clear, place the story nuggets somewhere in your presentation for your audience to discover and remember.

# Tip 6: BBP Beyond PowerPoint

When you're at a loss for words or are bogged down or frustrated with writing or communicating, open up a story template. The reliability and simplicity of the structure can break an intellectual or creative logjam by providing clarity and focus. People have reported using the BBP story template for a wide range of purposes beyond PowerPoint presentations, including to structure e-mail messages, curriculum design, radio spots, ads, and classroom outlines. Give it a try, and see what clarity it can help you uncover beyond PowerPoint.

## Tip 7: Build an Outline in a Brainstorm

Your Act II headlines have to come from somewhere. If they don't flow easily from your imagination, you might need to loosen things up with a little brainstorming. A number of excellent books and online resources such as *www.innovationtools.com* are available to help you to brainstorm new ideas either on your own or with your team. Whatever technique you decide to use, you need to understand the relationship between the fruit of your brainstorming labor and the story template process you undertake in Act II.

*Brainstorming* is the art of generating ideas for a particular purpose; it supports an environment of free-flowing thinking without constraints. *Presentation development* is the art of selecting and prioritizing ideas; it calls on a different set of skills, including critical thinking, selection, prioritization, and reasoning.

When you've finished your brainstorming exercises, the story template helps you to select the ideas that best support the focus of your presentation. As you begin to work on Act II, gather all of the brainstorming ideas you might have on hand, whether they're in the form of lists, note cards, whiteboard diagrams, or other formats. Then apply the process of writing your Act II headlines described in this chapter.

At times, you might need to switch back into a brainstorming mode when you're stuck on a headline or if your Act II structure isn't working. But when you've generated fresh ideas, it's time to switch back into story template mode so that you can select appropriate ideas that support the focus of your presentation.

Brainstorming and using the story template are different but complementary techniques, and when you alternate the two, you can have the best of both worlds—the correct selection of the freshest ideas that support your singular story.

## Tip 8: Tap Your Team's Talents

Consider working with your team to structure your ideas in Act II. By connecting a projector to your computer, you can display a number of software tools that allow you to work with your team to develop your Act II headlines. Or you can build your own tables or logic trees using Microsoft Office Visio® 2007, Microsoft Office OneNote® 2007, or PowerPoint 2007's organization chart feature.

If you don't have a projector or you prefer a hands-on approach, use a sheet of paper, a flip chart, or a whiteboard to draw your logic tree. Or write your draft Act II headlines on sticky notes and affix them to a wall to build a logic tree, as described in David Straker's *Rapid Problem Solving with Post-it Notes* (Fisher Books, 1997). Experiment with a range of techniques and tools until you find what works best for you and your team to focus and prioritize your ideas. When you've finished, return to your Word document and enter your headlines in the story template.

Some people think clearly and quickly at the top level, others at the detail level. If you're caught up in the detail, step back and ask a top-level thinker/organizer to help.

When it comes to creating the story template, you'll probably find that tapping into the talents of your team will build the best presentation possible.

## Tip 9: Take the Express Elevator

When entrepreneurs begin to approach investors to raise money for a venture, they're expected to have something called an *elevator pitch*. The idea is that they pitch their company within the length of time of an elevator ride. Even if you're not trying to raise money for your company, you might need to give your own version of an elevator pitch if you get a call from your boss before you give your presentation and she says, "I'm sorry, but I can't make it to your presentation—can you tell me quickly what you're going to say?"

In every case, you'll be clear about what you're going to say after you complete your story template. To respond to your boss, give your own elevator pitch by first summarizing your Act I headlines and then describing each of your Key Point headlines in Act II of your story template. This sets the context for the presentation and covers the high-level points. If your boss is interested in knowing more about any particular point, you can elaborate more as needed by providing more supporting information from the Explanation and Detail columns.

This handy technique is not just for elevator pitches and verbal summaries. If you have to write the marketing description for your talk, you've got the outline already written in the story template in the form of your Act I and Act II Key Point column headlines. If you want to let other people know the structure of your talk in advance, you can summarize it in the same way in an e-mail message. In all of these situations, your story template can keep you speeding along with effective communication.

## Tip 10: The Hierarchy in Your Mind

There are many reasons why the ancient concept of hierarchy still holds such power today. Some researchers believe that the mind uses hierarchical structures to store information in and retrieve information from long-term memory. For example, the idea of *chunking* is based on the idea that long-term memory applies a higher category to smaller pieces in working memory to bring them together and make them easier to handle. Some experts believe that a part of the brain called the neocortex retrieves information in a hierarchical way. And certainly the organizational technique of hierarchy is fully a part of most outlining systems, as well as many computer languages. When you write your Act II headlines, you tap into hierarchical power by bringing the structure itself from long-term memory and applying it to the organization of your slides, as shown in Figure 5-30. A hierarchy turns out to be a deep and memorable way to help you and your audiences get right to the heart of the matter.

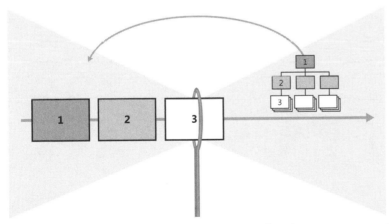

**FIGURE 5-30** Applying a familiar hierarchical structure from long-term memory to your slides helps make them easier to prioritize and put in a proper sequence.

CHAPTER 6

# Setting Up Your Storyboard and Narration

**IN THIS CHAPTER, YOU WILL:**

- Transform your script into a storyboard with preliminary backgrounds.

- Write out the words you'll speak during the presentation.

- Review the three ground rules for storyboarding.

**WHEN YOU** complete the Beyond Bullet Points (BBP) Story Template, you have in hand a complete and coherent story that sets the foundation for all of your slides. Your story is so clear that even if your technology fails during your presentation, you have the security of knowing that you can present using only a printout of the story template as your guide. But of course you'll want to use graphics in your Microsoft® Office PowerPoint® 2007 presentation, because research indicates that people learn better when you add graphics to your narration in a multimedia presentation.

In Chapter 4, you used a story thread to prepare new information for the eye of the needle of your audience's working memory, and in Chapter 5, you used the sharp tip of a triangle of hierarchy to determine the sequence and order of information along that thread. Now in this chapter you will focus on the two strands of that story thread. These two strands represent the two essential elements that you have to coordinate in any multimedia presentation—the visual and verbal channels, as described in Chapter 2.

You'll learn how to guide the visual and verbal strands over the next three chapters. Your challenge in this chapter is to set up your PowerPoint presentation in specific ways to guide these two strands through the entire presentation so that you don't split the attention of the audience or create wasteful redundancy. In Chapter 7, you'll explore the wide range of options you have to plan and sketch the graphics for your storyboard; in Chapter 8, you'll add the final graphics based on the sketches you choose; and in Chapter 9, you'll see the BBP approach applied to a range of different types of presentations that you can refer to for inspiration. You can expect that it will take some time to learn and apply the techniques described in these chapters, but as you develop your BBP skills, the process will go faster, and PowerPoint 2007 will become a handy tool for rapid visual prototyping of creative concepts. As you build presentations over time, you'll develop a personal library of styles that you can review for inspiration on future projects.

## What Will You Show, Say, and Do During Every Slide?

The prospect of managing everything you show, say, and do during every slide in a presentation can seem daunting at first. Even if you have written a clear and coherent set of headlines, as shown in Figure 6-1, how can you possibly fill all of the empty slides you will create from the story template with graphics, narration, and interaction in a quick and efficient way? And at the same time, how can you seamlessly integrate all of these complex elements during a live presentation? The answer lies in a different way of looking at PowerPoint—as a visual storytelling tool.

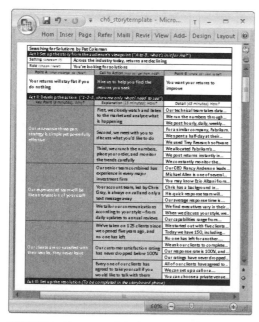

**FIGURE 6-1**  Your completed story template.

As mentioned in Chapter 3, if you were a filmmaker with a finished script, you'd probably hire a storyboard artist to sketch frames of selected scenes from your script. These initial sketches enable everyone on the production team to begin to see how the film will look so that they can start to turn the words from the script into spoken words and projected images. A storyboard is a powerful tool because it lets you see many frames from a story in a single view and consider how those frames relate to one another through a narrative. Without this important perspective, you would find it hard to see how the parts link together to become a coherent whole.

You won't need to hire a storyboard artist to create your storyboard; instead you'll adapt the basic techniques of creating a storyboard to your PowerPoint presentation to help you to organize the visual and verbal pieces of your story. This will shift your thinking of a PowerPoint presentation from individual slides toward slides related as frames in a strip of film. By setting up a new PowerPoint presentation in this way, you'll use the storyboard not only to plan your words and visuals but also to present them to the audience using a single media document that works across projector, paper, and browser.

# Preparing the Storyboard

As you complete the story template in Chapters 4 and 5, you're actually also formatting your information in a specific way that prepares it for a PowerPoint storyboard. The concise headlines that communicate each act and scene in the story template are the same concise headlines that will communicate clearly to the audience on your PowerPoint slides. Writing headlines for both the story template and the PowerPoint slides is the powerful fulcrum that allows you to leverage PowerPoint software beyond bullet points into a new world of visual storytelling. This process embeds your script in a storyboard and ensures that everything you say and show maps back to the structure and sequence of a story. It also ensures that you have broken up your ideas into bite-size pieces so that working memory can easily digest them.

Although you've finished with the story template for now, it's a good idea to print a copy and keep it handy while you set up and work on your PowerPoint storyboard. The story template gives you the significant benefit of seeing your entire story on a single page or two, but when you import your headlines into PowerPoint, you will break the link between story template and storyboard. If you make changes to the headlines or the presentation structure later in PowerPoint, it's always a good idea to update your Microsoft Office Word file so that you can still use the story template as an organizing tool.

# Reformatting Your Story Template Manually

> **NOTE** Once you learn how to reformat your story template manually, the process will take only a couple of minutes. If you want to skip these steps altogether, visit *www.beyondbulletpoints.com* for tools that can help you format your storyboard faster.

To prepare the headlines in your story template to become the headlines of your PowerPoint slides, you need to do some prep work on the story template. First save the Word document, and then on the Home tab, in the Editing group, click Select; then choose Select All to select all of the headlines in the template, and then press Ctrl+C to copy them. Next create a new Word document and save it on your local computer in a familiar folder, adding the word *Formatted* to the end of the file name. Position the cursor in this new document, and then on the Home tab, in the Clipboard group, click the Paste button, and on the drop-down menu, click Paste Special. In the Paste Special dialog box, select Unformatted Text, and then click OK. The resulting new document should look similar to Figure 6-2.

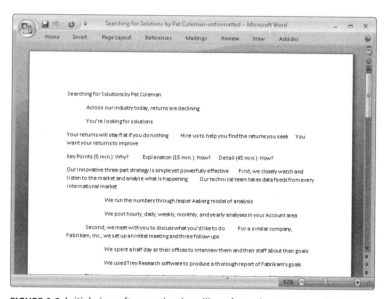

**FIGURE 6-2** Initial view after pasting headlines from the story template into a new Word document.

Delete the line containing the column headings and any extra text so that only your headlines remain. Remove any extra spaces between words and add new line breaks where needed so that you end up with only one headline per line. Last select your Call to

Action headline, and click and drag it to the line after your Point B headline—your final document should appear as shown in Figure 6-3. After you save the document, close it.

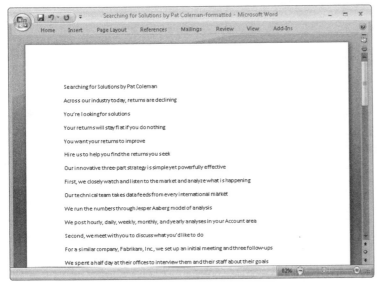

**FIGURE 6-3** Word document with extra spaces between words removed, new line breaks added, and only one headline per line.

## Using the BBP Storyboard Formatter

Now that you've reformatted your story template, the next step is to import your headlines into PowerPoint 2007. You'll do that with the BBP Storyboard Formatter—a specially formatted PowerPoint 2007 file that takes care of a number of technical steps for you so that you don't have to take the time to apply them manually.

> **NOTE** If you choose not to use the BBP Storyboard Formatter, manually apply the settings as described in the sections "Tip 1: Set Up the Office Theme Slide Master Manually" and "Tip 2: Set Up the Notes Master Manually" later in this chapter.

To use the storyboard formatter, copy the BBP Storyboard Formatter – Basic.potx file from the companion CD to a folder on your local computer. Locate the BBP Storyboard Formatter on your local computer, and double-click it. Because the file format is a PowerPoint 2007 Design Template, as indicated by the .potx file extension, double-clicking the file will open a new presentation based on the template's formatting. Your

PowerPoint file contains one blank slide and is now shown in Slide Sorter view. Name and save the new PowerPoint file on your local computer.

## WORKING IN POWERPOINT 2007

If you're new to Microsoft Office PowerPoint 2007, you'll notice that the interface looks completely different from earlier versions. The Ribbon at the top is probably the most noticeable new feature, but there are many other changes to the way the software works. This book aims to give you only the basics you need to know to get started with BBP in PowerPoint 2007—to learn more about the technical details of how to use the software, refer to one of the many how-to books, such as Joyce Cox and Joan Preppernau's *Microsoft Office PowerPoint 2007 Step by Step* (Microsoft Press, 2007).

On the Home tab, in the Slides group, click New Slide, and near the bottom of the drop-down menu, select Slides From Outline. Then, in the Insert Outline dialog box, find and select the formatted story template you just created—it should have the word *Formatted* that you added to the title—and then click Insert. (If you get an error message, you likely have your formatted Word document still open—in that case, return to the document and close it.)

These steps create a single PowerPoint slide for each of the headlines you wrote in the story template, with each headline now placed at the top of a slide, as shown in Figure 6-4. If there are any blank slides in the presentation without headlines, delete them.

At the lower right of the PowerPoint window on the status bar is a View toolbar with three buttons—when you click them from left to right, you will see the storyboard in Normal, Slide Sorter, and Slide Show views. Click and drag the handle on the Zoom toolbar to the left to decrease magnification of your current view and to the right to increase magnification. The indicator to the left of the Zoom toolbar displays the exact percentage of magnification—click this value to open the Zoom dialog box and make more precise adjustments.

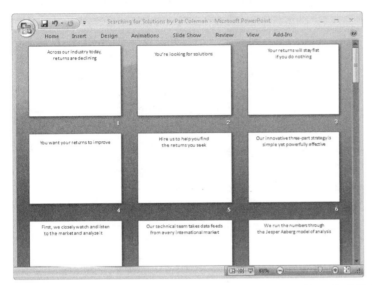

**FIGURE 6-4** Slide Sorter view of all of your headlines imported into the BBP Storyboard Formatter.

After you master the fundamentals of the BBP approach, you can customize the settings of the BBP Storyboard Formatter according to your needs. You can also save the template to your local computer to make it easily accessible when you create a new presentation; for details, see the section "Tip 3: Install the Storyboard Formatter on Your Local Computer" later in this chapter.

# Cuing Working Memory with Preliminary Slide Backgrounds

One of the big benefits of using the BBP Story Template is that you can easily see how all of your ideas relate to one another in the Word document. The story template is a particularly effective organizing tool for the Act II scenes because it shows you a visual hierarchy of your ideas. In each column, you write out the headlines in descending order of importance from top to bottom and add columns of information from left to right. But when you send the story template to the storyboard, you lose the template's ability to show you the hierarchy of your ideas. Every slide you see in Slide Sorter view looks as though it carries the same visual weight, and each slide follows the next in an undifferentiated sequence.

To be able to quickly see your built-in informational hierarchy in Slide Sorter view and begin to address the need to provide visual cues for working memory, you'll apply custom layouts with special backgrounds that indicate the presentation's organization. These custom layouts will be only temporary while you sketch your storyboard—later, in Chapter 8, you'll change these custom layouts or apply new ones. Using the BBP Storyboard Formatter, you'll apply a custom layout with a dark gray background to your Call to Action slide, a custom layout with a medium gray background to the Key Point slides, a custom layout with a light gray background to the Explanation slides, and a custom layout with a white background to the remaining Act I and Detail slides.

## FINDING YOUR SLIDES

Keep a printout of the Word version of the story template handy as you locate the corresponding slides on the storyboard. If you have trouble finding slides because the slides are too large or the headlines are too small, click and drag the handle on the Zoom bar to increase or decrease magnification of Slide Sorter view. Try counting slides if that helps—for example, once you have located a Key Point slide, you know that an Explanation slide follows directly after it, and you can count three Detail slides after that one to find the next Explanation slide, and three Detail slides after that to find the third Explanation slide.

To color-code these slides in Slide Sorter view, click Ctrl+A to select all the slides in the presentation. On the Home tab, in the Slides group, click Layout, and on the drop-down menu, click the layout titled Detail Sketches, as shown in Figure 6-5. Now apply the rest of the layouts in the order of the informational hierarchy of your slides, from top to bottom. Select the Call to Action slide, click Layout, and on the drop-down menu, click the layout titled CTA Sketch. Next select the first Key Point slide, hold down Ctrl and click to select the second and third Key Point slides, and then click Layout again, and on the drop-down menu, click the layout titled Key Point Sketches.

**FIGURE 6-5** Applying the Detail Sketches custom layout to all the slides in Slide Sorter view using the custom layouts included in the BBP Storyboard Formatter.

Next click the first Explanation slide, hold down Ctrl and select the rest of the Explanation slides, and then click the Layout button, and on the drop-down menu click the layout titled Explanation Sketches. Last click the first Setting slide, hold down Shift and select the Point B slide, and then click the Layout button, and on the drop-down menu click the layout titled Act I Sketches.

| NOTE | The companion CD for this book provides the Basic version of the BBP Storyboard Formatter, which includes the custom layouts you need to format your slides for sketching your storyboard—there are more advanced formatters available at *www.beyondbulletpoints.com*. If you choose to not use a storyboard formatter at all, follow the steps in the section "Tip 5: Apply Slide Backgrounds Manually" at the end of this chapter. |

Scroll through your slides as you read the headlines, and check them against the printout of your story template to make sure that you have applied the layouts properly. If you made a mistake, select the slide, click the Layout button, and select the correct layout to apply it. Your storyboard should now look like Figure 6-6.

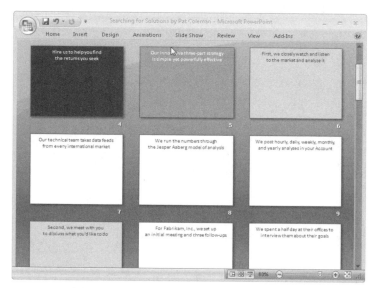

**FIGURE 6-6** Slide Sorter view, showing the Call to Action slide with a dark gray background, the Key Point slides with medium gray backgrounds, the Explanation slides with light gray backgrounds, and the Detail slides with white backgrounds.

As you scroll through the slides of the presentation in sequence, the change in color of the backgrounds from dark gray to medium gray to light gray to white indicates that you have made a transition to a new point that corresponds to Act I or the three columns in the storyboard. This transition should also be reinforced by your spoken words. Even though the shaded backgrounds are only temporary, already the contrast of the different shades of color calls attention to the three levels of hierarchy—the dark gray color calls attention to the most important Call to Action slide, the medium gray to the Key Points slides, the light gray next to the Explanation slides, and the white color to the Detail slides. Stick with these backgrounds for now so that you'll be able to sketch over the backgrounds as you work in the storyboard. In Chapter 7, you'll review and sketch a range of different color backgrounds, layouts, and graphics you can use to call attention to the different levels of information, and in Chapter 8, you'll apply them to the slides in their final form.

# Practicing Scaling to Time

As you saw in Chapter 5, if you complete all three columns of Act II, you have enough Key Point, Explanation, and Detail slides to fill about a 45-minute presentation. However, at the last minute, you might need to scale down your presentation from 45 minutes to 15 or even 5 minutes, and now you can practice how easy it is to do that with only a few clicks of the mouse. Follow these steps in Slide Sorter view to scale the storyboard to time by hiding the slides that you don't need to use in the presentation:

- If you're giving a 45-minute presentation, do nothing—all your slides will appear to your audience.

- To prepare a 15-minute presentation, hold down the Ctrl key and click the white Detail slides throughout the presentation. With all of the Detail slides selected, right-click any slide, and then select Hide Slide. Now only the Act I, Key Point, and Explanation slides will appear when you give the presentation; the Detail slides will be hidden. You can see the result by pressing the **F5** key to start the slide show from the first slide. Press the **Esc** key to return to Slide Sorter view.

- To prepare a 5-minute presentation, complete the tasks for a 15-minute presentation, but in addition to selecting the white Detail slides, select the light gray Explanation slides, and then right-click any slide and select Hide Slide. Now only the Act I and Key Point slides will appear during the presentation; the rest of the Act II slides are hidden. Test the result by pressing the **F5** key. Press the **Esc** key to return to Slide Sorter view.

When you use the Hide Slide feature, a hidden slide icon containing the slide number is displayed in the lower-right corner of each slide in Slide Sorter view. To reset the hidden slides to make them viewable again during a presentation, select the hidden slides, right-click any slide, and click Hide Slide again—the hidden slide icon will disappear. Keep in mind that hidden slides don't appear on screen when you run a presentation, but they will be printed unless you clear the Print Hidden Slides check box in the Print dialog box.

When you hide the slides as you scale to time, you maintain a single presentation file that has the flexibility to accommodate different-length presentations. Because of the hierarchy of ideas you wrote into Act II, you can scale your presentation up or down to time without losing the core integrity of the story—with only a few clicks of your mouse.

## Editing Your Headlines If Needed

As you practiced scaling to time in Slide Sorter view, you might have noticed that some of the headlines extend beyond the two-line limit or have text that is unevenly balanced between the two lines—to fix that, you'll need to master the basics of editing headlines, described in the section "Tip 4: Edit the Headlines" later in this chapter. In Normal view, scroll through all of the slides, and when you find a headline that exceeds the two-line limit of the title area, edit it down to size. Sometimes you can reduce a headline's length simply by deleting a word or two, without affecting its meaning. At other times, you might have to revise and restructure the wording of a headline to make it fit. You can position the cursor after any word in a headline and then press Enter—this places the rest of the words in the headline on the next line to more evenly distribute the words over the two lines. Always stick with the two-line limit for headlines to maintain consistency in the presentation, to leave ample room for visuals, and to challenge yourself to be as concise as possible.

## Reviewing the Storyboard

Congratulations! You have now officially moved beyond bullet points. Even before you've added a single visual, the PowerPoint file is embedded with a strong story, meaningful headlines anchoring every slide, preliminary backgrounds that indicate the presentation's structure, and a basic layout designed to hold graphical elements in the main area of the slides instead of bullet points.

Your new PowerPoint storyboard is inspired by the idea of a filmmaker's storyboard, but it's actually a much more sophisticated tool than its namesake. What you've created is the foundation for a complete, integrated, and coherent media document that manages both the words you speak and the visuals you show on screen.

# Planning for the Verbal Channel by Writing Down What You'll Say

No PowerPoint slide is an island, because it always exists in the context of your spoken words. To create a coherent presentation, you need to plan not only each slide but also the words you speak while you project the slide on a screen. Your primary objective in writing out your narration is to seamlessly integrate the soundtrack of your voice with the visual track of your slides so that you can avoid splitting the attention of your audience between the two. To ensure that you properly manage what you say with what you show on screen, click the View tab on the Ribbon, and in the Presentation Views group, click Notes Page. Scroll through all of the slides in the presentation, which will each look similar to Figure 6-7—starting in this view reinforces the concept that you're designing an experience consisting of both projected visuals and spoken words.

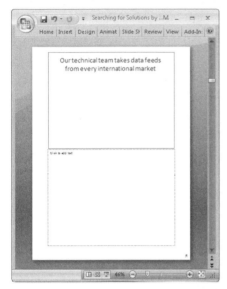

**FIGURE 6-7** Reviewing both projected visuals and spoken words in Notes Page view. (An outline has been added to the slide area to make it visible in this illustration.)

As mentioned in Chapters 2 and 3, the top half of the page shows what you see on the slide, and the notes area below shows your spoken words. (You won't see an outline around the slide as in Figure 6-7—it has been removed in the BBP Storyboard Formatter settings so that your printed notes pages handouts will look better.) The headline of the slide does double duty in Notes Page view—not only does it summarize the main idea that will appear on screen during the presentation, but it also summarizes the meaning of the entire notes page. If you're used to having a great deal of written information on screen, writing out your verbal explanation in the notes area gives you the confidence that you will cover the bulk of the information through the verbal channel, which in turn gives you the freedom to keep the visual channel simple, focused, and to the point.

> **TIP** ✓ An easy way to remember the essence of storyboarding is to imagine the audience saying to you, "Synchronize what you say with what I see."

To tap into the power of Notes Page view, review the slide headline in the top half of the page, position the cursor in the text box in the bottom half of the page, and then write out what you plan to say about this headline, as shown in the magnified view of the notes area in Figure 6-8. The text you write in the notes area represents what you'll say while the slide is displayed on the screen, normally for a period of less than a minute. If you find that you have more to say and your narration extends past the limits of the text box, go back to the story template and break up your ideas across more slides.

**FIGURE 6-8** A magnified view of the notes area in Notes Page view, displaying an idea being described in complete sentences and paragraphs.

Fully writing out your ideas in the notes area fleshes out the ideas and increases your confidence in the topic. It also helps you to develop a close connection with the headline, which will aid you later when you speak. During the presentation, the headline will show the audience in a glance the idea of the slide, and it will also prompt you to improvise on the detailed written explanation, with a relaxed voice that comes from knowing the topic so well.

If you're used to having text on screen as a reminder of what to say, you also have full confidence in knowing that whatever you write in the notes area now is also viewable to you alone as the speaker in Presenter view, as described in Appendix B on the companion CD. After you have completed the notes area of one of your current slides, it will look like the slide shown in Figure 6-9 in Presenter view—during a presentation, the text you wrote in the notes area is now visible to you in the speaker notes pane on the right.

**FIGURE 6-9** Presenter view of a Detail slide that has had text added to the notes area.

A valuable byproduct of starting to design in Notes Page view is that at the end of the design process, you have not only well-designed slides but also a useful handout. If you plan to share the presentation with your audience or others who were not present, it is important to write out what you'll say about the headline in complete sentences and paragraphs in the notes area so that your handout is complete and accurate when you print out both slide and text box together. Don't worry about the formatting of Notes Page view now—you can adjust that in Chapter 8, and you'll also have the option to place additional graphics in the notes area if you choose.

> **NOTE**
> You also have the option to add text to the notes pane when you are in Normal view by positioning the cursor in the notes pane below the slide area and typing—it's a common mistake to think that you're in Notes Page view when you use the notes pane in Normal view this way. The disadvantage to using Normal view to write out your notes is that you lose track of how each slide will look as a handout. You also might lose the perspective of your on-screen slide and your off-screen notes area as an evenly balanced visual-verbal unit that has to be seamlessly coordinated in order to most effectively make use of the dual-channels research reality described in Chapter 2.

For a quick presentation for which you don't plan to print handouts, write short notes to yourself in the notes area of the slides of the storyboard. For now, spell out as much of your explanation as you can at this stage of the presentation—if you're pressed for time, write what you can at this point and then expand on your text in more detail later. Or you can use a digital recorder to capture your thoughts as you're speaking about each slide and then transcribe the recording later and paste the text passages into the corresponding notes areas. You also might try using speech recognition software such as Dragon Naturally Speaking or one of the dictation services such as SpeakWrite Voice-to-Document Service that allow you to speak your narration into a telephone and then the service sends you an e-mail message with a transcription a short time later.

■ **REMEMBER  Start writing out your spoken words in the notes pane in Notes Page view so that you establish the complete context for what you'll say. You can continue to add notes in this view, as well as in the notes area in Normal view.**

Now that you've prepared and reviewed the PowerPoint file, it's time to start planning the presentation's visuals with a few sketches.

## Planning for the Visual Channel by Sketching Your Storyboard

Just as a filmmaker would, the best way to start getting visual in your storyboard is to sketch what you would like on each slide before you go looking for the actual graphics that you'll use. Creating sketches of the slides accelerates the design process because it keeps you from getting distracted amidst the many visual possibilities you'll find when you search through photo and graphics libraries. A series of sketches can also help you to select a consistent style, because you see all of the slides together and can consider a design for all of the slides at once.

**NOTE**  If you've never sketched your PowerPoint slides before, this might seem like an extra step that you don't have the time to take. But the investment you make in taking the time to sketch will actually save you time in the long run. Much of the frustration that comes from developing PowerPoint presentations, especially in an organizational context, comes from endless revisions to graphics. When you sketch your slides first, you get everyone involved to sign off on the sketches to make sure that they're what everyone wants. By getting agreement on the visual concepts now, you save frustration, inefficiency, confusion, and unhappiness later.

You have two ways to go about sketching your slides—either on a computer or on paper. By far, the best way to sketch ideas for your slides is using a Tablet PC, because it allows you to draw directly on the PowerPoint slides and easily edit and erase the "ink." There is tremendous value to having your sketches in electronic format, because you have a record of what you did that you can immediately e-mail to others to review. If you use a Tablet PC, you can also connect your computer to a data projector and project your PowerPoint storyboard on a screen as you sketch ideas with your team—this is a particularly powerful way to tap into the collective visual intelligence of the group, and into the visual creativity that is likely lying dormant within your coworkers.

If you have a Tablet PC, to start sketching your storyboard, open a slide in Normal view, click the Review tab on the Ribbon, and in the Ink group, select Start Inking. The Pens tab that appears gives you options for types of pens, colors, and weights. Read the headline, and think of the simplest way you can illustrate it. Now place the Tablet PC stylus on the screen below the headline (or use your finger or fingernail if you have a Tablet PC with a touch screen), and draw your illustration directly in the slide area as you would with a regular pen and paper, as shown in Figure 6-10. The Tablet PC lets you create your sketches using electronic ink, which you can easily erase, recolor, resize, copy, and paste.

**FIGURE 6-10** Slide showing a sketch made on a slide with the stylus of a Tablet PC.

As in this example, don't worry if you're not an artist—just do the best you can to capture the general idea of what you're looking for, even if it is the simplest stick figures, shapes, and arrows. In Chapter 8, you'll turn these simple sketches into professional, simple, and clear photographs, illustrations, and diagrams. If you can't draw even a stick figure, just sketch out the words to describe what you want on the screen. Don't try to make everything perfect at this point—you want to apply your more creative side here, and you will likely find that you can develop a sense of surprise, cleverness, and a visual sense of humor in your sketches to make sure the presentation doesn't get too stiff and impersonal. On the Slides tab in the Overview pane on the left, you can see the sketch you just drew in thumbnail size—the first illustration in the sequence of slides of your storyboard.

> **TIP** ✓ If you don't have a Tablet PC, you can still sketch on your PowerPoint slides using your computer and a mouse if you use the presenter tools available in Slide Show view, as described in Appendix B on the companion CD—the limitation is that your sketching will not be as smooth or natural with a mouse as it is with a Tablet PC stylus.

If you don't have access to a Tablet PC, the next best thing to use is paper. To sketch your complete storyboard, you'll need to print a paper copy. To do this, click the Microsoft Office Button, click Print, and then click Print again to open the Print dialog box. Click the Print What drop-down arrow, and select one of the following options:

- Select Slides in the Print What drop-down list to print an individual copy of each slide. You can tape these pages to a wall or assemble them in a loose-leaf notebook that you can flip through as you sketch ideas for individual slides.

- Select Notes Pages to print the notes pages. Assemble these pages in a notebook so that you can sketch visuals in the slide areas or take notes to add to the notes areas later.

- Select Handouts, click the Slides Per Page drop-down arrow, and click 1, 2, 3, 4, 6, or 9 to print the corresponding number of slides per page. Use these pages to sketch on multiple slides per page on the thumbnail images of the slides.

When you have selected a format, click OK to print. Although the examples in Chapter 7 were all sketched using a Tablet PC, you can apply most of the same techniques by sketching a paper storyboard.

> **TIP** ✓ To make sketching your paper storyboard more convenient by printing more than nine slides on a single page, see the section "Tip 8: Print Full-Page Storyboards" later in this chapter.

# Storyboarding Using Three Ground Rules

Whether you have an electronic version or a paper version, as you review and work with your new storyboard, three ground rules can help you and your audience to stay connected to the big picture.

## Rule 1: Be Visually Concise, Clear, Direct, and Specific

In Chapters 4 and 5, you wrote the headlines for your story template following the procedures in the section "Writing Headlines Using Three Ground Rules" in Chapter 3. Just as you strive to be concise, clear, direct, and specific with your words, you should strive to be the same with your visuals. Whether you use words or visuals to communicate, your singular goal should be to get across the most meaning in the most efficient way possible. When you sketch your storyboard, that means you should use the simplest illustration possible without any excess detail. Not only does a simple illustration help you make your visual point quickly, it also will guide you to avoid the extraneous detail that would otherwise clog the eye of the needle of working memory of your audience. When in doubt, leave it out of your sketches.

As you sketch, always pay special attention to the wording of the headlines as you read through them in Slide Sorter view to see whether you can reword them to tie them together more tightly. As you reword a headline in PowerPoint, go back and edit the headline in the story template as well. If you find that you start making many changes to slide headlines, go back to the story template directly to work out the structural issues you are having before returning to the storyboard.

## Rule 2: In Act II, Sketch Consistency Within Columns and Variety Across Columns

When you work with the storyboard, keep in mind that in Act II, *it's all about the hierarchy.* Act II of the story template is your disciplined guide that helps you make the tough decisions about whether to include or exclude ideas and automatically prioritizes for you every slide in a hierarchy from the most important to the least. When you apply preliminary layouts with color backgrounds to indicate the levels of importance of your slides, you can clearly see in Slide Sorter view how the hierarchy fits into the specific sequence of the slides of the presentation. And now you'll build on the rock-solid verbal foundation of Act II by using visual techniques to keep the hierarchy at the top of the minds of both you and your audience.

When you begin to sketch, the Act II structure will help you decide exactly what you want to accomplish visually on your slides, as shown in Figure 6-11. As you learned in Chapter 5, you want the audience to remember and apply your Call to Action and Key Point slides above all—if they walked away and remembered nothing else, these slides carry the most important information. You'll sketch on these slides the most memorable things you can say, show, and do to make these points stick—here you'll use memorable photographic icons, illustrations, or visual elements from your motif.

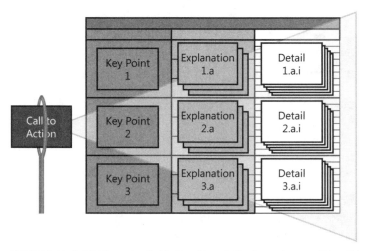

**FIGURE 6-11** Act II hierarchy, indicating the relative importance of the slides.

Next you'll sketch the second-most important Explanation slides, which the audience will likely remember—here you might use diagrams, charts, or other illustrations. And then you'll sketch the third-most important Detail slides, which the audience might not remember—here you'll include graphs, charts, screen captures, and other visual elements.

As you sketch the slides that correspond to the three columns of Act II, you want to keep a consistent look in terms of similar layout, style, and placement of headlines and graphics within each column, as shown in the slides that correspond to the headlines from the Explanation column in Figure 6-12. By sketching the slides from a single column together, as you'll do next in Chapter 7, you avoid concentrating exclusively on only single slides; instead, you focus on what is happening *across* slides. This makes sure that you approach the design of any slide by its context and relationship to other slides within its column, not as individual slides in isolation.

**FIGURE 6-12** Telling a visual story across three slides from the Explanation column.

In addition to sketching variety across slides from the same column of Act II, you also want to sketch variety *across the columns* of the presentation. You don't have to worry about how you'll do this—it will happen automatically as a result of the way you approach the sketching process in Chapter 7. But it's important to know what's happening in terms of variety as you sketch your storyboard. For example, the Explanation slides shown earlier in Figure 6-12 will not appear in direct sequence in the storyboard because they will be broken up by their subsequent Detail slides.

However, you do still want to tell this visual story across these Explanation slides even when they are broken up by the Detail slides, as shown in Figure 6-13.

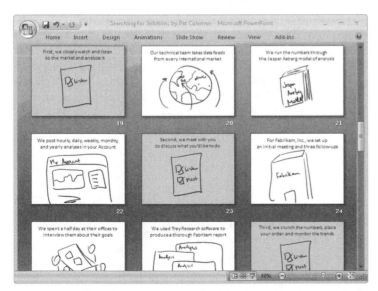

**FIGURE 6-13** Telling the story across each of the three slides from the Explanation column, even though they are separated in sequence by the slides from the Detail column.

In the sequence of slides as they appear in this example, you introduce the first Explanation slide and then follow the idea with its three Detail slides. You then present the second Explanation slide and follow the idea with its three Detail slides. This back-and-forth technique is helpful to your audience because with the first Explanation slide, you summarize what you are about to tell them, and then with the Detail slides, you do the actual telling. As you write out the narration in the notes area on the Explanation slides, you likewise should summarize the Detail slides to follow.

Think of the slides as cognitive stepping stones that are guiding and supporting the working memory of the audience along their path of understanding.

## Rule 3: Sketch Outside the Screen Too

You have in your PowerPoint file a powerful planning tool, with each slide representing one idea that you will convey at one point in the presentation as summarized by the headline. You will probably add graphics to most of these slides to illustrate the headlines, but you don't have to limit yourself to showing information on a slide exclusively with a graphic; you can use other media tools and techniques. For example, use a physical prop that you hold in your hands or pass around to audience members to communicate an Explanation slide, as shown in Figure 6-14. You might switch to a different software application on your desktop to communicate the headlines across three Detail slides. Or you might use a brief video clip to illustrate each of your three Key Point slides.

The storyboard will guide you as you decide whether to use different media—you will specifically choose to include different media based on the slide's headline and its location within the Act II hierarchy. For example, you wouldn't use your most memorable video clip on a Detail slide because you don't want your audience to remember the Detail slides over the Key Point slides—you would integrate and use the clip through the Key Point slides instead.

**FIGURE 6-14** Holding a physical prop while displaying a photo of it on the screen.

Even when you use other media, your PowerPoint storyboard will still be the foundation that guides the entire experience. On the slides where you use other media, in most cases, you'll keep just the headline on the screen to keep the meaning of what you're doing clear and in the context of the overall presentation. Or you may use a photo as a physical prop to ensure that everyone sees it clearly. You'll see an example of this technique shortly in Chapter 7.

**THREE GROUND RULES FOR STORYBOARDING**

Inspired by a filmmaker's storyboard, your PowerPoint storyboard helps you manage both the words you speak and the images you show. Follow these three ground rules to keep your storyboard coherent:

**Rule 1.** Be visually concise, clear, direct, and specific.

**Rule 2.** In Act II, sketch consistency within columns and variety across columns.

**Rule 3.** Sketch outside the screen too.

**BBP CHECKLIST: PREPARING THE STORYBOARD**

Does your storyboard:

❏ Include backgrounds that cue the Key Point, Explanation, and Detail slides?

❏ Provide you with the ability to quickly scale your presentation up and down to time?

❏ Contain notes in the notes area of what you'll say during each slide?

Now that you have an operational storyboard, here are 10 advanced things you can do with it.

# 10 Tips for Enhancing Your Storyboard

Your storyboard is a versatile tool to prepare and plan both your spoken words and your projected visuals during the presentation. Once you've mastered the basics, try using these 10 tips to enhance the storyboard.

## Tip 1: Set Up the Office Theme Slide Master Manually

If for some reason you decide not to use the BBP Storyboard Formatter, follow these steps to set up the basic formatting you'll need to start sketching the storyboard:

1.  Open and save a blank PowerPoint presentation, and as described earlier in this chapter, import the formatted story template headlines into PowerPoint following the **New Slide**, **Slides From Outline** sequence.

2.  In Slide Sorter view, on the **Home** tab, in the **Editing** group, click **Select**, **Select All**, and then in the **Slides** group, click **Layout**, **Title Only**.

3.  On the **View** tab, in the **Presentation Views** group, click **Slide Master**. In the **Overview** pane on the left, click the **Office Theme Slide Master**.

4.  In the **Slide** pane, right-click the **Title** box, and on the formatting shortcut menu, select **Calibri** for the font (or a different font if you prefer), select **40** for the font size, and make sure that **Centered** is selected.

5.  Right-click the **Title** box again, and on the second shortcut menu below the formatting menu, select **Format Shape**.

6.  In the **Format Shape** dialog box, select **Text Box**; on the **Vertical Alignment** drop-down menu, choose **Middle Centered**; in the **Autofit** area, select **Do Not Autofit**; and then click **Close**.

7.  On the **Slide Master** tab, in the **Close** group, click **Close Master View** to return to the previous view of the slides.

## Tip 2: Set Up the Notes Master Manually

Just as the Storyboard Master uses the Office Theme Slide Master to set the formatting for all of the slides, the Notes Master sets the formatting for all of the notes pages. By making a few adjustments to the Notes Master, you'll be able to use the notes pages to effectively plan both your slides and your spoken words.

**TIP** ✓ To save time formatting the Notes Master, use the Beyond Bullet Points Storyboard Formatter on the companion CD.

To format the Notes Master, follow these steps:

1.  Continue working on the same PowerPoint file you started in the section "Tip 1: Set Up the Office Theme Slide Master Manually," and on the **View** tab, in the **Presentation Views** group, click **Notes Master**. Right-click the **Slide Image** placeholder in the top half of the page, and on the drop-down menu, click **Size And Position**.

2.  In the **Size And Position** dialog box, on the **Size** tab, make sure that the **Lock Aspect Ratio** check box is selected, change the **Width** setting to **6"** (the **Height** setting will be automatically adjusted to **4.5"**), and then click **Close**.

3.  Right-click the border of the the **Body** placeholder in the lower half of the page, and on the drop-down menu, click **Size And Position**. If the notes area doesn't already have these settings, clear the **Lock Aspect Ratio** check box, make sure that **Height** is set to **4.5"** and Width is set to **6"**, and then click **Close**.

    On the **Notes Master** tab, in the **Placeholders** group, you can delete or add any other Notes Master placeholders, including **Header**, **Date**, **Footer**, and **Page Number**.

4.  Hold down Shift while you click both the **Slide Image** placeholder and the **Body** placeholder, and on the Home tab, in the **Drawing** group, click **Arrange**, point to **Align**, and click **Align To Slide**. Click **Arrange** again, point to **Align**, and click **Align Center**. Then drag the two placeholders to position them one above another. If you want to align any placeholders on the Notes Master more precisely, right-click the slide background, and on the shortcut menu, choose **Grid And Guides**, and then configure the settings of the grids and guides according to your needs, and click **OK**.

5.  Select the **Slide Image** placeholder again, and on the shortcut menu, click the **Line Color** down arrow, and then in the drop-down list, select **No Outline**.

6.  On the **Notes Master** tab, in the **Close** group, click **Close Master View** to return to the previous view.

# Tip 3: Install the Storyboard Formatter on Your Local Computer

If you want to make the BBP Storyboard Formatter available on your local computer every time you create a new PowerPoint file, save it in your PowerPoint Templates folder. To do that, follow these steps:

1. Double-click to open the BBP Storyboard Formatter that you saved to your computer earlier in this chapter.

2. Click the **Microsoft Office Button**, click **Save As**, and then in the **Save As** dialog box, click the **Save As Type** drop-down arrow, and choose **PowerPoint Template**.

3. PowerPoint automatically selects the location on your local computer where the default PowerPoint template is stored. To create a new presentation, click the **Microsoft Office Button**, click **New**, and then in the **Templates** area, select **My Templates**. In the **New Presentation** dialog box, you should see the template you just saved—select it and click **OK** to create the presentation.

# Tip 4: Edit the Headlines

PowerPoint provides two ways for you to edit headlines. The first method is to click the View tab and, in the Presentation Views group, click Normal. In this view, click in the title area of the slide, and then start editing. The second method is to view the presentation in Outline format. In Normal view, the leftmost pane of the PowerPoint window contains an Overview area with two tabs: Outline and Slides. Click the Outline tab to see a list of headlines and, to the left of each headline, a number and a small icon of a slide. Click in the text of the headline you want to edit. As you make changes to a headline on the Outline tab, the corresponding text in the title area of the slide to the right is updated. You can drag the vertical line at the right side of the Outline pane to increase or decrease its size to accommodate the width of the headlines. The Outline tab can be useful for reviewing all of the headlines of the slides in a list that you can read from top to bottom. Later you can print this outline to use as speaker notes.

# Tip 5: Apply Slide Backgrounds Manually

If you do not use the BBP Storyboard Formatter, you will not be able to use the built-in custom layouts to format the Key Point, Explanation, and Detail slides, but you can still format them manually. To quickly do this, follow these steps:

1. In Slide Sorter view, right-click the Call to Action slide, click **Format Background** on the shortcut menu, and in the **Format Background** dialog box, click **Fill** and then select **Solid Fill**.

2.  On the **Color** drop-down menu, click **More Colors**, select dark gray, and then click **OK**. Make sure that the **Transparency** bar slider is set to **0%**, and then click **Close**.

3.  Click the first Key Point slide, and then hold down Ctrl and click to select the second and third Key Point slides.

4.  Now right-click one of the slides, click **Format Background** on the shortcut menu, and in the **Format Background** dialog box, click **Fill** and then select **Solid Fill**.

5.  On the **Color** drop-down menu, click **More Colors**, select medium gray, and then click **OK**. Make sure that the **Transparency** bar slider is set to **0%**, and then click **Close**.

6.  Next click the first Explanation slide, and then hold down Ctrl and select the rest of the Explanation slides.

7.  Now right-click one of the slides, click **Format Background** on the shortcut menu, and in the **Format Background** dialog box, on the **Fill** tab, select **Solid Fill**.

8.  On the **Color** drop-down menu, click **More Colors**, select light gray, and then click **OK**. Make sure that the **Transparency** bar slider is set to **0%**, and then click **Close**.

Do nothing to the Act I and Detail slides.

Be sure to change only the background colors for now and otherwise leave the slides blank except for the headlines. If you were to include logos, other slide backgrounds, and other graphics on your storyboard at this point, they would constrain your design decisions and interfere with the way you will use backgrounds in this chapter to purposefully cue the working memory of your audience.

## Tip 6: Set Up Custom Layouts and Themes Manually

The BBP Storyboard Formatter on the companion CD includes built-in layouts that you apply to your Key Point, Explanation, and Detail slides. These were built using the custom layouts feature in PowerPoint 2007, which is described in more detail in Chapter 8—you'll be able to modify the current custom layouts at that point, or add new ones and apply them to your slides. The Key Point and Explanation slides also have background styles applied to them as part of the Storyboard Formatter custom theme that is included with the storyboard formatter. Learn more about modifying and creating themes manually by referring to a PowerPoint 2007 book that covers the topic in more detail.

## Tip 7: The BBP Storyboard Sketchpad

Visit www.beyondbulletpoints.com to download a blank BBP Storyboard Sketchpad that you can print and use to sketch ideas for the Act I and Key Point slides, as shown in Figure 6-15. When you print a copy, you'll need to write your headlines in the corresponding slides on the printout. Although this covers sketches for only eight slides, they are the most important slides, and you can collect a range of these sketches to inspire you about ways to develop your visual motifs.

**FIGURE 6-15** The BBP Storyboard Sketchpad.

## Tip 8: Print Full-Page Storyboards

Although PowerPoint allows you to print only up to nine slides per page on a handout, you can purchase an add-in for PowerPoint called the Handout Wizard that allows you to print as many slides per page as you want. This is particularly useful if you plan to sketch your storyboard on paper. For example, you can fit groups of 20 slides from your storyboard on 8½-by-11-inch sheets of paper by using the Handout Wizard to arrange them five slides across and four slides down, as shown in Figure 6-16. You can fit even more slides per page if you use 11-by-17-inch sheets of paper. The add-in places all of the slide thumbnails on a single PowerPoint slide that you can then print. For more information about the Handout Wizard add-in, visit *http://skp.mvps.org/how/*.

**FIGURE 6-16** A 20-slide storyboard ready for printing, created with the Handout Wizard.

# Tip 9: Create Nested Storyboards

What if you're not certain which of two stories you want to present until you're standing in front of the audience? The section "Tip 4: Multiple Stories, Multiple Templates" in Chapter 4 explored the possibilities of developing two related story templates in parallel. Both stories presumably relate to the same topic, so they should share the same Setting slide because this is a general statement about the context that everyone should agree is true. You can use this single slide as the starting point for whichever story you choose to present from that point forward.

To do this, create a separate PowerPoint file from each story template, and then copy and paste all of the slides from the second presentation to the right of the last slide in the first presentation. This creates a "nested" storyboard in which the second story sits in the same file as the first. Note the number of the slide that begins the Role slide of the second story.

When you present the Setting slide, ask the audience a question such as, "Which option do you prefer, 1 or 2?" Based on their responses, if you decide to stay on path 1 with the first story, you advance the slides as usual. But if you decide to take the alternative path 2, type the number of the Role slide of the second story and press Enter to go directly to that slide and begin that story instead.

The drawback of this approach is that you might have more than a hundred slides in the PowerPoint file to manage, so when you try it out, you'll need to balance the flexibility of a nested storyboard against the management challenges that large storyboards create.

## Tip 10: Rehearse with Your Headlines

Before adding sketches and graphics to the slides, which you'll do in Chapters 7 and 8, it's a good idea to rehearse the presentation with only the headlines on the slides. You might be more comfortable rehearsing alone at this stage, or you could rehearse with your team if you prefer to get some early feedback. To start, find a place to rehearse—either at your desk or in a conference room. Try to be aware of what you're doing with your body in relation to the computer and the screen.

Stand up to put yourself in a public speaking mode. If you use a remote control device, hold it in the palm of your nondominant hand so that you can advance the slides discreetly. Press the F5 key to begin the presentation from the first slide. Imagine the audience is in the room, and turn to face them. From the corner of your eye, glance at the first headline that appears on the screen, using it as a prompt to remind you what you wrote in the notes area. When you've nearly finished explaining what you want to say while that slide is displayed, discreetly advance to the next slide while you transition to the next topic with your spoken words, as prompted by the headline on the new slide.

Move your body around the room in a natural way when you want to emphasize a point or indicate your enthusiasm. Be aware of where you stand in relation to the screen—avoid being blinded by the light of the projector or standing in front of the projected image. Your goal should be to relate naturally to the audience using your body and voice and to use the screen to complement the presentation, not distract from it. Keep your hands at your sides except when you raise one or both of them in a gesture to support an important point.

Rehearsing using only the slide headlines increases your confidence in your topic and ensures that you're comfortable with the pace and flow of ideas. If you're working with a team, it's a great idea to run through a rehearsal like this to review the story, structure, and sequence of the presentation in slide form before proceeding to the next stage.

CHAPTER 7

# Sketching Your Storyboard

**WHEN YOU** put stylus to screen or pencil to paper to sketch your slides, it's a revolutionary moment in terms of Microsoft® Office PowerPoint® approaches. Think of the way you use PowerPoint according to the conventional approach—you open up a slide with a predesigned background, type a category heading such as **Our Company** in the title area, and then type a list of facts about the company below, maybe adding a small photo of your company building to spice things up. But now you are doing something completely different. There are no words to type—the headline already on the slide summarizes your point, and the off-screen text box holds the words that you will speak aloud. With just a clear headline on the blank slide before you, the only thing left to do now is to tap into your visual thinking skills to illustrate the headline.

## What Do I Sketch on Each Slide?

Sketching literally puts you in a different frame of mind, especially if you spend most of your day working with words and numbers. If sketching is completely new to you, you might find it difficult at first, and the prospect of sketching your entire storyboard, as shown in Figure 7-1, might be daunting. But just take it one slide at a time—this chapter guides you through the sketching process and shows you a range of specific sketches that you can draw on any one of your slides or across several of them. The sketches in this chapter relate to the specific example from the story template, but you can apply them to many types of presentations, as shown in the upcoming examples in Chapter 9. Be patient as you practice your new visual thinking skills—as you tackle the first few slides, your creativity will start to flow and you'll get the hang of sketching in no time.

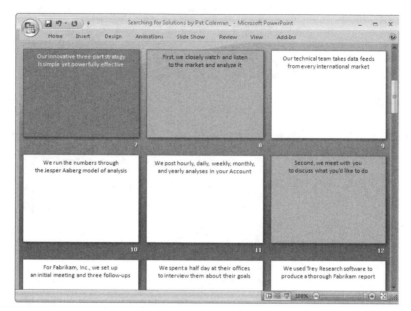

**FIGURE 7-1** This chapter will guide you through the process of sketching every slide in your storyboard.

Just as you wrote the verbal essence of your presentation in the story template, your focus now is to sketch the visual essence in the storyboard. Again, don't worry about the artistic quality of the sketches—they are only temporary placeholders for the graphics you'll add to each slide later. So let's get started at the start, by reviewing a range of sketching possibilities for your Act I slides.

# Sketching the Act I Slides

As you saw in Chapter 5, the first five slides of your presentation accomplish the crucial work of orienting the audience to your story and making the experience personal and relevant to them. When you import your headlines into PowerPoint, an additional slide is inserted in front of these five slides—a Title slide is automatically created from your title and byline, as shown in Figure 7-2. Now you will sketch illustrations for the Title slide along with the Act I slides to powerfully complement the clear and coherent flow of ideas you set in motion in the beginning of your story.

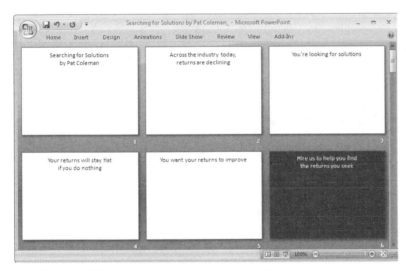

**FIGURE 7-2** The Title and Act I slides in the storyboard.

If you're using a Tablet PC, as you work through this chapter, you'll always review the slides to sketch in Slide Sorter view first, then click on an individual slide to sketch it in Normal view, and then return to Slide Sorter view to review your work. If you're using a paper storyboard, sort the printouts of slides in whatever way works best for you.

## Sketching the Title Slide

The Title slide will be the first thing to appear on the screen as you begin your talk, so it should intrigue the audience and set the visual tone of the presentation to come. In this instance, sketch a magnifying glass to illustrate "searching," as indicated in the title, "Searching for Solutions." As shown on the upper-left slide in Figure 7-3, sketch your organization's logo in the corner and perhaps add a note to use your company's colors on this slide.

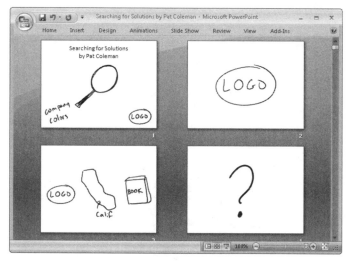

**FIGURE 7-3** A sketch of a Title slide (upper left) and three sketches of a possible Introductory slide: one with only the logo of your organization, another with three small icons, and a third with only a question mark.

## Sketching an Optional Introductory Slide

One of the most overlooked parts of the presentation experience is your introduction to the audience. A good introduction raises an audience's interest in the presentation and establishes your authority to give the talk in the first place. To make sure that your story gets off to a solid start, plan the way you'll be introduced by inserting an optional Introductory slide directly after the Title slide. In Slide Sorter view, position the cursor to the right of the Title slide in the presentation, and on the Home tab of the Ribbon, in the Slides group, click New Slide, and then select Blank on the drop-down menu.

What you sketch on the Introductory slide depends on who will be introducing you. If someone else will introduce you as a representative of your organization, sketch your organization's logo on the slide, as shown on the upper-right slide in Figure 7-3. In this case, only the logo will appear on screen while that person introduces you. If you're an expert in your field, sketch a photo of the cover of a report or book you've written.

In the notes area of this slide, write the introduction you would like the person who introduces you to read. Make it brief and informal, and include your relevant credentials as they relate to the topic of the presentation. This isn't about boosting your own ego—to be in the right frame of mind to listen to the presentation, the audience needs to know that you're the right person to be giving this talk. When you meet with the person who will introduce you, provide a printed Notes Page version of this slide to show what will be displayed on the screen along with the script of your introduction.

If you will introduce yourself at the start of your presentation, try sketching three visual icons that symbolize who you are in the context of the presentation. For example, as shown on the lower-left slide in Figure 7-3, sketch the logo of your organization, which will appear as you describe what you do there; then sketch the shape of the state of California, which will appear while you describe your upbringing in the state to your California audience; and then sketch the cover of your favorite book or movie, which will appear as you describe how that book or movie shaped who you are today. These three simple images are intended to prompt you to speak naturally, unlock your personality, and connect with your audience. When you add graphics later, animate the images so that they appear in sequence as you click your remote control.

If you're speaking to a small group or are conducting a workshop, consider inserting an additional Introductory slide asking your audience members to introduce themselves—to illustrate it, simply sketch a question mark, as on the lower-right slide in Figure 7-3. When the question mark appears on screen, ask the audience members to introduce themselves and relate one thing they would like to accomplish. As each person speaks, use a Tablet PC to write the names and responses on the screen, or write them on a flip chart. This approach demonstrates to the audience that you will listen to them, that you agree to accomplish certain tasks over the course of the presentation, and that you have created a record of the conversation. Review the same screen or flip chart again at the end of the presentation to make sure that you covered everything.

## Sketching the Setting Slide

Now you'll sketch the Setting slide, which orients the audience to the context of the presentation.

### Picture a Strong Start

As you probably remember from Chapter 4, the first five slides work their magic by appealing primarily to emotion. One of the most effective ways to enhance your appeal to emotion is by adding a full-screen photograph to the slide. If that's the way you want to go in this example, sketch a photo of a magazine cover with a headline about declining returns, as shown on the upper-left slide in Figure 7-4.

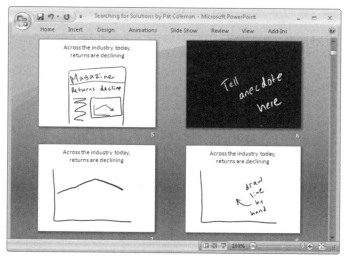

**FIGURE 7-4** Four ways to sketch the same Setting slide: a photograph of a magazine cover, a brief anecdote with a black screen, a chart, and only the axes of the chart—the line will be drawn by hand.

**TIP**　If you want to explore more than one sketch option for any slide in your storyboard, select the slide in Slide Sorter view, and then click **Ctrl+D** to duplicate it. Now try a different sketch on the duplicated slide, or create several slides and compare them side by side before you decide which sketch you like best.

## Tell a Story

Another way to start strong is to tell an anecdote—a brief story—while you display no graphic at all on the slide. In this case, the anecdote should communicate the point of the headline of the slide—be sure that your story lasts no more than a minute or two, because you have many more slides to present. If you want to include a longer anecdote that relates to more of the presentation, return to the story template to see how to weave the story through the Key Point, Explanation, or Detail slides.

Since you won't need a graphic if you're telling a brief verbal anecdote during the Setting slide, you could simply sketch the words *Black out screen* on the slide. Or take care of things now: Right-click the slide, and then select Format Background on the shortcut menu. In the Format Background dialog box, click Fill in the left pane, click Solid Fill in the right pane, and in the Color drop-down list, click Black. Make sure that the Transparency control is set to 0%, and then click Close. If you're using a Tablet PC, sketch a note to yourself using white ink reminding you to tell your anecdote here, as shown on the upper-right slide in Figure 7-4. You'll remove the note later. Making the background of any slide black in your storyboard ensures that when you review the presentation in Slide Sorter view, you see exactly where among the sequence of slides you will fade to black and what happens on the slides immediately before and after.

When you advance past the Title slide to the black slide, say something like, "I know you're expecting me to start with bullet points, but I'm going to start with a story instead." Your spoken words and the blank screen work together to create a sense of surprise, focusing attention intensely on you and what you say next—a good example of a strong way to start.

## Start with a Chart

When you decide what to sketch, it's important that you choose the visual elements that are the best fit for an audience. If you're presenting to executives in the financial industry, as in this example, it might not be a good fit to start with a sketch of a full-screen photograph on the Setting slide. A better fit would be to sketch the meaningful visuals these executives are more accustomed to seeing—charts and graphs. When you sketch a chart that everyone in the audience instantly recognizes (as in the example shown on the lower-left slide in Figure 7-4), you quickly connect with the audience because you're speaking the same visual language.

## Start with a Simple Line

To make the chart concept even more powerful, integrate other media in the Setting slide to increase engagement and make the experience more interesting. For example, sketch only the two axes of a chart on the slide, as shown on the lower-right slide in Figure 7-4. When you show the chart axes, say something like, "I know you all are familiar with what is happening in our industry, especially after the last Trey Research report." After a pause, position the stylus on the screen of your Tablet PC and draw a line traveling upward and then downward as you say, "Things have been good, but now they are turning in another direction." Since people don't usually write directly on screen during a presentation, this technique is sure to be memorable and catch everyone's attention. If you don't have a Tablet PC, do something similar by drawing the chart axes on a flip chart before your talk and then placing the chart near the podium. When you're ready, move to the flip chart and draw a similar line there.

## Start with a Video

Using a video is a great way to capture everyone's attention at the start of a presentation, especially when you present to large groups. If you have the resources to produce a video clip, make it brief to illustrate the headline on the Setting slide, or perhaps extend an extra bit of time to cover the headline of the Role slide. Sketch a note on the corresponding slides to indicate that's what you'll do there.

# Sketching the Role Slide

Next, on the Role slide, sketch something that engages the audience in the setting and puts them in the middle of the action. If you sketched a photograph on the Setting slide, as shown earlier on the upper-left slide in Figure 7-4, use the same sketch on this slide. During the presentation, write directly on the photograph using the stylus of your Tablet PC, crossing out the word *decline* and then writing on the screen *increase!*, as shown on the upper-left slide in Figure 7-5. If you don't have a Tablet PC, later add to this slide a text box with the word *decline* using the Text Box tool available in the Text group on the Insert tab of the Ribbon.

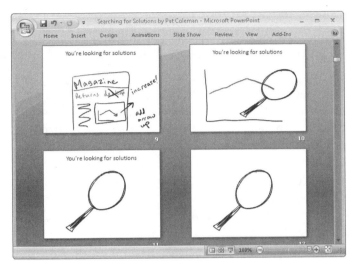

**FIGURE 7-5** Four ways to sketch the Role slide: using the Setting slide's photograph and updating the headline, using the Setting slide's chart and adding a magnifying glass, showing only the headline and the magnifying glass, and hiding the headline.

In a similar way, if you sketched a chart on the Setting slide, as shown on the lower-left slide in Figure 7-4, use it again on the Role slide. Sketch a small magnifying glass over the chart to illustrate the "searching" theme from the headline, as shown on the upper-right slide in Figure 7-5. Carrying over the same graphical element from the preceding slide helps to tell the story visually across the two storyboard frames. Your verbal explanation will keep the story flowing too, as you transition between the two slides by saying something like, "Although we all can agree that the returns are declining, we can also agree that you want to do something about it." Advance to the Role slide, and say, "Like everyone else, you've been searching for the next thing to do."

## Prompt with a Simple Photo

Try something a little different by sketching only a magnifying glass on the Role slide, as shown on the lower-left slide in Figure 7-5. This turns the slide into a visual prompt in which a photograph alone prompts you to unlock your natural voice. If you keep the photograph simple, the audience members will use their imagination and see themselves in the role and in the setting you verbally and visually describe.

## Hide the Headlines

To unlock even more visual power from the magnifying glass in the last example, hide the headline, as shown on the lower-right slide in Figure 7-5. When the headline is not visible on the screen, you increase the audience's reliance on you to explain why you are showing this image. To sketch this slide, simply draw a line through the headline. Or go ahead and take care of this now: right-click the border of the title area, and on the short-cut menu, click White in the Font Color drop-down list to make the font color match the background of this slide. When you do this, the headline remains on the slide but is hidden from the view of the audience unless you change the font color to something that's visible. Even though the headline is hidden to the audience, when you're working on the slide in Normal view, you can select the text of the headline and it will become visible so that you can read it and confirm the point you want to make here. To use this hidden headline technique effectively, use Presenter view so that you can see the off-screen notes area attached to the slide, or otherwise become so familiar with the slide that the photo alone prompts your memory about what to say next.

## Tap into the Power of Paper

Although you use a projector to show your slides on the screen, consider what paper can do for you too. Especially for an audience such as financial executives who likely want to see detailed data, quickly establish credibility by handing out a printed detailed analysis when you display one of the Act I slides. Here you would say something like, "We crunched the numbers and they're all here, but out of respect for your limited time, we've pulled to the top what we thought would be most relevant to your situation, which will be the focus of this presentation." Your handout could be printed copies of your presentation in Notes Page view, Microsoft Office Excel® spreadsheets, or whatever other format your data is in. If you like that idea, sketch a note on the slides where you plan to do that.

# Sketching the Point A and Point B Slides

As described in Chapter 4, the Point A slide engages the audience by describing a challenge they face, and the Point B slide motivates the audience by affirming what they want in light of the challenge. This gap between Point A and Point B forms the dramatic tension that you propose to resolve in the rest of the story. Just as the wording you choose for the Point A and Point B headlines can spell the difference between hitting or missing the mark with your audience, what you choose to sketch here will make the difference too. Because these two slides are so critical to the entire presentation, sketch them as a pair, as shown in Figure 7-6, as you carefully consider how to connect with the emotions of the audience and confirm that they care about the problem that exists in this gap between A and B.

**FIGURE 7-6** It's critical that you hit the mark of the Point A and Point B slides, both verbally and visually.

## Use an "Emotional" Chart

Just as with the Setting slide, it might be a good match with the financial executives in the room to use a chart on these two slides. Sketch a chart of the company's flat returns on the Point A slide, as shown on the upper-left slide in Figure 7-7. On the Point B slide, sketch several dotted arrows pointing up toward a range of possible improved returns, as shown on the upper-right slide in Figure 7-7. Although charts are normally considered purely objective displays of information, this chart is sure to stir up emotions if the executives are unhappy with the numbers at Point A and would like to get to Point B. The use of this particular chart in this context makes an emotional connection with this audience, although in other contexts and to other audiences, the same chart might not work. As with all presentations, sketch the graphics that are the best fit for your own audience.

**FIGURE 7-7** Two ways to sketch the pair of Point A and Point B slides. Top row: Sketch a chart on the Point A slide, and then sketch additional lines showing returns going up on the Point B slide. Bottom row: A split-screen layout starts with a photo on the left on the Point A slide; a second photo is added to the Point B slide.

## Double Your Impact by Splitting the Screen

Emphasize the dramatic tension that exists between Point A and Point B by sketching two contrasting photographs in juxtaposition. To do this with a Tablet PC, sketch a line down the middle of the Point A slide to indicate that you are going to place two photos side by side. To the left of the line, sketch the photograph that you would like to represent Point A—for example, a photograph that shows a downward arrow, as shown on the lower-left slide in Figure 7-7. Add the same sketch to the Point B slide, and then to the right of the midline, sketch a contrasting photograph—in this case, an upward arrow. When you show the slides in sequence, the Point A slide introduces the first photograph as you explain it, and then on the Point B slide, the second photo appears. Depending on which photographs you use for the two sides of the split screen, this pair of contrasting images can communicate the tension between A and B more powerfully than words ever could.

## Interact at Points A and B

A presentation is a live experience, and you can amplify the liveliness in the room by using a range of old and new techniques to help the audience feel even more involved. Of all the places in a presentation where you plan to interact with your audience in the storyboard, the Point A slide is a particularly good one. When you interact with your audience here, open a conversation to get the critical information you need to confirm that you are on track. If you hear from your audience that you are off track with your Point A slide, adapt your verbal narration or follow a different track through the material. (See "Tip 9: Create Nested Storyboards" in Chapter 6 for more information.) You can interact here and elsewhere in your storyboard in a number of ways.

## Take a Poll

To engage your audience using the Point A slide on the upper left in Figure 7-7, try one of the oldest and simplest techniques to prompt interaction: ask a question. Sketch a question mark on the chart. The Point A headline is "Your returns will stay flat if you do nothing." When you show this slide to a smaller group, ask an open-ended question such as, "Do you agree or disagree with that?" and then have a conversation about it. When you show the slide to a larger audience, ask the question, "How many of you **agree** with that?" and then hold up your hand to signal the audience to raise their hands. Quickly count the number of hands and tell the audience the results of the poll as you move on to the next point, "It looks like about two-thirds of you agree. Well, today we're going to talk about . . ." Taking a quick poll like this makes the audience feel like they're part of the conversation and also gives you a gauge of where the audience stands in relation to the topic. You can vary this technique with larger audiences by providing the audience with interactive polling devices, which some companies build specifically for PowerPoint. When you ask the audience a question, the results of the poll are displayed directly on your Point A slide in the form of a chart that summarizes the polling results.

## Introduce the Motif

So far, you've focused on numbers and charts to start off strong with the financial executives. If this approach is a match with your audience, another way to go is to sketch out a motif as it plays out over the Point A and Point B slides. If you chose to incorporate a motif through the headlines of your story template, now you'll extend this recurring theme from your written words to the sketches of your slides. For example, if you use a puzzle motif in the story template, the Point A headline might read, "You're hearing conflicting pieces of advice that leave you uncertain" and the Point B headline might be "Seeing the big picture will help you decide how to improve the returns." As shown in Figure 7-8, sketch three puzzle pieces on the upper-left Point A slide to visually refer to the "conflicting pieces." Sketch the pieces coming together on the upper-right Point B slide to form the "big picture."

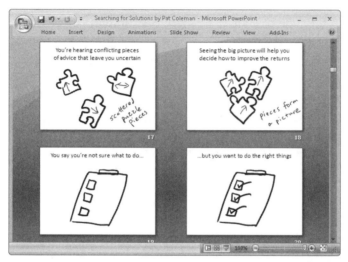

**FIGURE 7-8** Two ways to sketch the pair of Point A and Point B slides. Top row: Introduce the motif of scattered puzzle pieces, and then show the pieces coming together to form a picture. Bottom row: The Point A slide shows a clipboard with empty check boxes, and the Point B slide shows the check boxes selected.

An alternative motif might have a Point A headline that reads, "You say you're not sure what to do . . ." and a Point B headline that reads, ". . . but you want to do the right things." As shown in the bottom row in Figure 7-8, sketch the clipboard with empty check boxes on the Point A slide, and then sketch check marks in the same boxes on the Point B slide.

Later the Point A and Point B slides would be a good place to add subtle animation because these slides serve the important function of capturing the audience's attention in Act I. As shown in the top row in Figure 7-8, sketch a note to animate the puzzle pieces to appear and then scatter on the Point A slide and then come together to form the picture on the Point B slide. And as shown in the bottom row in Figure 7-8, the check boxes on the clipboard could appear on the Point A slide, and then the check marks could appear one by one on the Point B slide. Whatever motif you choose, you'll have a sense of how that motif can start playing out visually as you sketch the additional slides of the storyboard.

## Unlock Information with a Visual Prompt

To use interaction to obtain useful information from your audience, sketch a simple photo object that relates to your topic on one or both of the Point A and Point B slides, and then use the photo to prompt conversation about specific topics. For example, if your Point A headline reads, "You're hearing conflicting pieces of advice," sketch the names of your company's competitors on the screen and then hide the headline. Then, when the names appear on the slide, you might say, "We understand you've been talking to many other companies about this. What sorts of things have you been hearing?" Not only does this technique demonstrate to your audience that you will listen from the start and that they can participate in the conversation, but it also opens the door for you to hear information from the audience that might be useful to you.

## Link the Act I Slides with a Single Chart or Photograph

To tie together even more tightly the slides in this example, consider sketching one image across all of Act I. Figure 7-9 shows how to do this. The Title slide includes a sketch of a magnifying glass, then the Setting slide shows a chart of the industry returns declining, and then the Role slide shows the chart and magnifying glass. The Point A slide keeps the industry returns line of the chart but now adds the specific company's data— to do this, use a different color ink on either your Tablet PC or on paper to distinguish the different lines in the chart. The Point B slide illustrates what the company wants to achieve by showing three arrows pointing upward. The final Call to Action slide adds the magnifying glass directly over the upward arrows and shows the logo of your company.

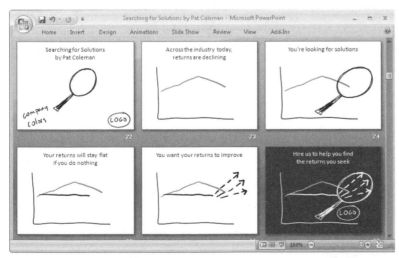

**FIGURE 7-9** Telling a visual story using a single chart across all of the Act I slides.

This is a good example of how your PowerPoint slides are no longer like pieces of paper filled with lists of facts. Now your slides are like frames in a filmstrip, moving at a pace of about one frame per minute, with your voice providing the soundtrack to a clear and compelling story. Although to the audience, your presentation is a single smooth and seamless experience, in fact you have packed a great deal of information into these frames and have covered the five essential elements that ensure that you always start strong, as described in Chapter 4: orienting, interesting, engaging, motivating, and focusing your audience.

**TIP** You could also build the same sort of visual story across the frames of Act I by sketching a single photograph, copying it to each slide, and then sketching additional elements on each slide. If you present using a Tablet PC, sketch graphical elements directly on the photograph for more impact.

If you want to increase the visual impact of these Act I slides, sketch a note on the slides that you plan to hide the headlines so that only the graphics are visible to the audience. As described earlier, when you present slides without headlines, the simple graphics make the audience rely on you to describe the slides' meaning, which creates an engaging interdependence between speaker and audience. This is an effective technique to use on your Act I slides while you make an emotional connection with your audience.  Later, on the Act II slides, you'll usually want to keep your headlines visible to your audience to guide their attention through the much larger volume of information.

Although in this example the Call to Action slide shown in Figure 7-9 was sketched as part of the group of Act I slides, be sure you visually integrate it with the important Key Point slides, as you'll do next.

**TABLET PC SKETCHING TIPS**

The best way to sketch a visual story across slides using a Tablet PC is to work backward from the last slide to the first. For example, in the sequence of slides shown in Figure 7-9, first sketch all the elements you want to include on the lower-right Call to Action slide. On the Review tab, choose Start Inking, and on the Pens tab, click Select Objects, hold down the **Ctrl** key while you click to select the Ink objects you want to include, and then right-click and select Copy. Go to the preceding slide, right-click and paste the Ink objects, and then on the Pens tab, click Eraser and move the mouse pointer over the parts of the sketch you don't need. Then copy this sketch, and follow the same steps as you work backward through the slides. Designing the last slide in the sequence first ensures that the final slide is organized and composed in a way that works—if you were to build from the first slide to the last, you would probably end up making changes to the last slide's layout. Working backward through the sequence also saves time because you don't need to keep resketching the same elements on the slides in the sequence. Unfortunately, inking on your Tablet PC works only in Normal view and not in Slide Sorter view, so you will need to frequently switch back and forth between the two views to see how the story is flowing visually across slides.

# Sketching the Call to Action and Key Point Slides

Your next job is to sketch the most important group of slides in the presentation—the Call to Action and Key Point slides. If you're using a Tablet PC, to see the Key Point slides together, zoom out in Slide Sorter view, and then locate the Key Point slides. Drag each one in sequence so that they follow the Call to Action slide, as shown in Figure 7-10. When you've finished sketching, you'll drag these slides back to their original positions. You don't have to do this every time you sketch, but it is helpful as you're honing your storyboarding skills. It's important that you see and work with these four slides together as a visual package because when each slide appears in its sequence in the storyboard, it should cue the audience that these are the most important slides in the presentation. If you're working on paper printouts, flip through the storyboard to see where these slides are.

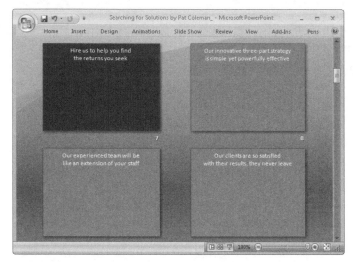

**FIGURE 7-10** The dark gray Call to Action and medium gray Key Point slides should be the most visually memorable in the storyboard.

The Call to Action headline summarizes the Key Point headlines, and in turn the Key Point headlines summarize the Explanation headlines and the Explanation headlines summarize the Detail slides. Because the Call to Action headline sits at the top of the informational hierarchy, as described in Chapter 5, it is really the verbal summary of the entire presentation. Likewise, what you sketch on the Call to Action slide should be a visual summary of the Key Point slides and of the entire presentation—if you had only one slide to show, this one would be it.

This group of slides formed by the Call to Action and three Key Point slides (CTA+3) is so important, you'll want to sketch the group using the most creative, memorable, and powerful techniques you can come up with. If you have a marketing background, on these slides, you will apply the most powerful "branding" techniques you know—the set of techniques you use to visually distill a message and integrate it through an experience. The only difference here is that you're not applying these techniques to your corporate identity; instead, you're applying them to the highest level of ideas in your presentation.

Following are a range of techniques to "brand" the top level of your thinking on your CTA+3 slides. These sketching ideas are some of the basics—as you become comfortable with sketching, try out your own ideas, or invite a graphic designer to give you a hand.

## Tripling Your Impact with Three Panels

A simple yet effective visual technique is to sketch full-screen photographs to illustrate each of the Key Point slides. Full-screen photographs can be a good fit on the CTA+3 slides if they function to make the ideas of the headlines memorable. In the example shown on the upper-right slide in Figure 7-11, the first Key Point slide refers to "three-part strategy," so the sketch of the photograph includes a clipboard with a piece of paper that has three check boxes. The second Key Point slide, on the lower left, refers to an "experienced team," so that sketch illustrates a photo of the team. The third Key Point slide refers to the clients being "satisfied," so the sketch is of a photo of a client survey with *100%* written on it, along with some clients' logos around the document.

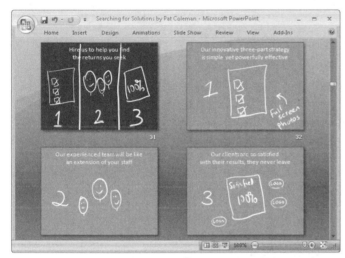

**FIGURE 7-11** Sketches of the Call to Action slide with a three-panel layout and the Key Point slides with full-screen photographs.

Now that you've sketched three photographs on the Key Point slides, use these elements to sketch a *triptych*, or a single slide with three vertical graphical elements placed side by side. To create a triptych on the Call to Action slide (upper left), draw two vertical lines through the slide to create three panels, and then sketch in each of the three panels a key visual detail from each of the three photographs that were sketched on the Key Point slides. As shown in Figure 7-11, sketch the numbers *1*, *2*, and *3* below each of the three photographs on the Call to Action slide, and sketch the corresponding numbers on each Key Point slide. As you present them in sequence, these sketches form a tight, crisp visual package across these most important slides.

## Propping It Up

A classic technique in oral presentations is to show a physical prop and explain how the object relates to the presentation. The CTA+3 slides are a good place to integrate a prop, especially when you tie in that prop with your motif. For example, hold up a numbered puzzle piece when you present each Key Point slide to carry through a puzzle motif. Or better yet, pass out to your audience their own numbered puzzle pieces they can hold—they will literally carry the main message of the presentation out of the room in their hands, and undoubtedly in their long-term memories too. If you plan to use a physical prop, sketch a photograph of it on the CTA+3 slides—during the presentation, you'll show the photo of the prop on the screen while you display the prop physically in the room.

## Adding It Up with Icons

Another way to go with your sketches is related to the three-panel photographs approach, except here you sketch simple icons that represent the essence of your idea in a basic visual form. For example, as shown on the third Key Point slide on the lower right in Figure 7-12, sketch the "innovative three-part strategy" as the numbers *1-2-3* in a box, the "experienced team" as a group of three face symbols, and "our clients are so satisfied" as a piece of paper with the figure *100%* on it. Sketch only the first and second icons on the second Key Point slide, and only the first icon on the first Key Point slide. It would be fine to use the same graphic on the third Key Point slide and on the Call to Action slide—sketch a note to differentiate the Call to Action version later by adding animation to that slide only.

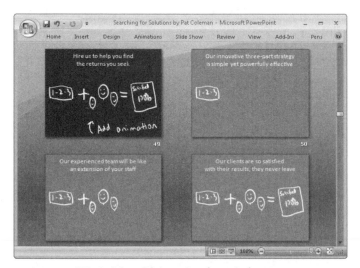

**FIGURE 7-12** CTA+3 slides with icons in a formula format.

As shown here, you build a *visual formula* out of the icons by sketching a plus sign after the first icon and an equal sign after the second element. You can also sketch the numbers *1-2-3* or the letters *A-B-C* alongside each icon to relate that familiar organizational structure to the audience and build the formula *1+2=3* or *A+B=C*. If your headlines support the concept, create an unexpected formula that will play out in the presentation such as 1+1=11, which will intrigue your audience as they wait to see how you will explain what it means.

## Using Video, Sound, or Motion Graphics (Carefully)

If you plan to use video, audio, or motion graphics in your presentation, these forms of media stand out so significantly from the even pacing of your presentation that you want to use them carefully and strategically. Before you use them, consider the research study described in Chapter 2 that found when you remove extraneous information from a multimedia presentation, you increase learning. Remember, in Act II it's all about the hierarchy in your storyboard, and your measure of success is if your audience can recall and apply the information on your Key Point slides. If you can use video, sound, or motion graphics to illustrate the Key Point headlines, go ahead and sketch these elements on the Key Point slides. Be very careful about using these types of media in another part of the presentation if you don't use them on your Key Point slides—you would be unsuccessful in your presentation if the audience remembered your trendy video on the Detail slides but not the message of your Key Point slides.

## Blacking Out the Screen

Earlier in this chapter, you learned about displaying a blank screen for the Setting slide while you tell an anecdote, creating a sense of surprise after the Title slide, when the audience expects to see bullet points on screen. Now that you've sketched a number of other slides, consider fading to black to emphasize the Key Point slides. Visuals projected on a screen can be spellbinding, but when you break that spell by blacking out the screen, you focus the audience's attention completely on you and your ideas at a specific moment. This creates an abrupt shift in the presentation with dramatic effect that works well to emphasize your three Key Point slides.

To plan for this, sketch the letter *B* on the corner of your Key Point slides. You'll remove the note later when you add graphics to the slide, but for now it's your cue that after you present the first Key Point slide, you'll press the **B** key on your keyboard, or the appropriate button on your remote control, to turn the screen to black. Then, as all eyes turn to you, you'll emphasize verbally the key point. When you've finished, you'll press the **B** key again to return to the Key Point slide before moving on. (Alternatively, press the **W** key to turn the screen to white.) Later, when you get to the second and third Key Point slides, you'll do the same.

## Raising Interest with Your Layouts

A striking way to set up your CTA+3 slides is to use a distinctive layout to make them stand out among all the other slides in the storyboard. In Chapter 6, you set up a preliminary medium gray background on the Key Point slides when you set up the storyboard. You can change those placeholder backgrounds to something more striking—for example, by using a split-screen layout on the Key Point slides. This layout style, shown in Figure 7-13, is a quick and easy way to set up these slides for sketches, and it's a particularly good fit for using icons as described earlier in this chapter.

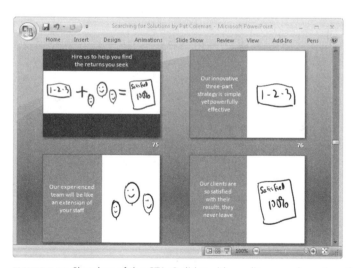

**FIGURE 7-13** Sketches of the CTA+3 slides with a split-screen layout on the Key Point slides.

In Chapter 8, you'll explore PowerPoint features to set up and apply different layouts to the different levels of the storyboard. For now, if you want to quickly set up these slides to see how they look when you sketch on them in split-screen layout format, go to Normal view for the first Key Point slide. On the Insert tab, in the Illustrations group, click Shapes and then select Rectangle. Position the cursor in the upper right of the slide, click and drag until the rectangle fills half the screen, and then right-click the box and add a white fill. Then click and drag the headline to the left and click and drag the sizing handles to fit the headline, as shown on the upper-right slide in Figure 7-13. Copy and paste the rectangle to the other two Key Point slides, and adjust the headlines. On the Call to Action slide, add a horizontal white rectangle to the middle of the slide to distinguish this slide from the Key Point slides, as shown on the upper-left slide in Figure 7-13. Once you have the temporary layouts in place on the CTA+3 slides, sketch on the slides as usual.

## Keeping the Motif Flowing

Your sketches will start to really strengthen your visual story if you have used a motif throughout your story template. For example, carry the puzzle motif from the Act I slides to the Call to Action slide, as shown on the upper-left slide in Figure 7-14. Beginning with the third Key Point slide on the lower right, sketch three puzzle pieces together with the numbers *1-2-3*, then put the first two puzzle pieces on the second Key Point slide on the lower left, and then put the first puzzle piece on the first Key Point slide on the upper right. You can still add photos to the slides if you want—sketch a photo of a document on the first Key Point slide on the upper right, the people photo on the lower-left slide, and the customer survey form and logos on the lower-right slide.

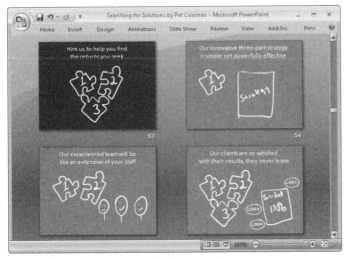

**FIGURE 7-14** Sketches of the CTA+3 slides with a puzzle motif.

The photos in this example might or might not be full-screen, depending on the actual photos you use. They could also be simple photo objects with the backgrounds cut out. Or if you want to get really creative, bring the puzzle motif and the photos together by sketching each photo inside a puzzle piece.

## Integrating the Interaction

Just as the Point A and Point B slides are good places to ask questions and prompt dialog, other good places to do that are just before the second and third Key Point slides. To plan for audience interaction at these points, go to Slide Sorter view after you sketch your Key Point slides, select Key Point 1, and then click **Ctrl+D** to duplicate the slide. Drag the duplicate Key Point 1 slide to just before the Key Point 2 slide. Now select Key Point 2, duplicate it, and drag the duplicate to just before Key Point 3. After you present the Explanation and Detail slides that follow Key Point 1, you'll see the Key Point 1 slide again, and there you'll pause to ask for questions. When you've finished, advance to the Key Point 2 slide. Pause again after the Key Point 2 slide, and then advance to Key Point 3. You also might choose to duplicate these slides in Chapter 8, after you've added graphics to visually reinforce the Key Point slides at the end of the first and second Act II scenes.

## More than One Speaker

Some organizations feature multiple speakers during a presentation—if you plan to do that, put each of three speakers in charge of one of the three Act II scenes. Hand over the microphone to the next speaker when it is that person's turn to present the assigned Key Point, Explanation, and Detail slides. The change of speaker adds emphasis to each of the Key Point slides, but because the presentation is constructed from a single underlying story template, the people in the audience experience a single story that makes sense to them. Make a note on each Key Point slide of the name of the assigned speaker if you plan to do this.

## Going Back to A and B

As always, keep on the lookout for ways to visually link frames across the storyboard. For example, if you sketch on your Tablet PC the split-screen photographic approach for the Point A and Point B slides, as shown on the left and middle slides in Figure 7-15, carry over the photographs to the Call to Action slide. Here, sketch an arrow over the two photographs to literally show that you will be taking your audience from Point A to Point B, and sketch the numerals *1 2 3* over the arrow, as shown on the right slide in Figure 7-15.

You will develop this 1-2-3 numerical structure in the sketches of the Key Point slides to come. The more you can sketch a singular visual story across the acts and levels of the storyboard like this, the more elegant your presentation will become.

**FIGURE 7-15** Sketches showing how to carry over the split-screen approach from the Point A and Point B slides to the Call to Action slide.

Now that you've explored the CTA+3 sketches, in Slide Sorter view, drag the Key Point slides back to where they belong in sequence. Review the storyboard to see how these slides guide the working memory of your audience across the levels of the storyboard— first with the first Key Point slide, then with the Explanation slides, and then with the Detail slides, with each level of the slide design carrying the visual story forward from the preceding one.

Next you'll explore a visual way to link the rest of the slides to come—by sketching a navigation bar.

## Sketching an Optional Navigation Bar

You can tie together the slides of the presentation even more tightly with a visual navigation bar at the bottom of the screen. In the conventional PowerPoint approach, the space at the bottom of a screen usually contains the presenting organization's logo. You can certainly sketch your own organization's logo to illustrate the point of any single slide in the storyboard if the headline calls for that, or you can sketch the logo on the Introductory slide, as described earlier. But you would not sketch your logo on other slides because doing so adds extraneous visual information for working memory to process, which impairs learning, as described in Chapter 2. (Besides, putting your logo on every slide sends the wrong visual message that every slide is all about you, when it is really all about the audience.)

A much better way to use the small space at the bottom of the Explanation and Detail slides is to visually cue your audience to the organization of, and current location within, the presentation. For example, if you use a puzzle motif through the presentation, after you sketch the first puzzle piece on the first Key Point slide, add a small horizontal bar at the bottom of the subsequent Explanation and Detail slides, and then sketch a small puzzle piece throughout these slides, as shown in Figure 7-16. You'll learn how to set up and apply navigation bars using custom layouts in Chapter 8.

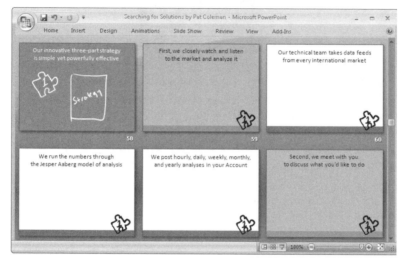

**FIGURE 7-16** The light gray Explanation slides and white Detail slides now include a navigation bar with a single puzzle piece.

After you add a second puzzle piece to the second Key Point slide, add a similar puzzle piece to the navigation bar through the rest of the Explanation and Detail slides in this section, as shown in Figure 7-17. Then, after you add a third puzzle piece to the third Key Point slide, add three similar puzzle pieces to the navigation bar through the rest of the Explanation and Detail slides in that section.

As the audience views the slides in sequence, the navigation bar appears the same, until you reach the slides in the subsequent Key Point section, when they see a new puzzle piece appear to cue them that they are in a new section.

**FIGURE 7-17** The second Key Point slide and the Explanation slides and Detail slides with a navigation bar with a second puzzle piece added.

## Sketching the Explanation Slides

Your next job is to sketch the second-most important slides in the presentation—the Explanation slides for each scene of Act II. In Slide Sorter view, zoom out to locate the light gray Explanation slides, and then drag each one in order to follow their corresponding Key Point slide to see them together, as shown in Figure 7-18. When you've finished sketching, you'll drag these slides back to their previous positions. As with the CTA+3 slides, it's important that you see and work with these four slides together as a package—just as each Key Point headline summarizes the Explanation headlines to come, each Key Point slide should visually summarize its Explanation slides.

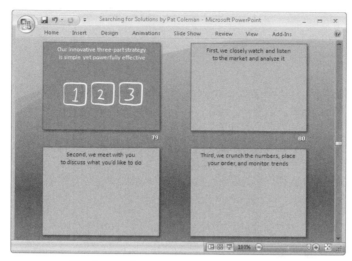

**FIGURE 7-18** The first medium gray Key Point slide and its corresponding light gray Explanation slides.

Look at the sketch you created for the Key Point slide, and then read your Explanation headlines and imagine how to sketch the story forward across these slides. If you can sketch a single visual story across the Explanation slides, you should. But it might be that the Explanation slides are independent facts that are tied together only by the preceding Key Point slide and not to one another. If the Detail slides stand alone as independent ideas, sketch a standalone illustration for each one and use other techniques to visually tie the Explanation slides together, such as a similar split-screen layout or with a navigation bar running through the Explanation slides, as described earlier.

## Explaining Ideas by Building a Diagram

A common problem in conventional PowerPoint presentations occurs when a diagram or chart is too complex to be understood—or at least not understood all at once on a single slide. If your audience is new to the information in any diagram or chart, you can easily overwhelm the limited capacity of the working memory of your audience and impair learning. You address the underlying root of this problem by breaking down Key Point headlines in the story template into smaller pieces as you write the Explanation and Detail headlines, which later become the foundation for individual slides that appear on screen for less than a minute while you narrate each slide.

Because you have used this approach of breaking down complicated ideas into smaller pieces, instead of explaining a great deal of information in a diagram on a single slide for many minutes, you can explain the same information in smaller pieces for less than a minute each, across a series of slides. This ensures that you present new information evenly over the sequence of slides of any explanation, showing and saying only the correct information at the correct time to ensure that you do not overload or split the attention of the working memory of your audience between what you are saying and showing at any moment.

After you have broken up an idea into smaller pieces across a set of Explanation headlines in the story template, building a diagram across the corresponding series of Explanation slides is an effective way to illustrate your ideas if you are describing a process or how the parts of something relate to the whole. For example, you might sketch on your Key Point slide a simple diagram with three numbered boxes to illustrate the "three-part strategy," as shown on the upper-left slide in Figure 7-19. Carry through this simple structure by sketching three similar boxes on the third Explanation slide. Sketch number labels below the boxes, and then sketch an eye icon in the first box to illustrate "we closely watch and listen," a clock icon to illustrate "we meet with you," and a row of small numbers from a spreadsheet to illustrate "we crunch the numbers," as shown on the lower-right slide in Figure 7-19. Sketch an arrow to show the motion in the diagram from left to right. Next sketch the same first two boxes on the second Explanation slide (lower left) and only the first box on the first Explanation slide (upper right).

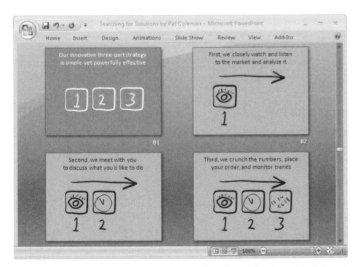

**FIGURE 7-19** Sketches of a Key Point slide and Explanation slides showing a diagram carried across the slides.

Review these four slides. You show first a simple 1-2-3 illustration that introduces and summarizes the topic. Then you show and narrate the first headline with the first part of the diagram and build the diagram over the next two slides. Notice that the third Explanation slide has more detail than the Key Point slide. You generally want the Key Point slide as simple as possible so that you don't overwhelm the working memory of your audience with too much new information too quickly. As you develop the diagram over the three Explanation slides, the final slide is easy to understand because each element has been appropriately introduced both verbally and visually, piece by piece.

Although this example diagram is a basic one, when you apply the same approach to other types of diagrams, you will make sure that you properly synchronize the verbal and visual channels of working memory, as described in Chapter 2. When you present your slides this way, you also align with the research-based *temporal contiguity principle* described in Richard E. Mayer's research, which is based on studies that show that people understand information better when animation and narration are presented together rather than animation first and narration second.

**TIP** If you find that your headlines don't quite map to the sequence in which you want to present information, return to the story template and adjust the headlines there first, and then return to PowerPoint to edit the headlines accordingly.

## Building a Chart Across a Series of Slides

After you have broken up an idea into smaller pieces across a set of Explanation headlines in the story template, building a chart across the corresponding series of Explanation slides is an effective way to illustrate your ideas if you are describing quantitative information. With the sequence of headlines in place in the storyboard, you'll know exactly what you want to communicate before you start building the chart. Again, this is where the wording of the headlines in the story template will define what you sketch. Build a chart across a series of Explanation slides if the headlines contain specific quantitative explanation, such as "The industry average returns are 20%" and "Your average returns are 10%" and then "We can help you close the gap." If your headlines don't explain a chart but you would like them to do so, return to the story template to see how to revise the headlines to make the chart work.

**TIP** If you have difficulty sketching the Explanation slides, sketch the Detail slides first and then return to the Explanation slides. This approach can be helpful because the Explanation slide summarizes the Detail slides to come, and if you sketch the Detail slides first, you can use them to come up with a visual summary for the Explanation slide.

## Sketching a Visual Organizer

Earlier in Figure 7-8, the sketch of a clipboard with check boxes served to visually carry an idea across the Point A and Point B slides. Try a similar concept using check boxes to visually organize your ideas across your Explanation slides. On the upper left in Figure 7-20, the Key Point slide features a sketch of a piece of paper with three completed check boxes to illustrate the three-part strategy. Sketch the first Explanation slide (upper right) with only one check box and the word *analyze* from the headline, and then on the second Explanation slide (lower left), add a second check box and the word *meet* from the headline. On the third Explanation slide (lower right), add a third check box with the word *monitor* from the headline.

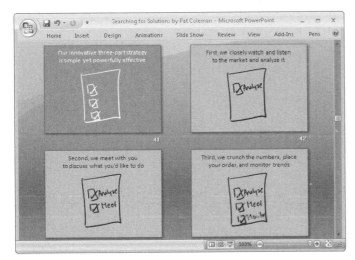

**FIGURE 7-20** Sketches of a Key Point slide and Explanation slides using a checklist to visually tie them tightly together.

As they appear in sequence, the Key Point slide introduces the simple visual concept of the three check boxes, the first Explanation slide introduces the concept of analyzing from the headline, the next slide builds on the preceding one and adds the concept of meeting, and then the third slide builds on the preceding slide and adds the concept of monitoring. When each Explanation slide is dragged back to its position in the storyboard, it introduces another layer of meaning to the visual checklist story and at the same time ties together the Detail slides that follow.

## Completing the Explanation Slides

Many of the sketch possibilities you have reviewed so far in this chapter can also be a good fit with the rest of the Explanation slides. For example, simply sketch a few words on an Explanation slide, as shown on the upper-right slide in Figure 7-21, to note that you'll include the names of "every major firm" on the slide. Sketch a personal digital assistant, as shown on the lower-left slide, to illustrate "only a text message away," or sketch several photographs, including a phone and a computer screen, to illustrate "communications according to your style," as shown on the lower–right slide.

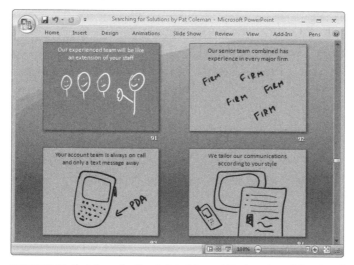

**FIGURE 7-21** Sketches of a Key Point slide and Explanation slides that show photographs, text, and a screen capture.

## Using a Screen Capture

For a quick illustration, consider sketching a screen capture. Almost anything that can be viewed on a computer screen can be captured and displayed on a slide, including pictures of your desktop, Web pages, documents, and more. The sketch on the lower-right slide in Figure 7-21 includes a screen capture of an e-mail message to illustrate a type of communication.

Another good use of a screen capture is to convey more detailed quantitative information available in other documents. For example, each dollar amount or other piece of quantitative information included in a headline is likely derived from an Office Excel spreadsheet or another data source that reflects the detailed analysis that produced it. You could probably spend an hour discussing the details of any single figure, but if you did that, you wouldn't have time to cover any of the other points in the presentation. Instead, sketch a screen capture of a close-up of a spreadsheet on a slide, and when you display the slide, explain that the detailed data is contained there. Sketch a note on the slide that you will also bring printouts of the spreadsheet providing the detailed financial analysis and explanation that back up the headline. Now the headline communicates the main idea that you want to get across, the tightly cropped screen capture of the spreadsheet indicates that you can back up your point, your verbal explanation conveys what you intend, and you have backup in the printouts.

## MY DIAGRAM DOESN'T FIT!

If you have a diagram that you've used in other presentations and you'd like to fit it into your new BBP presentation, go to the story template and figure out where the pieces of the explanation of the diagram fit into the overall story. If the diagram contains information that is new to the audience, you need to break it up into smaller pieces in order to ease the new information through the working memory of your audience. As you use the story template to explain the diagram, think of the three main parts of the diagram and describe them in the Key Point headlines. Then complete the story template as before, breaking up each Key Point piece into smaller pieces in the Explanation headlines and then breaking each Explanation subpiece into smaller pieces in the Detail headlines. When you return to the storyboard to revise the storyboard headlines, you'll have laid the groundwork for a series of slides that explains the new information in the diagram piece by piece, slide by slide—rather than all at once.

When you've finished sketching the Explanation slides, in Slide Sorter view, drag each slide back to where it belongs in the sequence of the storyboard. Now look at the storyboard and see how these slides guide your audience across the sections of the storyboard—first with a Key Point slide, followed by an Explanation slide, and then the Detail slides, all carrying the visual story forward.

# Sketching the Detail Slides

Your last job is to sketch the third-most important slides in the presentation—the Detail slides that follow each Explanation slide. In Slide Sorter view, zoom in to see a set of Explanation and Detail slides together, as shown in Figure 7-22. It's important that you see and work with these four slides together as a package, because when you write out an Explanation headline in Act II, it summarizes the Detail headlines that come next. Similarly, each Explanation slide should be a visual summary of the Detail slides.

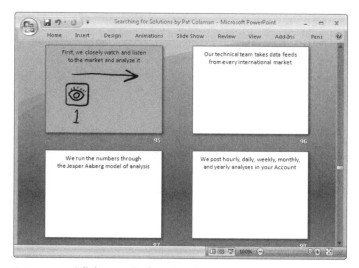

**FIGURE 7-22** A light gray Explanation slide and the following three white Detail slides.

Look at the sketch of the Explanation slide, and then read the following Detail headlines and imagine how to sketch the story forward across the Detail slides. If you can sketch a single visual story across the Detail slides, you should. But it might be that the Detail slides are independent thoughts that are tied together only by the preceding Explanation slide—in that case, sketch standalone illustrations for each Detail slide.

You should be getting the hang of things by now, as you've already sketched many of the elements that you can also sketch on the Detail slides. Some of the techniques for creating illustrations can be used at any level of the storyboard, depending on what your headlines say. Here are some of the techniques you can use to sketch the Detail slides:

- **Use photos, screen captures, or other graphics.** As in the previous levels, sketch photographs for your Detail slides such as a book cover photo, as on the lower-left slide in Figure 7-23, or a screen capture such as a Web page, as on the lower-right slide. If a photo alone doesn't work, you might include additional informational elements that you will add to the photo such as the arrows on the globe on the upper-right slide.

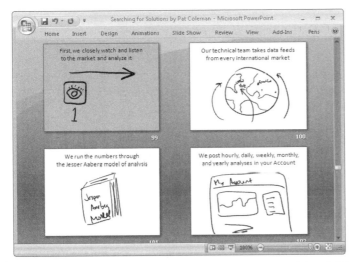

**FIGURE 7-23** An Explanation slide with part of a diagram and Detail slides with a photo and added arrows, a photograph, and a screen capture.

- **Use a chart, graph, or diagram.** You can sketch a chart, graph, or diagram on a single slide or across three Explanation or Detail slides, depending on what your headlines say. The bottom-row Detail slides in Figure 7-24 feature sketches of charts to illustrate single headlines.

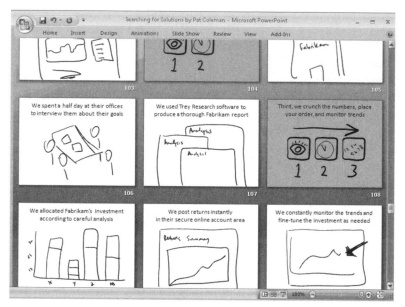

**FIGURE 7-24** Explanation slides with parts of a diagram and Detail slides with photographs, screen captures, and charts.

## Switching to Other Media

In many instances, you might want to switch out of PowerPoint and into another software application to demonstrate an activity. For example, an instructor would switch over to Office Excel to demonstrate how to use one of its features, or to Office Word to show how to edit a document. The Explanation headline on the upper-left slide in Figure 7-25 reads "First, we closely watch and listen to the market and analyze it." Here you can sketch an additional graphic or use the headline alone by clicking on the title box in Normal view and dragging it to the center of the screen.

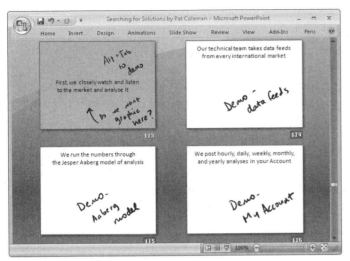

**FIGURE 7-25** An Explanation slide showing where you'll switch to another software program. The Detail slides are hidden while you use the other program before returning to the Explanation slide.

The three Detail slides could easily be illustrated with a live demonstration of the technical feeds (upper right), a review of the actual analysis model (lower left), and a tour of the account page features (lower right)—sketch a note to that effect on each slide, as shown in Figure 7-25. Next click the first Detail slide and hold down the Ctrl key as you select the second and third Detail slides, and then right-click and select Hide Slide. Now the audience will not see the three hidden slides, but you know in the planning phase that the headlines are there to guide the points you will make over the next three minutes.

During the presentation, when you arrive at the Explanation slide (upper left), verbally explain the point of the headline. When you're ready to switch to the first live demonstration, hold down the Alt key while you press the Tab key, and then in the window that appears, press the Tab key again until you select the corresponding software application that is open on your desktop, and then release the Alt key. After you've shown what you need to illustrate the headline, press Alt+Tab again until you select the software application that is open on your desktop that corresponds to the second hidden slide (lower left). After you've shown the demonstration, press Alt+Tab again until you select the software application that is open on your desktop that corresponds to the third hidden slide (lower right). (If you have the Microsoft Aero™ color scheme enabled on a Windows Vista® computer, instead of Alt+Tab, hold down the Windows key and repeatedly press Tab to use a 3-D interface to select applications.) When you've finished with the third application, press Alt+Tab and return to PowerPoint, where you'll see the Explanation slide again. The headline here summarizes the point you made during the demonstrations; from here, advance to the next slide, which will be the following Explanation slide.

With this technique, you're using PowerPoint as a tool to manage what's happening on-screen and off-screen as well. As always, the headlines of the slides should establish the ideas you want to communicate at any and every point in the presentation. You can use the same technique to manage a number of other non-PowerPoint media, including:

- A flip chart, whiteboard, or chalkboard.

- A document projector.

- Video clips, audio, or motion graphics.

- A physical prop.

- Paper handouts.

## Adapting Your Sketches to Your Profession

As you're thinking about what other sketches to include on your Detail slides, review the optional Act II headings in the section "Tip 3: Tailor Your Act II Column Headings to Your Profession," in Chapter 5. For example, if you're a market researcher, your Detail slides will probably include sketches of screen captures that illustrate your analytical tools, brief video clips from focus groups, and of course charts, graphs, and diagrams. If you're a lawyer, your Detail slides will contain sketches of your specific evidence, such as screen captures of your "hot documents," photographs, short clips from video depositions, and scientific drawings. If you're selling a software product, your Detail slides will probably include sketches of the various sections of your product demonstration.

# Sketching Your Story Template

It might take some time to learn the new skills of sketching your slides across frames and across levels. If you're having a tough time figuring out how to sketch diagrams, charts, and other Explanation or Detail slide elements, you might find it helpful to leave PowerPoint for a few minutes and review a printed copy of your story template. Read through the headlines from top to bottom in the Explanation column, and sketch directly over the column how you want to illustrate each Explanation slide—for example, with a diagram, as shown in Figure 7-26. Then read through the headlines in the Detail column, and sketch how to illustrate each Detail slide—for example, with a demonstration, a video clip, or a chart. Here it might be easier to see that the sketch of each Explanation slide should be a summary and introduction of the adjacent Detail headlines to the right.

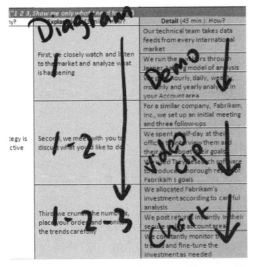

**FIGURE 7-26** Sketch what you want to illustrate directly on a printout of the story template.

TIP    Sketching directly on the story template connects you back with the verbal story you wrote and helps you see what you're trying to accomplish from a different perspective. To sketch directly on the story template while you work with a team, place a screen capture of the story template on a PowerPoint slide and mark it up while it is displayed on a screen in the room.

Keep this technique in mind when you're writing the story template for the first time and as you go forward with your sketches in the storyboard.

## BBP CHECKLIST: SKETCHING THE STORYBOARD

Do your storyboard sketches show clearly:

❏ Where your Act I, Key Point, Explanation, and Detail slides are?

❏ How you tell your story across frames, at each level of the storyboard?

❏ Which graphics that you'll use?

❏ Where you will use interaction, props, and other media?

# Ready, Set, Sketch!

Now that you have a range of techniques in mind, start sketching the rest of your storyboard. Sketch each and every slide in the entire storyboard first, even if you already have some finished graphics that you know you want to use—that way you don't get caught up in the visual details of individual slides that prevent you from spending time on the rest of the slides. After you have a sketch for every slide in place, you'll review the entire storyboard in Slide Sorter view in Chapter 8 to assess how much time you have to add graphics, where you need to spend your time first, what resources you have to get things done, and who you can ask for help if you need it.

This process might seem challenging now, but the more you storyboard, the more skilled you'll become. Just as you do when you write the story template, it helps to bring in other people to collaborate with you on the storyboard. If you're using a Tablet PC, you can project the storyboard on a screen and sketch together; if you're using paper, you can tape printed copies of individual slides on the wall and collaborate that way. And just as you do when you verbally edit the story template, look for ways to visually edit, tighten, and improve your storyboard.

When you have a fully sketched storyboard in hand, it's time to turn the sketches into finished graphics as you complete your final PowerPoint storyboard in the next chapter.

CHAPTER 8

# Adding Graphics to Your Storyboard

**IN THIS CHAPTER, YOU WILL:**

- Review the three ground rules for adding graphics.
- Apply custom layouts to the different sections of the storyboard.
- Add graphics to every slide of your storyboard.

PEOPLE SAY a picture is worth a thousand words, but if you're not a professional illustrator, where exactly do you get that picture? Turning words into visuals can be a daunting task for anybody, especially if you're used to putting mostly bullet points on your Microsoft® Office PowerPoint® slides. Fortunately, you've already done significant work to prepare the way for this moment—you have in hand a storyboard that includes all the slides in your presentation, and each slide includes a sketch that indicates the specific graphic you want to add. As always with the Beyond Bullet Points (BBP) approach, your focus is on helping your audience effectively understand new information, so your next task is to add the specific graphics to the storyboard that help make your visual point on each slide, without overwhelming the working memory of your audience with excessive new visual information.

## Which Graphics Do I Add to Each Slide?

Like completing the story template, adding final graphics to your storyboard is both easy and hard. It's easy because all you need to do is use your sketch as a guide to "fill in the blank" below the headline on each slide with the graphic that the sketch describes. But it's also hard because you have a potentially unlimited range of graphics and styles to choose from, and you have to find the ones that are the best match with both you and your audience. Especially if working with graphics is a new skill for you, this project might feel daunting right now. But think of approaching this task just as you would any other project—by first assessing the current state of the project, then figuring out what needs to be done, and then making a plan for how you're going to accomplish that. This chapter will help you through the process of adding graphics to your storyboard step by step, helping you to break up the project into smaller, more manageable tasks.

## Defining Your Design Constraints

PowerPoint 2007 is an easy-to-use and powerful media tool that can produce impressive results. But if you're like most people who use PowerPoint, you're not a graduate of a design school. In addition, every design project has constraints that will limit what you can do—as much as you might want to take your time creating a work of art, the reality might be that you have only until tomorrow or next week to create a PowerPoint masterpiece. It's important that you know up front what limits you have so that you can plan your project accordingly. You can do that by asking a few questions:

- **What is the scope of the project?** Look at your presentation in Slide Sorter view, as shown in Figure 8-1, to get a sense of the number of graphics you will need to find. It's a good idea to first identify where you will *not* need graphics so that you can eliminate those from your count. For example, if you're giving only a 15-minute version of your presentation, you will hide the 45-minute version slides, as described in Chapter 6, and focus your efforts only on the other slides you need. Likewise, if you'll be switching over to another software application to present the ideas on some of the 45-minute version slides, you won't need to add graphics to those slides either because you'll hide those slides as well.

- **How much time do you have?** Next determine how much time you have to get the job done. If your presentation is a report for this afternoon, you will have to do the best you can with the resources at hand, but if it's a presentation for a new product launch in three months, you obviously have more time to invest and to bring other people in on the project. Consider whether you have any additional deadlines before you need the final version of the PowerPoint file, such as marketing or legal approval. All of these factors will determine whether you have a couple of hours, a day, a couple of days, a week, a month, or longer to get the project done.

**FIGURE 8-1** Review the fully sketched storyboard.

- **Where can you get graphics?** This chapter will show you a wide range of ways that you can get graphics for your slides, but one of the most useful resources you will use is a stock photography Web site. Stock photography Web sites feature a database that you can search to locate photographs, as well as illustrations, motion graphics, and video. It's important that you properly obtain a license or otherwise get permission to use graphics if you do not already hold the rights to use them. Stock photography Web sites are set up to make the licensing process easy. The cost of licensing photographs ranges from free to hundreds of dollars or more. In this chapter, you will use a stock photography Web site called iStockphoto, which has a database of more than 2 million images that you can search; you can license most of the photos for use in your presentations for only a few dollars each. You can find a number of similar stock photography Web sites by doing a Web search for terms such as "stock photography presentations."

- **What's your budget?** If you have a budget of $0, you will be limited to only free graphics, screen captures, and any graphics you can create yourself. If you have a budget of $20, you can license 10 photographs from iStockphoto for $2 each; if you have $500, you can hire a freelance graphic designer for perhaps 10 hours; and if you have $10,000, you can commission a video that you integrate into your Key Point slides and elsewhere through the storyboard.

- **What other resources do you have available?** If you have the skills, you can create original illustrations yourself in another software program, or you can shoot your own photographs and edit them with image editing software. If you don't have these skills, consider other people you can ask for help, such as an in-house design team or your coworkers. If you have the budget, you can outsource the entire task of adding graphics to a professional graphic designer.

Whatever constraints you have, you don't need design training to produce effective results with your new PowerPoint storyboard. This chapter will introduce and demonstrate a number of new tools and basic design techniques that you can start applying to your PowerPoint presentations today.

# Adding Graphics Using Three Ground Rules

The most important thing to keep in mind when you add graphics to your storyboard is that you're not just designing *slides*; you're designing a complete *experience* that manages the visual and verbal channels for the working memory of your audience. It's easy to become absorbed in the details of fonts, graphics, and animations on the slides while losing track of your spoken words and how the entire experience helps the audience to understand your message. To make sure you keep on track, keep three ground rules in mind while you're working with graphics.

## Rule 1: See It in Seconds

In Chapter 7, you sketched your storyboard across adjacent slides and sketched the hierarchy across levels. This process ensures that when you view the entire presentation in Slide Sorter view, you can see exactly how you manage the attention of your audience *across time*. Within that context, you now will focus on the individual slides to see how you can best manage your audience's attention in any particular *moment of time*, both visually and verbally. The best place to understand the design of your slides is in its complete context of screen and narration—that is, in Notes Page view. As illustrated in Figure 8-2, the Notes Page view composition is built on three levels of information hierarchy.

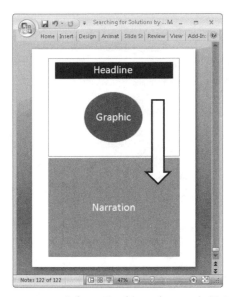

**FIGURE 8-2** Information hierarchy seen in Notes Page view.

The top of the hierarchy is the on-screen headline, which summarizes the point you make at this moment; the second level of the hierarchy is the on-screen graphic, which visually explains the headline; and the third level of the hierarchy is the off-screen narrative explanation in the notes area, which further explains both the headline and the visual element with your spoken words. When you work with graphics in this chapter, never forget the role of your narration. Not only does your voice provide a rich stream of information, but also you will use it during your presentation to emphasize the relative importance of information. For example, when you raise the volume of your voice, you indicate that what you are saying now is more important than what you said in a lower voice just before. Other classic techniques of public speaking can also be used to add emphasis, such as using intonation and pauses for effect. Although you will be working on individual slides in Normal view, it's a good idea to return frequently to Notes Page view during the process of adding graphics to view the slides in the context of their verbal narration.

Keeping in mind how your voice will seamlessly integrate with the graphics you add to each slide, Figure 8-3 shows the built-in hierarchy of the default layout for your slides in Normal view. When you display any layout on the screen, you want your audience's eyes to go first to the most important information on the slide—the headline that summarizes your point. The headline communicates the topic clearly to the audience, reminds you as a speaker what you want to say, and keeps both parties focused on a specific topic.

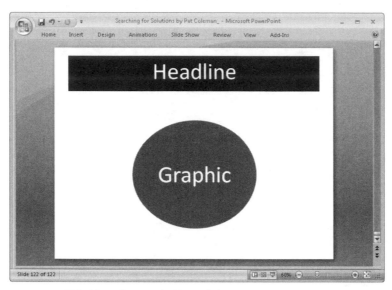

**FIGURE 8-3** Slide hierarchy seen in Normal view.

Next you want your audience's eyes to move to the second-most important element on the slide—the graphic. Whatever graphic you add here should illustrate the headline and help your audience literally see your point by using the power of the visual channel of working memory. The graphic should pack as much meaning as possible into visual form and still be simple enough to be quickly digestible. On the default layout when you first import your headlines into PowerPoint slides, the position for the graphic is centered on the screen, where it is easy to see and understand—you can adjust this layout according to what you sketched for each hierarchical level of the storyboard. If you do adjust some of the slide layouts later, you should keep them simple and include white space if possible to give your audience visual breathing room to easily process the new information.

Although the basic layout for the slides is simple in style, it is sophisticated in its effect because the audience scans the headline and graphic and quickly understands the idea. This "verbal-visual reading" of the slide should get your point across in seconds so that the working memory of your audience can now pay attention to you and what you're saying. Later in this chapter, you can reinforce this reading sequence by using a simple animation technique to display the headline first and then the graphic briefly thereafter. The goal is to help your audience quickly digest the slide—even if you display the slide for only a few seconds and then black out the screen, your audience should be able to articulate the main point of that single slide as you intended. After the slide initially sets the stage this way by quickly conveying the meaning of the headline, the slide now shifts in function to a reinforcing backdrop while you verbally explain the point in more detail over the next minute.

## Rule 2: Align the Aesthetics with the Audience

Life would be easy if you could choose any graphics to add to your slides, but unfortunately there is the matter of *aesthetics*—how your audience thinks your graphics look. You might personally prefer the style or composition of a particular graphic, but in truth, it doesn't matter as much what you think as what your audience thinks. For better or worse, your aesthetic choices can present a major obstacle to communication if you don't get them right. You can create a clear underlying structure in your story template, but if people are paying attention to what they see as your bad choice of graphics, they're not paying attention to your message. Not only is effective learning at stake, but also your credibility. In the days before PowerPoint, you established credibility through your verbal introduction, your ideas, your authority, and your physical appearance. Now, with PowerPoint, you have an additional need to establish a *visual credibility*—without it, you and your presentation will be perceived as amateurish and without substance.

Because the beauty of the graphic is in the eye of the beholder, you really need to know the beholder of your presentations—your audience. As you research your audience to determine how to focus your presentation across the first five slides of Act I, you also want to find out as much as you can about their aesthetic preferences as well. If you've been in a particular profession or industry for a while, you probably already have a sense for what is perceived as acceptable aesthetics. For example, if you're presenting to corporate executives, you'll take your aesthetic cues from a company's marketing materials, annual report, and office environment. But if you're presenting to a jury, you'll take your cues from the juror questionnaires, popular culture, and the local area. Whoever your audience might be, it is essential that you choose the graphics appropriate to the group so that your graphics do not stand in the way of your message. As a secondary consideration, you also need to be personally comfortable with the aesthetics so that you can deliver the material confidently and naturally.

Although the general aesthetic preferences of your audiences and their cultures might vary, when you work with BBP, you know you'll use a minimalist style because adding anything extraneous will add unnecessary cognitive load on the working memory of your audience. That said, even if something is simple, it can be an aesthetic mismatch with your audience.

As you search stock photography databases for graphics that are a good aesthetic match with your audience, scan through as many as time will allow so that you get a full sense of the spectrum of possibilities. For example, the headline from the storyboard shown on the upper left in Figure 8-4 reads, "Our innovative three-part strategy is simple yet powerfully effective," and the sketch from Chapter 7 indicates that you'd like to use a clipboard image. When you visit a stock photography Web site such as iStockphoto and search for "clipboard," you will get more than 1,400 results—which presents you with more than 1,400 potential graphics you could use for this slide. It's possible that many of the graphics here might work—or that none of them will.

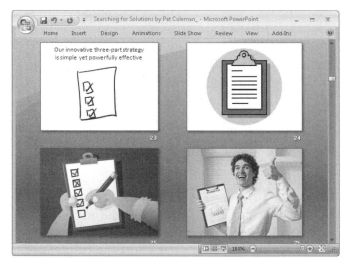

**FIGURE 8-4** Aesthetic mismatches for a presentation for financial executives.

| | |
|---|---|
| **TIP** ✓ | The general guidelines for choosing graphics are to keep things as simple and unadorned as possible, and when in doubt, take it out. Always review the graphics with other people on your team and gather their opinions to get a range of perspectives that will help you to choose the aesthetics for your graphics that work best for both you and your audience. |

When you're searching for an aesthetic match of a graphic with your audience, your focus should not be on whether you think a particular graphic is good or bad, but rather on whether a specific graphic will do the job of communicating the point of a specific headline to your specific audience. Scrolling through the search results reveals that many of the graphics probably are an aesthetic mismatch for the audience of the sample presentation in this book—senior financial executives. For example, the clip art example of a clipboard on the upper right is done in a cartoon style that might make your message come across as not being serious as the topic at hand. The clip art example on the lower left includes hands that are marking up the clipboard, but it's an aesthetic mismatch because the image also is in a cartoon style and comes across as too playful and not aligned with the aesthetic style of most marketing material in the more conservative financial services industry.

Using a photograph of someone holding a clipboard is in the realm of possibility, but this example on the lower right is too playful for the context, and it's also hard to see the clipboard because it is such a small percentage of the screen area. This is a good example of why you need to be careful when using a photograph that has a person in it, especially on a Key Point or an Explanation slide. The photo of the person in this example will distract attention away from the point of the headline and prompt thoughts in the viewer's mind such as, "I wonder if I should know this person," or "We never walk around with our thumbs up in our office," or "I'm personally not a fan of his haircut." Again, this is not about whether these example graphics are good or bad, because they all would work perfectly well within other contexts, just not for this audience of financial executives.

> **TIP** ✓ An important consideration when you're using graphics from commonly used sources is to be careful not to use images that you've seen everywhere else, because if an image is perceived as trite or overused, it will distract from your headline as well.

Although none of these examples from the search results are an aesthetic match with the financial executives, there are others that could work. For example, the photograph of the clipboard on the upper left in Figure 8-5 is simple enough to serve as the basis for a graphic in the presentation. A design constraint of this chapter includes not working with photo manipulation software, but you can still do simple things to make this image work if all you have is a preexisting photograph such as this one. Add three square boxes using PowerPoint drawing tools to create the check boxes (upper right), and then add the check marks (lower left). Shift the photo to the right half of the screen, add a black rectangle to the left, and then shift the headline to the left and change its font color to white (lower right).

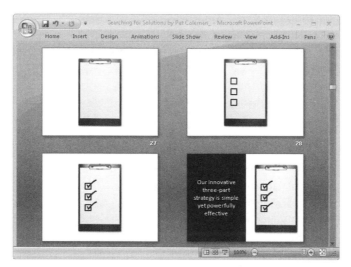

**FIGURE 8-5** A closer aesthetic match for this audience.

The final slide on the lower right is a closer aesthetic match with a financial services audience than the clip art and photo examples shown earlier in Figure 8-4. A professional designer might do an even better job with this slide. But accepting the constraints of doing it yourself and using only existing photographs and PowerPoint drawing tools, you can adapt and improvise like this in order to make the best of what you have.

**NOTE**   Choosing an unpolished aesthetic style can be a savvy and sophisticated strategy at times. If everyone presents the same slick, polished, and flawless style, everyone's presentations will look the same. If you choose something simple to contrast with the norm, you could break through the visual boredom and succeed at making a memorable impression. There is of course a risk that using a technique like this might not work if your audience expects the same aesthetics as they see everywhere else, so you would need to be confident that you could make this choice work for both you and your audience.

Definitely, the considerations of innate taste, talent, and skill come into play when you find, create, or add graphics. You might find that you are naturally good at finding graphics that align with the aesthetics of your audience. But you also might discover that your talents lie elsewhere—if so, it's best to enlist the help of your coworkers or designers to help you find the best graphics for the job, or use some of the professionally designed graphics created for BBP presentations that are available at *www.beyondbulletpoints.com*.

## Rule 3: Defend Your Foundation!

At this stage in your BBP presentation, you've worked hard to create a strong foundation all the way from the words and structure of your story template through to your sketches. But if you're not careful to defend the foundation you've built, things quickly can start to unravel if you break the mechanisms that make BBP work so well. The main temptation is to add more to a slide than what you need to make your graphical point. You might begin by adding a simple graphic, but soon you likely will be tempted to add more on the slide. But as Chapter 2 explains, research indicates that the more extraneous information you add, the more you increase the load on working memory and decrease learning. Every bullet point you add back to the slide, every additional color, and every extra visual detail can potentially clog the eye of the needle, the limited capacity of your audience's working memory to process new information, so relentlessly keep out anything that does not convey the meaning of the headline. Keep subtracting from—not adding to—your slides, and keep in mind that adding obscures, subtracting clarifies. If you find yourself continuing to add more to a slide in order to make your point, most likely there's a problem with the structure and sequence of your ideas, and you should return to the story template to address the section of the presentation where the slide originates.

Although you might be able to control your own inclinations to keep adding more visual detail to your slides, the biggest risk to your solid presentation foundation is from others who pressure you to keep adding information to your slides. For example, you might choose a simple illustration for a slide, as shown on the upper left in Figure 8-6— an image of a globe, along with three arrows created using PowerPoint drawing tools to illustrate the headline "Our technical team takes data feeds from every international market."

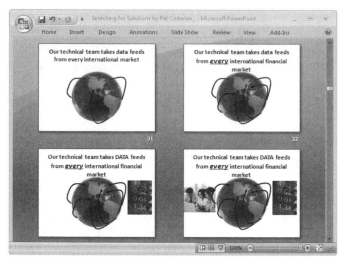

**FIGURE 8-6** A BBP graphical foundation as it is eroded over time.

Then you invite your boss over to your desk to ask for his opinion. He thinks that you should really emphasize how much you take data feeds from every international market. He asks you to make the word *every* bold and underlined, and to add three more arrows to show more of the international market. Then he says that he wants you to clarify the headline by adding the word *financial* to *international market*, which extends the headline from two lines to three (upper right). Not sure whether the slide is exactly right, he calls his boss over for her opinion, and she says that you should emphasize the credibility of the data referenced in the headline, and she asks you to change the word *data* to uppercase and then add a photo of data of some sort (lower left). Then the vice president of technology happens to walk by and says that the slide looks unbalanced and that you should add a photograph of an IT team (lower right).

In spite of everyone's good intentions to make the slide better, the combined additions made it much worse. As the old saying goes, "If you emphasize everything, you emphasize nothing." The headline on a BBP slide already sits in the most prominent position on the original slide (upper left), so there's no need to add any embellishment to make it stand out—there is an easy flow as the audience sees the headline, looks at the graphic, and listens to the speaker. The emphasis on individual words disrupts easy reading of the headline (lower right) and creates unnecessary visual competition about where to look first. The same happens when you add three more arrows to the globe and the two additional photographs—they have transformed what was once a clear and easily viewable slide into a distracting hodgepodge. The audience can no longer easily see the meaning of the entire slide in seconds, as in Ground Rule 1. The group process has broken the foundation of the BBP approach and rendered the slide ineffective.

Not only does breaking the BBP foundation impact an individual slide, but it also disrupts the sequence of slides. It's easy to get lost in the individual slides instead of seeing the big picture of the story template. For example, for BBP to work, you should have the same font style and size of headlines on all your slides to ensure that each slide is easy to read and links together visually. Within the hierarchy levels of your storyboard, you should have consistent placement of headlines as each slide flows visually from one to the next. You break the consistency in the BBP approach *only for specific reasons*— for example, when you disrupt the flow of ideas to indicate that the next idea is more important than the others, as determined by the story template. But in this example, the organization broke the consistency *for no reason*—the unnecessary details added to the headlines do nothing to help the big picture of the presentation, and instead hurt it. The situation can get even worse if you start adding new slides to your storyboard and rearranging them without reflecting the changes in the story template. Soon, the internal pacing and flow of the presentation begin to unravel too.

The graphical way to fix the problems shown in Figure 8-6 is easy—remove everything except the minimum visuals needed to illustrate the headline, as in the original slide (upper left). But the organizational fix will take a bit more work. People's urges to add extraneous detail are most often related to habit or myths, such as thinking that the more you add, the more people will learn; or that you need to add pizzazz to catch someone's attention; or that you need to entertain people instead of helping them learn. To protect your hard-earned BBP foundation, stand firm on your research-based grounding from Chapter 2 as you help other people to understand that "Less is more" is more than a slogan—it's a strategy and tactic for getting results in your presentations.

## THREE GROUND RULES FOR ADDING GRAPHICS

Adding graphics is the crucial last step in designing the storyboard. Follow these three ground rules to make sure you get the graphics right:

**Rule 1:** See it in seconds.

**Rule 2:** Align the aesthetics with the audience.

**Rule 3:** Defend your foundation!

# Starting the Production Flow

As you look at the sketch on each slide of your storyboard, consider how you can locate and find a graphic to replace it, according to the resources you have available. Aim for a first draft of your storyboard, not a finished product. Don't spend too much time on any single graphic—you could easily spend all day on one slide and get nothing else done. Instead, put something on the slide for the first draft, even if it's not exactly what you're looking for, and come back to work on the imperfect things later. Work in a sequence that will make most efficient use of your time, beginning with getting others to help you.

> **NOTE**   This book assumes that you know the basics of PowerPoint 2007, such as using drawing tools and inserting, resizing, and cropping photographs. If you need a tutorial or a refresher on how to use the software, a number of basics books are available, such as Joyce Cox and Joan Preppernau, *Microsoft Office PowerPoint 2007 Step by Step* (Microsoft Press, 2007). To review the basics of working with photographs, see "Tip 2: The Photo Basics: Size, Crop, and Compress" later in this chapter.

## Assigning What You Can

If you have coworkers who can help you find or create graphics to add to your storyboard, get them started first so that the other work is under way while you do your work. A good way to provide these coworkers with the information they need is to click the Microsoft Office Button, point to Save As, choose PowerPoint Presentation, and then create a new version of the PowerPoint file with another name. In the new PowerPoint file you created, delete all the slides that your coworkers won't need to see. Now, when your coworkers open the file, they will have the specific slides you have assigned to them, and if you ask them to view the slides in Notes Page view, they will see the headline that summarizes your point, the detailed off-screen narration, and the sketch you added to the slide in Chapter 7. They can replace the sketch with a graphic, and when they e-mail the file back to you, you can insert the new slides, copy and paste the entire slides, or copy and paste just the graphics from the slide area. If you have the resources to have graphics custom-made, assign those now in the same way, providing the designer with the slides—see "Tip 5: Design for Your Designer" later in this chapter for additional advice about working with designers.

## Getting the Graphics You Already Have

Next get the things done on the project that you can do quickly, to reduce the scope of the project. For example, if you already have on hand 10 preexisting graphics out of the 40 you need, adding them now to the storyboard means that you're 25 percent done, which will give you a better handle on the situation. The first place to go to get graphics is your existing BBP presentations, if you have any. You'll be building a library of BBP presentations over time that will help your production process go faster each time. This library will save you effort as you build BBP presentations from scratch less and less. If you don't have previous BBP presentations, you might have some graphics in other presentations that you can use if they are simple and illustrate the point of a headline— but if they are overly complex, or otherwise don't align with the BBP foundation of your storyboard, don't use them.

## Getting the Graphics You Can Easily Find

There are many resources for finding photographs for your presentations. If you're a good photographer, take your own photographs using a digital camera. But it's most likely that you'll want to visit a stock photography Web site. In photo databases, you'll usually search for graphics based on keywords you enter into a search box, such as "clipboard." You'll then see a search results screen similar to the one from the iStockphoto Web site shown in Figure 8-7. It's worth the time to learn how to use advanced search tools to more capably find what you're looking for. A Web site such as iStockphoto has more than two million graphics, and the search results for common terms will often produce hundreds or thousands of results. Narrow your search using advanced search features based on specific parameters, such as color, vertical or horizontal orientation, or popularity ratings. When you're looking for photos that have white backgrounds, include the term "isolated" in your search terms. When you see a photo that's close to what you want but not an exact fit, click on it to examine the photo details page, where you might find related images or access to the artist's portfolio.

**FIGURE 8-7** Search results at the iStockphoto site.

As you consider where to get graphics, you probably have more readily available graphics than you think, especially if you work in an organization—for example, many marketing departments have libraries of photographs that are already licensed for use in presentations. In every case, make sure that you get any permission needed to use the photographs in your presentation and that the photographs are optimized for presentation, not print, use.

TIP

Visit the companion Web site to this book at *www.beyondbulletpoints.com* for more ideas on how to find and add graphics to your BBP presentations—this online community is dedicated to making the graphic design process faster and easier for you, so be sure to review the range of tools, training and techniques, and templates to make your job easier and faster.

## Creating the Graphics You Can

PowerPoint includes a range of drawing tools that you might already know how to use, such as creating shapes, lines, arrows, callouts, charts, and graphs. You can add any of these elements as a simple graphic on a slide or use the drawing tools to add other graphical elements such as callouts to existing photographs. And if you know other illustration software or know people who do, you have that many more resources.

# Applying Custom Layouts to Your Storyboard

PowerPoint 2007 offers some new features that will make your job of adding graphics to your BBP storyboard much easier than in earlier versions of the software. Just as you began setting up the storyboard by creating distinctive layouts in Chapter 7, the best place to begin working in PowerPoint 2007 now is with the new Custom Layout feature, which will help you set up the sections of the storyboard that correspond to the sections of your story template.

In Chapter 6, you applied layouts with different backgrounds to the Key Point, Explanation, and Detail slides so that you could see them clearly in Slide Sorter view and practice scaling your presentation to time. These visual cues indicate to your audience's working memory which slides are more important than others as you present them in sequence. In Chapter 7, you reviewed different ways to sketch these slide layouts to build on this foundation and keep the hierarchy of the presentation clear. Your goal now is to use PowerPoint 2007 features to create the slide layouts you sketched and apply color to them to call attention to the most important slides first and then to the second-most and third-most important sets of slides.

The completed Key Point, Explanation, and Detail slides from the example presentation shown in Figure 8-8 demonstrate how both layout and color work together to indicate the relative importance of these slides.

Apply a layout that calls attention first to the Key Point slides.

Call attention second to the Explanation slides.

Call attention third to the Detail slides.

**FIGURE 8-8** Custom layouts applied to the Key Point, Explanation, and Detail slides.

The Key Point layout (left) features both a distinctive split-screen layout with a solid color rectangle on the left and a photograph on the right. Like the Key Point slide layout, the Explanation slide layout (middle) is also a split-screen, except here the rectangle on the left is a lighter color. Last, instead of using a split-screen, the Detail slide layout (right) retains a horizontal shape with no color box. The gray bar at the bottom of the Explanation slide distinguishes it from the Key Point layout but also provides visual continuity across the Detail slides, which have the same gray bar with a navigational element—a small clipboard with a number *1* indicating that this is within the section of the presentation that follows the first Key Point slide. As shown in this example, next you will manually design custom layouts like these and apply them to the Key Point, Explanation, and Detail slides in your presentation.

**TIP** You can see the photos that were used in the example presentations in Chapters 8 and 9 and obtain a license to use them in your own presentations by visiting a special area set up for BBP readers at the iStockphoto Web site at *www.istockphoto.com/beyondbulletpoints.php*.

Although this book is printed in black and white, color is also something you need to consider when designing the layouts for the levels of your presentation. According to widely accepted principles of color theory, some individual colors such as red or high-contrast combinations of colors such as black and white call attention to themselves before others. With that in mind, you might choose a black fill color for the rectangle to contrast with the white background on the Key Point slides because you want the eye to go first to these slides out of all the slides. You might then choose beige for the Explanation slides and then leave the Detail slides plain white. Or you could choose red for the Key Point, blue for the Explanation, and white for the Detail slide layouts.

Your choice of colors should always align with the hierarchy of your ideas. If you consider integrating your organization's colors into your custom layouts, be careful when you do that, because those colors might conflict with your goal of guiding the working memory of your audience. For example, you might use red in your company colors, but using a red element on your Explanation and Detail slide layouts will call attention to that element instead of the headline and the graphic, which will erode the way your slides are working to guide the attention of the audience.

TIP

✓

You might run into resistance from others in your organization when choosing colors to indicate the hierarchy of importance of the ideas in your presentation. If that is the case, you might need to defend your BBP foundation by holding a meeting to relate to others the importance of verbal and visual hierarchy in communicating effectively to an audience, perhaps showing BBP and non-BBP versions of the same presentation to demonstrate how BBP uses color to guide the audience's attention and orient them to the presentation's organization.

## COLOR CONSIDERATIONS

Most general graphic design books provide information about how to use color, or you can refer to a book specifically about color, such as Lesa Sawahata, *Color Harmony Workbook: A Workbook and Guide to Creative Color Combinations* (Rockport Publishers, 2001). As you explore color, keep in mind that the colors you choose for slide backgrounds can influence emotion and mood; another consideration is how the colors will work on the specific projectors you will use. If you want to get an early start on exploring color even before you work on your slides, fill in the backgrounds of the three columns of Act II of the story template with the colors you plan to use in the corresponding storyboard slide layouts.

You can choose from a range of predesigned custom layouts at *www.beyondbulletpoints. com*, or you can have a graphic designer create layouts for you, or you can design layouts yourself manually by following a few basic steps, as described next.

## Creating Layouts Manually

To create custom layouts for your various levels of slides, on the View tab, in the Presentation Views group, click Slide Master. In the Overview pane on the left, you will see the built-in layouts that you can apply to your slides. You can add any custom layouts here that you want, and as always, the best place to begin is with the most important slides in the presentation.

## Creating the Key Point Slide Layout Manually

As you explored with your sketches in Chapter 7, there are many possible ways you can use layouts to make your set of Key Point slides stand out from the others. One quick and easy way to make these important slides stand out is to apply a split-screen layout to them. To create a custom split-screen layout to apply to your Key Point slides, follow these steps:

1.  In the **Overview** pane, right-click the large Office Theme Slide Master slide. When you select any Slide Master in the **Overview** pane, all of its editable elements appear in the large view of the Slide Master in the slide pane. The Office Theme Slide Master determines the formatting of any new Slide Masters and custom layouts you will create. You can adjust the font type, size, and color if you want to apply those changes to all slides going forward, but do not delete anything from this particular Slide Master. When you have finished, in the **Overview** pane, right-click the Office Theme Slide Master, and select **Preserve Master**.

2.  In the **Overview** pane, position the cursor directly below the Office Theme Slide Master slide, and then right-click and choose **Insert Layout**.

3.  Right-click the custom layout you created, choose **Rename Layout**, and in the **Rename Layout** dialog box, type **Key Point** and then click **Rename**.

4.  In the slide pane, right-click the large view of the Slide Master and select **Grid And Guides**, and in the **Grid And Guides** dialog box, under **Guide Settings**, select the **Display Drawing Guides On Screen** check box, and then click **OK**.

    This gives you temporary guides to help align objects on a slide, which you can remove by following the same steps and clearing the check box. See PowerPoint Help to learn more about how to use temporary guides.

5.  On the **Slide Master** tab, in the **Master Layout** group, clear the **Footers** check box, and then click **Insert Placeholder**, click **Picture**, and drag a rectangle to fill the entire right half of the slide.

6.  Next, on the **Insert** tab, in the **Illustrations** group, click **Shapes**. Click **Rectangle**, and drag a rectangle to fill the entire left half of the slide.

7.  Right-click the rectangle, and specify a fill color—in this example, black.

8.  Hold down the Shift key as you select both the rectangle and placeholder, right-click, and then click **Send To Back**.

9.  Select the title area, and drag it down and to the center of the rectangle on the left, using the resizing handles as needed. Change the text in the title area to read

**Click to edit Key Point headline**. If you need to change the contrast of the font color to make it readable against the color you chose for the rectangle, right-click the title area, and change the Font color—in this example, to white, as shown in Figure 8-9.

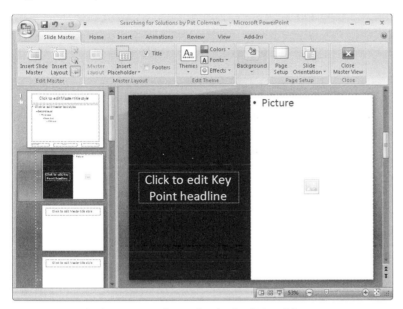

**FIGURE 8-9** Designing a custom layout for the Key Point slides.

**10.** On the **Slide Master View** tab, click **Close Master View** to return to Normal view.

> **TIP** ✓ Instead of inserting and designing new custom layouts, you can also rename and redesign the existing storyboard sketch layouts that you applied to your slides in Chapter 6. To do that, select and rename the Key Points Sketches custom layout to Key Point following the instructions in step 2 of the preceding procedure, and then make your design changes. When you have finished, return to Slide Sorter view, and you'll see that the layouts of the Key Point slides have been updated automatically according to the design changes you made.

Now that you have designed the Key Point custom layout, select a Key Point slide, and on the Home tab, in the Slides group, click Layout. The Office Theme window will now include the Key Point custom layout you created, as shown in Figure 8-10.

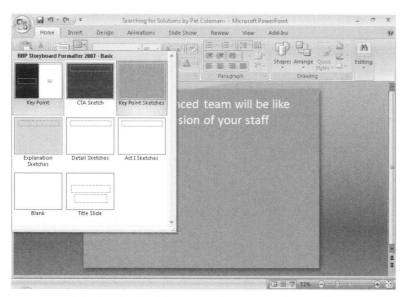

**FIGURE 8-10** Selecting the Key Point custom layout to apply to a slide.

Click the Key Point layout, and the formatting will be automatically applied, as shown in Figure 8-11.

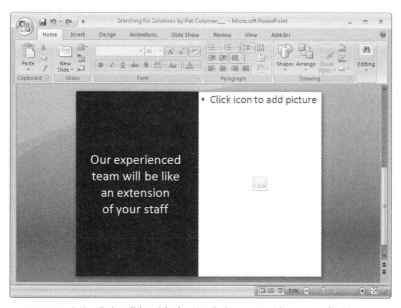

**FIGURE 8-11** A Key Point slide with the Key Point custom layout applied.

There are two ways to insert a photograph in the Picture placeholder on the right half of this slide. The first way is to find a picture and copy it and then click the Picture place-holder—not the Picture icon—and click Paste. The second way is to click the Picture icon in the center of the Picture placeholder to display the Insert Picture dialog box, as shown in Figure 8-12. When you find a photo you plan to use, it is good practice to save it in a familiar folder on your computer or network so that you can easily locate it and click Insert.

> **NOTE** If you used a Tablet PC to sketch on your PowerPoint slides, be sure to delete the sketch from the slide before or after you've added your graphic.

**FIGURE 8-12** Selecting a photograph to insert.

Whichever method of inserting a photo you use, the photo automatically fills the Picture placeholder that you added to the custom layout, filling the right half of the screen. Although the original photo is horizontal, the Picture placeholder has automatically cropped the photo to fill the vertical space. If sizing photos is not your talent, this feature has taken care of things for you. To resize or recrop the photo the way you want, select the picture, as shown in Figure 8-13, and use the tools on the Picture Tools tab to make adjustments.

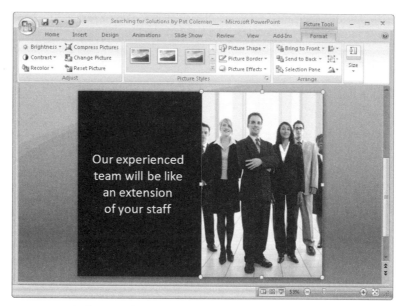

**FIGURE 8-13** A photograph automatically cropped and inserted into the Picture placeholder.

## Creating the Explanation Slide Layout Manually

Next, follow similar steps to create a custom layout that you will apply to all the Explanation slides, based on what you sketched in Chapter 7. Again, using a split-screen layout for all the Explanation slides in this example presentation is only one way to go, but in this case, a similar layout will complement the Key Point slide layout. To create another custom split-screen layout to apply to all your Explanation slides, follow these steps:

1. On the **View** tab, click **Slide Master**.

2. In the **Overview** pane, position the cursor directly below the Key Point layout you created earlier, and then right-click it and choose **Insert Layout**.

3. Right-click the custom layout you created, choose **Rename Layout**, and in the **Rename Layout** dialog box, type **Explanation** and then click **Rename**.

4. On the **Slide Master** tab, in the **Master Layout** group, clear the **Footers** check box. When you click **Insert Placeholder** to add a placeholder on the right half of the slide, take a look at the range of other types of placeholders that you can use in the custom layout. On the Key Point custom layout shown earlier, the sketches indicated that there would always be a photo on the Key Point slides, so selecting a Picture placeholder was a good fit and provided the added feature of

automatically cropping photos to fit the space. But here on the Explanation slides, if you want flexibility beyond just photographs, choose **Content**, as shown in Figure 8-14—this will allow you to insert a range of types of content on the slides where you apply this layout.  Alternatively, you don't have to use a placeholder at all in your custom layout—in that case, you can later add graphics manually to your slides.

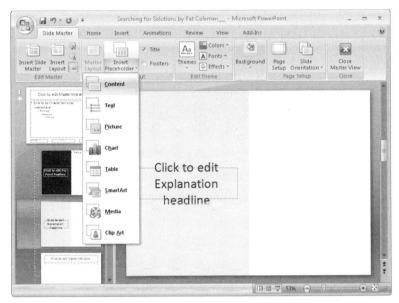

**FIGURE 8-14** Designing a custom layout for the Explanation slides—the Insert Placeholder drop-down menu shows a range of options.

5. As you did in the Key Point layout, add a rectangle to fill the left side of the slide. In keeping with color theory, fill this rectangle with a different color that in combination with the layout will call attention to these Explanation slides second, after the Key Point slides. As you did earlier with the Key Point custom layout, select the rectangle and placeholder and send them to the back, drag the headline over the box on the left side, and change the font color if you need to make it more legible. Change the text in the title area to read **Click to edit Explanation headline**.

**TIP** ✓  If your Explanation custom layout will have the same layout as the Key Point custom layout, instead of inserting a new layout, you can duplicate the Key Point layout, rename it, and then make the appropriate adjustments.

## Creating the Detail Slide Layout Manually

Now create a custom layout for the Detail slides. Because the Key Point and Explanation slide layouts are first and second in visual prominence in Slide Sorter view, you don't need to create a split-screen layout here on the Detail slide layout to make these slides stand out. To create a custom layout to apply to all your Detail slides, follow these steps:

1. On the **View** tab, click **Slide Master**.

2. In the **Overview** pane, position the cursor directly below the Explanation layout you just created, and then right-click and choose **Insert Layout**.

3. Right-click the custom layout you created, choose **Rename Layout**, and in the **Rename Layout** dialog box, type **Detail** and then click **Rename**.

4. On the **Slide Master** tab, in the **Master Layout** group, clear the **Footers** check box. Leave the layout as it is, except insert a Content placeholder, and drag the placeholder to fill the slide below the headline; then delete the text from the Content placeholder. Change the text in the title area to read **Click to edit Detail headline**. Next you can add something to the custom layout that will cue your audience to the presentation's organization—an optional navigation bar, as shown in Figure 8-15.

**FIGURE 8-15** Designing a custom layout for the Detail slides.

## Adding an Optional Navigation Bar Manually

To create a navigation bar in the Detail slide layout, insert a rectangle shape, and drag and size it to fit across the bottom of the slide. Placing the bar will not interfere with the simple visual reading of the slides, and its gray color will not call attention to it. Add the same bar to the Explanation slide layout you created earlier so that the bar visually links the Explanation and Detail slide layouts.

If you want to use an additional element to help viewers navigate the presentation, add a small icon in the lower-right corner. The magnification of the lower-right corner of the Detail slide layout, shown in Figure 8-16, shows a simple clipboard that offers a subtle visual cue to guide your audience through this section of the presentation. Its small size ensures that it doesn't interfere with the overall composition of the slide. To add a bit more navigational assistance, add the number *1* to the clipboard to indicate the first section of this part of the presentation. If you do that, you will need to duplicate this Detail custom layout twice, rename the new layouts, and then add a *2* and a *3* to the duplicate layouts to apply to the other corresponding sections. If you're tempted to add your corporate logo here to the navigation bar, don't—it only adds extraneous information to the screen that neither illustrates the point of the slide headlines nor cues the audience about the presentation's organization.

**FIGURE 8-16** A zoomed-in view of a navigational element in the lower-right corner of the Detail slide layout.

If you do create your own custom layouts and navigational elements manually, each time you do so, you will be building material that you can add to a BBP library that you can access and apply to future presentations—for more information about the library concept, see "Tip 6: Build a BBP Layout Library" later in this chapter.

## Adding Optional Animation Manually

To reinforce the principles described in the section "Rule 1: See It in Seconds" earlier in this chapter, you can introduce information on the screen in the same order you want your audience's working memory to process it—first the headline that you want the audience to quickly read, and second the graphical element that you want the audience to see immediately afterward. You can do this efficiently when you set up the custom layout with placeholders. For example, in the earlier Key Point slide layout, select the Title placeholder and the Picture placeholder, and then on the Animations tab, click Custom Animation. In the Custom Animation panel, select Add Effect, point to Entrance, and then click Fade. In the Start drop-down list, select After Previous, and in the Speed drop-down list, select Fast, as shown in Figure 8-17. On the Slide Master tab, click Close Master View.

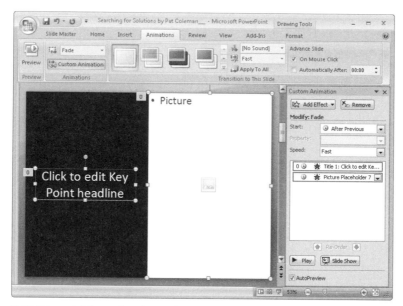

**FIGURE 8-17** Adding animation to the headline and placeholder in the Key Point slide layout.

Now every slide that uses the Key Point slide custom layout with a photo placeholder will automatically fade in the headline first and the picture immediately afterward—the sequence in which you want the audience's working memory to process the new information. Introducing the headline and graphic in this way adds a consistent and subtle movement to the screen without drawing attention away from your message. For the animation to work on your slides, you will need to insert graphics using placeholders as described earlier—if you add graphics to the slides manually, you will need to add animation to each one manually.

> **TIP**  Although they are not essential, you can also create custom layouts for your Title and Act I slides; alternatively, you can skip this step and later use the PowerPoint default Title Slide layout for your Title slide and the default Title Only layout for your Act I slides.

## Adjusting the Notes Master Layout

When you finish making changes to your custom layouts, on the View tab, in the Presentation Views group, click Notes Master. Here you can add any more graphical elements that you want to appear later when you print notes pages of your presentation as a handout. For example, add the logo of your company to appear in your printed handouts by inserting it in the lower-left corner of the Notes Master layout, as shown in Figure 8-18, or include a page number in the lower-right corner.

**FIGURE 8-18** Designing the Notes Master.

Including your company logo on the Notes Master so that it appears on printed handouts would not distract from the visual-verbal balance that you have established with the slide area, selected in Figure 8-18, and the notes area below.

When you have finished making any changes here, on the Notes Master tab, click Close Master View.

## Applying, Reviewing, and Refining the Layouts

Whether you use predesigned custom layouts or design the custom layouts yourself manually, test them now by applying them to specific corresponding slides in your presentation.

1. In Slide Sorter view, press Ctrl+A to select all the slides in the presentation.

2. On the **Home** tab, in the **Slides** group, click the **Layout** button to display a drop-down menu of your custom layouts, and then select the **Detail** slide layout to apply it to all your slides.

3. Next click the Title slide, click **Layout**, and apply the **Title** slide layout, and then hold down the Ctrl key while you click the Act I slides and apply the **Act I** slide layout if you have one or the **Title Only** slide layout if you don't.

4. Hold down the Ctrl key again while you select each of the Key Point slides, click **Layout**, and then click the **Key Point** slide layout.

5. Hold down Ctrl while you select the Explanation slides, click **Layout**, and then click the **Explanation** slide layout.

After you finish applying custom layouts, the slides of your storyboard should appear as shown in Figure 8-19. Now that you have custom layouts in place, you have a foundation for the graphics that you will add to individual slides next.

**FIGURE 8-19** Examples of Key Point, Explanation, and Detail slides with the corresponding custom layouts applied.

Custom layouts will give you tremendous flexibility as you get to know them better and find ways to make your graphical work easier and faster. The great thing about custom layouts is that experimenting is easy—if you create a layout that you don't like or that doesn't work, or if you make a mistake, it's easy to return to the layout in Slide Master view and make changes there that will be automatically updated on the corresponding slides built from the master. If a slide is not updated, select the slide, and on the Home tab, in the Slides group, click the Reset button to reset the slide to its default settings. When you have a set of custom layouts you like, you can copy and paste them from the Overview pane in Slide Master view to other presentations, save them in your presentation to use again later, or post them for others to use at *www.beyondbulletpoints.com*.

## POWERPOINT 2007 THEMES

The custom layouts you create are linked to the default PowerPoint 2007 Theme that controls the colors and fonts in your presentation—you can learn more about themes in most general books on PowerPoint 2007. If you would like to save a theme on your local computer so that you can apply it to a presentation later, on the Design tab, in the Themes group, click the More down arrow to the right of the Theme window, and at the bottom of the All Themes pull-down menu, click Save Current Theme, type a file name, and click Save. After you follow these steps, the next time you scroll over the Theme thumbnails in the Themes group on the Design tab, the new theme should appear. If you want to share the theme with someone else, it is attached to the presentation you applied it to. You can also send a theme with a file as a PowerPoint template. To do so, click the Microsoft Office Button, point to Save As, click Other Formats, and provide a file name. Under Save As Type, select PowerPoint Template, and then click Save. When other people click on the PowerPoint 2007 template file, PowerPoint 2007 will open a new file from the template that includes the theme.

# Adding Graphics to the Call to Action and Key Point Slides

When you apply custom layouts to your storyboard, you now have a graphical foundation established for all of your slides. The next step is to add graphics to the Call to Action and Key Point slides you sketched in Chapter 7, as shown in Figure 8-20. The

Call to Action slide sketch (upper left) features a three-panel photographic layout that calls attention to itself as the most important slide in the presentation. As you learned in Chapter 7, if you had only one slide to show in a presentation, this one would be it because it both visually concludes Act I and visually summarizes the Key Point slides to come. Each of the three Key Point slides features a split-screen layout along with one of the three graphics from the three panels of the Call to Action slide.

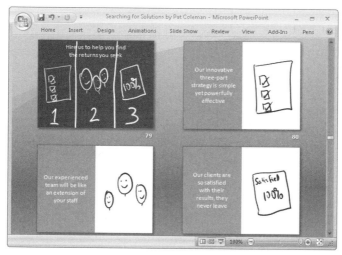

FIGURE 8-20 Original sketches of the Call to Action and Key Point slides.

If the three-panel Call to Action slide layout is one that you think you might use again, create a custom layout as you did earlier, but rename this one CTA. When you create the custom layout, shift the headline to the center of the slide. Insert three Picture placeholders side by side—the dimensions for each Picture placeholder are 7.5 inches to fill the slide vertically and 3.3 inches to fill one-third of the 10-inch slide horizontally. Animate each of the placeholders to appear when clicked. After you create and apply the custom layout to the Call to Action slide, insert photographs in each of the Picture placeholders—the images will be automatically cropped to fit and will appear as shown on the upper left in Figure 8-21. Insert the same three photographs separately into the corresponding Picture placeholders on the Key Point slide layouts (upper right, lower left, and lower right).

**FIGURE 8-21** The Call to Action and Key Point slides with graphics added.

As you learned in Chapter 7, photographs are a good fit for these most important slides because they connect at an emotional level and are more memorable than text. Because these photos have the same style and are an aesthetic match with the audience, they present an especially distinctive impression that drives the story visually through the storyboard. Notice that the original sketch of the third Key Point slide in Figure 8-20 (lower right) was of a customer satisfaction survey. There were no graphics in the database search that matched the sketch, so the final slide in Figure 8-21 (lower right) uses a picture of a stock chart instead to illustrate "results" in the headline. You won't always find the perfect graphics to match your sketches, and when that is the case, improvise and find the best match you can within your budget.

# Duplicating and Positioning Key Point Slides 1 and 2

Now that you've created the Key Point slides, an effective technique to keep these most important concepts continually fresh during a 45-minute presentation is to duplicate them at the end of each corresponding section. To do that, in Slide Sorter view, hold down the Ctrl key as you click the Key Point slides 1 and 2, and with the two slides selected, press Ctrl+D to duplicate these two slides. Now drag the duplicate Key Point slide 1 directly in front of Key Point slide 2, and then drag the duplicate Key Point slide 2 in front of Key Point slide 3. With these duplicated slides in place, after you present the Explanation and Detail slides for Key Point slide 1, you'll see Key Point slide 1 again to serve as a visual summary of the material before moving on to Key Point slide 2. The same thing will happen after the Key Point slide 2 section, except you'll see the duplicate Key Point slide 2 again before moving directly to Key Point slide 3.

# Creating the Act III Slides

As you'll recall from writing your story template in Chapters 4 and 5, you never got around to writing Act III of your story—the resolution. You will quickly take care of the end of your story now with a couple of mouse clicks. A classic way to end a story is to back out the way you came in, and you can end your story the same way by holding down the Ctrl key while you select your Point A and Point B slides along with your Call to Action slide. With these slides selected, press Ctrl+D to duplicate the three slides. Now drag these duplicated slides to the end of the presentation, following the last Detail slide of Act II. Here you might differentiate these slides graphically from their Act I counterparts by hiding the headlines, as shown in Figure 8-22.

**FIGURE 8-22** The Point A, Point B, and Call to Action slides duplicated as the closing Act III slides, with the headlines hidden.

When you reach the Point A slide in the closing Act III of the presentation, you can say something like, "You'll remember we started today by looking at your flat returns [advance to Point B slide] and agreeing that you want your returns to improve. That's been our focus today—figuring out exactly how you can get from a flat line to an upward-sloping line. Well [advance to Call to Action slide], today we've shown that we can help you to improve your returns in three ways. First, our innovative three-part strategy will . . ."

These familiar images connect back to the core problem of the story you began and visually reinforce the messages you want your audience to remember. Just as you start strong visually and verbally, these same slides can help you end strong visually and verbally. You can change the order of the slides and otherwise adapt, innovate, and improvise verbally. Whatever you plan to say in your strong ending here in Act III, make sure to make the appropriate updates in the notes area of the corresponding slides that you duplicated.

# Preparing Slides That Don't Require Graphics

Now that you have taken care of the most important slides in the presentation, the next thing to do is to take care of the slides that don't require graphics or that will be using off-screen media. The storyboard sketches in Figure 8-23 show four examples of these slides—blacking out a screen on an Act I slide (upper left), displaying a physical prop (upper right), switching to another application on an Explanation slide (lower left), and hiding an example Detail slide that you'll cover during a demonstration (lower right).

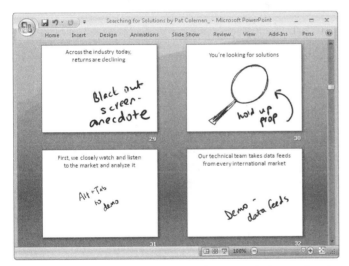

**FIGURE 8-23** Example sketches of slides that use techniques other than graphics on PowerPoint slides.

As described in Chapter 7, you can black out the screen, as shown in Figure 8-24 (upper left), by right-clicking and formatting the background color as black or by inserting a black rectangle to fill the screen. You could also use another dark color to fill the screen or rectangle, but in any case, make sure that the headline color is the same color as the background so that the headline will not appear on screen. If you plan to use a physical prop, either black out the screen or drag the headline down to the middle of the screen (upper right). Another option is to take a photo of the prop and insert it on the slide. (If you're looking for sources for props, try art supplies stores like Blick Art Materials [*www.dickblick.com*], hardware or toy stores, and theatrical design companies.) Although there is only text on this slide, keep in mind that you and your prop will be the visual elements that illustrate the headline.

To switch to an application on an Explanation slide, drag the headline to the center (lower left). Again, although this slide contains only text, it serves as the headline that introduces your activity next as you switch applications. If you're then showing a demonstration in another application, be sure to hide the corresponding Detail slides (lower right), as described in Chapter 7—when you right-click and choose Hide Slide, you'll see that the number of the slide in the lower-right corner has a line through it.

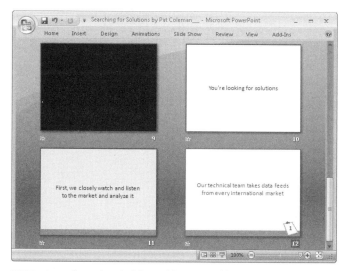

**FIGURE 8-24** Completed slides, without graphics.

## Adding Graphics to the Act I Slides

Now start at the beginning of the presentation and add the graphics to your Act I slides that you sketched in Chapter 7. Those sketches are shown in Figure 8-25.

In the completed example shown in Figure 8-26, the PowerPoint chart on the Setting slide (upper left) conveys the shape of the line in an extremely simple way without detail. The usual detail in a chart is not needed here because in this specific context, the reason you chose this image is that everyone in the audience is already familiar with the chart and agrees that the data is true. Here the purpose is not to analyze the graph as you will likely do on a Detail slide later in the presentation, but rather to visually cue the audience as quickly as possible to the topic and establish the setting. The Role slide features a simple magnifying glass (upper right), and the headline is hidden to unlock more visual power. The Point A slide (lower left) again is a simple PowerPoint chart, and in the Point B slide (lower right), three dashed arrows were added to the Point A chart using PowerPoint drawing tools to show returns improving.

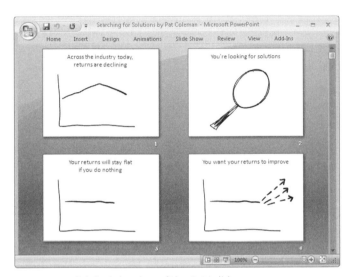

**FIGURE 8-25** Original sketches of the Act I slides.

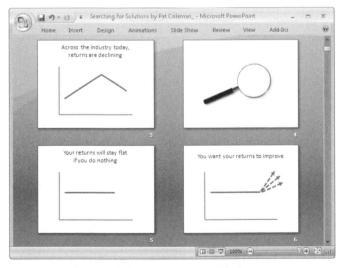

**FIGURE 8-26** The Act I slides with graphics added.

## Adding Graphics to the Explanation Slides

As described in Chapter 7, the sketches of your Explanation slides might guide you toward adding a photograph, logo, diagram, chart, or other illustration on the individual slides. Figure 8-27 shows a Key Point slide with graphics that you've already added (upper left), and the sketches of its three related Explanation slides.

Locate and add graphics that correspond to these sketches on each of these slides, as shown in Figure 8-28. Notice that the clipboard graphics are telling a story, slide by slide, as they explain the initial Key Point slide—in turn, each Explanation slide will visually introduce and summarize its subsequent Detail slides. You would apply a similar technique of building a visual story step by step if your story template and sketches call for the use of a diagram or chart on the Explanation slides.

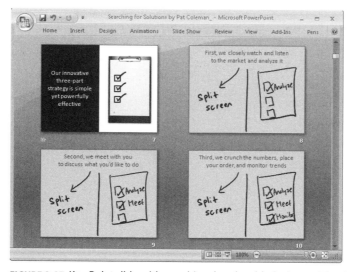

**FIGURE 8-27** Key Point slide with graphics already added, along with original sketches of the related Explanation slides.

When your Explanation slides feature the same underlying graphic—in this example, the blank clipboard—use custom layouts to make adding graphics easier, as described in "Tip 3: Use Custom Layouts to Add the Same Graphic to Related Slides" later in this chapter.

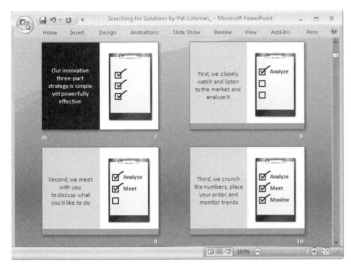

**FIGURE 8-28** The Explanation slides with graphics added.

# Adding Graphics to the Detail Slides

For a 45-minute presentation, the bulk of your work when adding graphics involves the Detail slides. As described in Chapter 7, you might have sketched photos or screen captures to add to these slides, as shown in Figure 8-29.

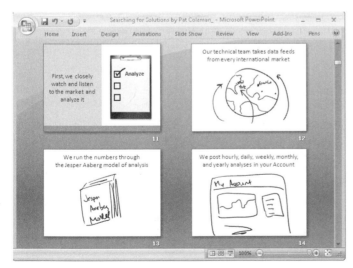

**FIGURE 8-29** Explanation slide with graphic added (upper left), along with original sketches of the related Detail slides.

If you use images from iStockphoto.com, these slides might look like the slides on the upper right and lower left in Figure 8-30 after you have added the graphics you found.

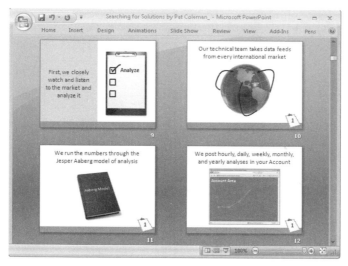

**FIGURE 8-30** The Detail slides with photographs and a screen capture added.

One of the simplest and most overlooked sources for graphics for Act II is your computer screen. To create a shot of your screen, press Print Screen (usually labeled PrtScn on your keyboard), and then on a slide in Normal view, right-click and choose Paste to place the image on the slide. Click on the image to access the Picture Tools and Format tabs, where you can make adjustments to the screen capture. Commercial screen capture programs such as SnagIt (*www.techsmith.com*) allow you many more options for customizing your shots, such as adding a subtle drop shadow. Use a screen capture to illustrate a concept—for example, a screen capture is a great way to show a Web page without presenting the actual details of the text on that page, as shown on the lower right in Figure 8-30. If you do want to show the details of a screen capture, crop out everything that's not essential to the idea and make sure that the portion of the image that contains the details is large enough to be read by people at the back of the room.

Other graphics that you might add on Detail slides such as those shown in Figure 8-31 include a company logo, a photograph, and more screen captures.

If you sketched a chart on a Detail slide, it might look like the slide on the upper right in Figure 8-32 in its final state. Although many of the guidelines and much of the writing and research related to charts deals with displaying them on paper, PowerPoint charts are usually projected on a wall with a live presenter explaining them. Because there is the added element of a synchronized verbal explanation in the live presentation environment, charts designed on a slide can generally be simpler than those displayed on paper without a live presenter.

**FIGURE 8-31** More Detail slides with a logo, a photograph, and screen captures added.

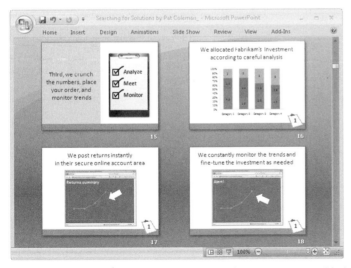

**FIGURE 8-32** More Detail slides with a chart and screen captures added.

With the BBP approach, you're always certain that the main point of a chart is fully explained by the headline—that's because you always clarify the point you want to make in the form of a headline before you select the chart to explain it. If someone was not present to hear your narration, you provide them with a handout of a Notes Page version of the slide that includes the headline, chart, and off-screen notes area explanation. Displaying the chart over a series of slides that are mapped to a sequence of headlines, as described in Chapter 7, helps to introduce the new information in smaller pieces at an appropriate pace for the audience to understand.

To keep a chart free of clutter and focused on the data at hand, simplify its formatting by removing excess lines, graphical treatments, colors, and grids. Avoid adding unnecessary ornamentation or special effects that can inhibit the audience's ability to understand information, as described in Chapter 2. Strive for a minimalist style that will allow the numbers to speak for themselves. When you need to show your numbers using a chart, consider consulting one of the books that can help you to display data effectively, including Stephen Few, *Show Me the Numbers: Designing Tables and Graphs to Enlighten* (Analytics Press, 2004).

The screen captures (lower left and lower right) in Figure 8-32 include arrows created using the PowerPoint drawing tools to highlight important information that visually explains the headline.

## Fine-Tuning and Finishing Up

Now that you have a first draft with a graphic on every slide, go back and review what you have with an eye toward refining your presentation and making it better.

### Adding Graphics to the Title and Closing Credits Slides

In a film, the opening title sequence establishes the mood and tone of the story to come. You can achieve a similar effect by adding graphics to the Title slide. Apply the same style to the Title slide that you did to the other slides in Act I. For example, if you use the photographic design technique for the Act I slides, use the same style for the Title slide. Then apply the same technique you use for the Title slide to a Closing Credits slide that will remain on screen when you finish your presentation. To create a closing slide now, on the Home tab, click New Slide, and on the drop-down menu, click Blank. Now add a simple image or a line of text that you want the audience to remember after the presentation. This slide might include your organization's name, your contact information, a Web address, or a simple image that conveys the theme of the presentation.

# Reviewing and Adding Graphics to the Notes Pages

The BBP Storyboard Formatter you used to create your slides in Chapter 6 includes formatting of the Notes Master that balances the notes pages equally between the amount of space you dedicate to the slide you show on screen and the amount of space you dedicate to the notes area, which holds the ideas you explain with your narration. The line around the slide placeholder was removed to open up the white space on the printed notes page. The Slide Master and Notes Master both have white backgrounds, and because neither the slide nor the notes areas will be bounded by lines, the headline of the slide summarizes the idea of the entire printed page.

To preview how the notes page version of any slide will look when printed, click the Microsoft Office Button, point to Print, and then click Print Preview. In Print Preview view, click the Print What drop-down arrow and click Notes Pages. When you've finished previewing, click Close Print Preview to return to the previous view. You can add more graphics to the notes pages if you choose, such as the chart shown at the bottom of Figure 8-33.

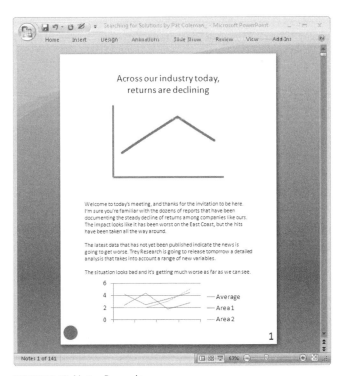

**FIGURE 8-33** Notes Page view.

When you finish making adjustments or adding graphics to all the slides, return once again to Notes Page view of each slide to review the notes areas and make sure that your written words are clear and concise. Begin with the first notes page: read the head-line, review the visual, and then read the notes area to make sure that everything flows smoothly. When you've read the last line in the notes area, scroll down to the next notes page and make sure that it reads smoothly as a continuation of the story from the previous notes page. It's a good idea to print the entire document as notes pages at this point so that you can check the wording and flow.

## Reviewing and Finalizing the Storyboard

Congratulations on completing your PowerPoint storyboard! Your final presentation should look something like the one shown in Figure 8-34.

**FIGURE 8-34** Completed storyboard with graphics added to all the slides.

Now that you've reviewed the complete presentation, it's always a good idea to have someone with fresh eyes take a look at the presentation to verify that you didn't miss anything, make a typographical error, or misstate something. When you prepare the presentation for review, plan to send it as notes pages so that it can be cleared not only for what appears on screen but also for the information covered in the notes area.

## SAVE YOUR POWERPOINT FILE IN PDF FORMAT

The 2007 Microsoft Office system includes a new feature that allows you to save documents in the popular PDF format. Saving your PowerPoint file in PDF format allows you to send a version of the presentation electronically in a form that does not allow others to alter it. To save a presentation as a PDF file, visit the Microsoft Download Center at *www.microsoft.com* to download the free 2007 Microsoft Office Add-In, Microsoft Save as PDF or XPS. After you install the add-in, open a PowerPoint presentation, click the Microsoft Office Button, click Save As, and then select PDF Or XPS. In the Publish As PDF Or XPS dialog box, select the file name, and in the Save As Type drop-down list, select PDF. Click the Options button, and in the Options dialog box, under Publish What, select Notes Pages. (Because you make use of both the slide area and the notes area, you'll usually want to send the full notes pages, rather than the slides alone.) Configure any other settings you want, and then click OK to close the Options dialog box. Last, in the Publish As PDF Or XPS dialog box, click Publish to create the PDF.

## BBP CHECKLIST: ADDING GRAPHICS TO THE STORYBOARD

Do your final graphics:

❑ Clearly illustrate each headline in the simplest way possible?

❑ Show consistency within levels of the presentation hierarchy and variety across levels?

❑ Keep your slides free of any extraneous visual information?

❑ Align with the aesthetics of your audience?

You've come a long way since you started on the road to the BBP approach in Chapter 1, and the detailed example presentation in this book should help you start applying the BBP approach to your next presentation. Next Chapter 9 will show you a range of presentations you can review for additional inspiration, and Chapter 10 will provide some ground rules and tips to consider when you deliver your presentation to an audience.

As you get familiar with adding graphics, take a look at these 10 tips for improving on the basic techniques described in this chapter.

# 10 Tips for Enhancing Your Storyboard

Your storyboard is a versatile tool to prepare and plan both your spoken words and your projected visuals during the presentation. Once you've mastered the basics, try using these 10 tips to enhance the storyboard.

## Tip 1: Clip Your Ideas

A great way to keep a fresh supply of creative visual ideas is by keeping a clipping file. Whenever you see an interesting layout, photograph, illustration, graph, or other visual idea in a newspaper, magazine, book, or other printed material, cut it out or copy it and place it in a folder in your file cabinet. Or for an electronic clip folder, create a folder in Microsoft Office OneNote® 2007, and use the clipping tool to save an electronic image of the item. The next time you're stuck, refer to your paper or electronic file folders for creative inspiration.

## Tip 2: The Photo Basics: Size, Crop, and Compress

Whatever photo you choose to add to a slide, you might find that it doesn't fit on the slide the way you want it to or that it is an inappropriate file size for a PowerPoint presentation. To fix these problems, you'll need to apply the three most important techniques you'll use to work with photographs: sizing, cropping, and compressing.

When you insert a photograph on the slide, it might fill only a portion of the screen, communicating only a portion of its visual potential. To increase its communicative power, resize the photo to fill the entire screen. To do that, click the photo. Round sizing handles will appear at each of the four corners of the photo—drag one of them to enlarge the photo so that it fills the entire slide area. Be careful not to drag one of the square sizing handles that appear on the sides of the graphic, because dragging them will distort the photo as you resize it. You always want to preserve the image's original proportions so that your audience does not notice any distortion.

Review the picture to make sure that it's crisp and clear at its current size. If it isn't, find another image. Never use a photo that is unfocused, grainy, blurry, or otherwise unclear—you'll distract from your message and diminish your visual credibility. People are used to seeing sharply focused photographs in professional media, and if you don't deliver the same in your slides, they'll think less of the presentation, no matter how good the story.

After you resize the photograph and verify that it's clear and focused, you might find that it extends over the edges of the slide. If so, you'll need to crop the image to keep only the portion you want in the slide area. Click the picture, and the Picture Tools and Format tab will appear, giving you access to the picture tools. In the Size group, click Crop, which will turn the sizing handles into cropping handles. To crop one side of the photograph, drag the cropping handle on that side toward the center of the photo to eliminate the part of the photo you don't want to keep.

The last tool to apply is Compress Pictures, available on the Format tab in the Adjust group when you click a picture. It's not uncommon for a single high-resolution photograph to be hundreds of megabytes in size, unnecessarily bloating the PowerPoint file. This huge image file can create problems when you try to e-mail the PowerPoint file or share it with other people. Solve this problem before it happens by making sure that the photographs are compressed to the smallest size needed for them to appear clearly on screen. Select the picture, click the Compress Pictures button, click Options, select the Target Output you prefer—the lower the ppi, the smaller the file size—and then click OK.

## Tip 3: Use Custom Layouts to Add the Same Graphic to Related Slides

If related slides in your presentation share the same underlying graphic, use the custom layout feature to apply them consistently to the corresponding slides. For example, let's say you sketched a clipboard across three Explanation slides, as shown in Figure 8-35. Based on these sketches, you know that you'll need the same underlying graphic of a clipboard and three check boxes on each slide.

**FIGURE 8-35**  Three Explanation slides with the same graphical foundation.

For this example, after you find the graphic of a clipboard, locate the Explanation slide layout that you designed earlier in this chapter, in the section "Creating the Explanation Slide Layout Manually." Right-click the Explanation slide layout, and select

Duplicate Layout. Right-click the duplicate layout that you just created, and select Rename Layout, naming the layout Explanation-Clipboard. Delete the Picture placeholder if you have one, and then add the clipboard graphic and three small boxes using the PowerPoint drawing tools. When you have finished, on the Slide Master tab, click Close Master View.

In Slide Sorter view, hold down the Ctrl key as you select the Explanation slides that need a clipboard graphic, and then on the Home tab, in the Slides group, choose Layout. This will display an Office Theme window, as shown in Figure 8-36, that includes the Explanation-Clipboard layout you just created.

**FIGURE 8-36** Applying a predesigned custom layout.

Clicking the Explanation-Clipboard layout option in this example applies all these changes to the selected slides, as shown in Figure 8-37, saving you the time and effort of adding the graphic to each slide yourself. For these particular clipboards, all you need to do next is add a check mark and a text box to each slide's graphic to match your sketches.

You won't always have graphics that you can apply to multiple slides using custom layouts, but when you do, this technique helps you to make sure that your slides look good and also makes sure you don't accidentally alter the foundation graphics since they can only be changed in the custom layout.

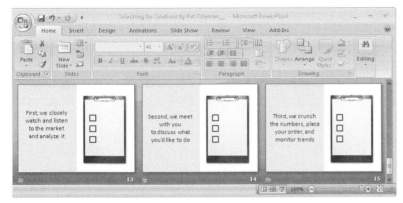

**FIGURE 8-37** A click of a button automatically formats the slides and adds the same foundation graphic to each one; next, more graphics are added to each slide.

## Tip 4: Try Three Treatments

You don't know what you have until you see it, and that's especially true with graphics. That's why you should create a range of options for yourself before you decide what to do with the design of your slides. When a professional design firm starts a job for a client, it's common practice to present the client with three design options. From the perspective of the firm, this gives designers a free hand to express their creativity by trying three completely different treatments. From the perspective of clients, this gives a range of options that they can review and select from based on what works for them. From the perspectives of both parties, this provides a way of stepping back from the emotional attachment anyone has to the different designs and gives a point of reference and comparison that can be used in deciding which design direction to take.

This time-tested method will serve you well when you design your PowerPoint storyboard. Select the sketches for the Key Point slides from the presentation you've created, and try three completely different design treatments. Show the design treatments to your team, and test them on people unfamiliar with the presentation and ask for feedback. When you're satisfied with a design that will work for the audience, extend that design across all of the slides in the presentation.

## Tip 5: Design for Your Designer

If you have the resources, invite a professional designer to help you design your slides and storyboard. Bring the designer in early—if possible, while you write the story template—so that the designer can absorb and learn from your thinking process. Working with the designer from the start avoids the frustration that graphic designers feel when someone hands them a PowerPoint presentation with the instructions to "make it pretty," and the designer has no ability to clarify the structure. In that scenario, no one is happy. Instead, the story template places responsibility for the clear structure of the story squarely on the presenter. The resulting storyboard shows the designer the order in which you want the ideas to appear and how you'll reinforce the message through the presentation. Discuss how the Key Point, Explanation, and Detail slides form the hierarchy of a presentation, and explain that you want the backgrounds and layouts of these slides to cue the audience's working memory to the presentation organization. Always walk through the slides in Notes Page view to make sure that the designer can see the relationship between the projected image on screen and your spoken words.

When everyone is in agreement, ask the designer to provide you with three completely different visual treatments of key slides in a test file that you select from Acts I and II. Then you can compare the treatments and choose the elements and styles that are the best fit with you and your audience. Ask questions to be sure that you understand why the designer is proposing a particular treatment. Through your interaction, you're sure to spark new creativity and understanding that will set the stage for a well-designed presentation. Because the designer doesn't have to take on the unnecessary job of figuring out what you want to say and in what order, you'll accelerate the design process and avoid possible confusion. Instead, the designer is freed up to do what a designer does best—designing. Using this approach, you can develop a smooth process that's sure to result in a PowerPoint presentation that gives everyone involved a rewarding communication experience.

## Tip 6: Build a BBP Layout Library

If you have colleagues who are also using BBP, consider pooling your resources to create a BBP design library. If your organization uses Microsoft Windows® SharePoint® Services, you could use it to create a collaborative Web site for people who are willing to share their PowerPoint files. For example, you could create document library folders labeled Key Point Layouts And Slide Examples, Explanation Layouts And Slide Examples, and Detail Layouts And Slide Examples. Anyone who created a presentation using one of those design techniques would then post it in the corresponding folder. You and the members of your team would no longer have to begin presentations from scratch; instead, you'd have a library of ideas ready for you to check out. If your organization uses Microsoft Office SharePoint 2007 and enables the Slide Library feature, you will find additional features that you can use to share and collaborate using your BBP slides.

## Tip 7: Build a BBP Charts Library

Many individuals and organizations use a relatively limited range of PowerPoint diagrams and charts to explain the information that relates to their work. Instead of formatting diagrams and charts from scratch every time, it's a good idea to design a single set of commonly used graphics that carry a clear and consistent design according to the best design principles. Whether you design the set of charts yourself or hire a professional information designer to help, standardizing the way you display quantitative information can both save you time formatting and ensure that you maintain the integrity of the data you display.

## Tip 8: Call Out Additional Information

To add a label to a graphic, on the Insert tab, in the Illustrations group, click Shapes, and then in the Callout group, select the style you want. After you add the label to the slide, you can modify it by adding text and adjusting the formatting as you would with any PowerPoint shape.

## Tip 9: Sketch It All, *Live!*

If you are a decent storyboard sketcher, consider something completely different and present your PowerPoint slides with only the headlines and no graphics added at all. When you present live, use a Tablet PC to sketch a graphic to illustrate each headline as you go along. It will be a deeply engaging and interesting experience for the audience, plus you can save the sketches you made with the PowerPoint file and send the illustrated file to everyone who attended.

## Tip 10: Develop a Single Illustration, Slide by Slide

If you're feeling particularly ambitious, try developing a single illustration across the entire presentation. You will have to plan this carefully in the story template, but the basic idea is that you introduce one piece of the graphic, one slide at a time, as you verbally explain each piece, until everything in the illustration comes together into a single graphic at the end of the presentation. This technique literally helps you explain the big picture to your audience.

CHAPTER 9

# Reviewing a Range of BBP Examples

**IN THIS CHAPTER, YOU WILL:**

- Review a range of presentation examples using the Beyond Bullet Points (BBP) approach.

- See how the core BBP principles look when applied to different topics.

- Get inspired by seeing how to apply new techniques to your presentation.

**SO FAR,** this book has demonstrated how you can apply Beyond Bullet Points (BBP) in depth to a single presentation example. Chapter 4 showed you how Act I of the story template helps you choose the specific ideas that you'll present to your audience's working memory in the first five slides of a presentation, and Chapter 5 showed you how Act II guides you through the process of setting the priority and sequence of the rest of the slides. Chapter 6 offered instructions on how to set up your storyboard and narration in Microsoft® Office PowerPoint® 2007, and Chapter 7 illustrated some of the many ways you can sketch your storyboard. Finally, everything came together in Chapter 8 as you set up custom layouts that align with the priority of your slides and you added the specific graphics that are a good fit for you, your headlines, and your audience.

Although these chapters used a single presentation example, you can apply the same underlying BBP process to unlock a clear message from any topic and guide the working memory of your audience to clear and memorable understanding.

# What Other Examples Can I See?

The verbal and visual variations that you can create using BBP are literally endless. This chapter shows you more examples of BBP in action as it is applied to a wide range of topics and purposes, showing what a presentation might look if you were to:

- Introduce a case to jurors in an opening statement with The Trial.

- Keep your team on track toward completing a project with The Plan.

- Summarize your market research findings to your clients with The Analysis.

- Update and gain the support of your boss for your activities with The Report.

- Teach your students about a new topic with The Class.

- Sell the services of your company to a client with The Pitch.

Because of space limitations, the examples in this chapter show selected portions of story templates, storyboards, and slides, focusing primarily on the critical Act I, Call to Action, and Key Point slides rather than on the Explanation and Detail slides that will contain your own specific photos, charts, graphs, screen captures, and diagrams. Every presentation was built using the same process in this book, but each looks and feels very different. Likewise, your own presentations will reflect your own understanding of your specific audiences that determines the words you write in the story template, the graphics you add to the storyboard, and the way you deliver the experience.

As with the financial services example presentation in the earlier chapters of this book, the example presentations in this chapter adhere to the design constraint of a limited budget to show you what you can do with a stock photography Web site and your own creativity—if you have a larger budget or work with a professional graphic designer, you probably can do even better. If you find that adding the graphics to the storyboard is fun and relatively easy for you, that's only because of the hard work you accomplished in the story template. If adding graphics is not your strength, work with others who can help, and be sure to visit *www.beyondbulletpoints.com* for a continually fresh stream of graphical ideas designed to make that part of your job easier.

# Introducing a Case with The Trial

This book began with the example of a headline-making BBP presentation used in a courtroom in Chapter 1, and it's worth taking a quick peek under the hood to see what made the first slides of that presentation work so well. Although you might not present the opening statement in a trial, when you explore the thought process behind this example, think of how you will write your own clear and concise words in Act I of your story template and apply equally effective yet simple visual techniques to your own storyboard.

# Act I: The Classical Storytelling Foundation

Chapter 4 explained that at the beginning of your presentation, you are faced with the formidable challenges not only of setting up the framework that will help the working memory of your audience understand what is to come but also of making an emotional connection. Mark Lanier, the plaintiff's attorney who presented the opening statement using BBP as described in Chapter 1, accomplished both goals by the way he structured his ideas in Act I of his story template, as shown in Figure 9-1, which established the story thread and pattern that would help the jurors sew up understanding of the case.

| The Trial by Mark Lanier | | |
|---|---|---|
| **Act I:** Set up the story from the audience's viewpoint ("A to B, what's in it for me?") | | |
| **Setting** *(Where am I?)* | Bob Ernst is dead | |
| **Role** *(Who am I here?)* | You get to be like CSI detectives and follow the evidence | |
| **Point A** *(What challenge do I face?)* | **Call to Action** *(How do I get from A→B?)* | **Point B** *(Where do I want to be?)* |
| The evidence will lead you to the pharmaceutical company | Follow the three parts of the case to bring justice for Mrs. Ernst | You'd like to bring justice to the situation |
| **Act II:** Develop the action ("1-2-3, show me only what I need to see") | | |
| **Case Theme** *(5 minutes):* How? | **Explanation** *(15 minutes):* Why? | **Evidence** *(45 minutes):* Why? |

**FIGURE 9-1** Act I of The Trial presentation example.

Although the specific words in Act I are brief, they're a good example of how a sequence of concise statements works dynamically to create the underpinnings for a compelling visual story in PowerPoint. When you work on your own Act I statements, keep in mind the absolute importance of getting Act I right. If you know your audience well and you write the correct words, you'll hit your target, as the attorney did in this example; if you put too little effort into Act I and get the words wrong, you'll miss the mark.

**NOTE**  Notice that the Act II category headings have been changed in this example from Key Point to Case Theme and from Detail to Evidence—other examples in this chapter are also tailored to the presentation content, as described in the section "Tip 3: Tailor Your Act II Column Headings to Your Profession" in Chapter 5.

# A Photographic Setting Slide

The Setting headline in the story template, "Bob Ernst is dead," quickly oriented the jurors to the context for the trial—Bob Ernst had died of a heart attack. As described in Chapter 1, this clear and direct statement is the foundation for the Setting slide, which in this example included three variations of a single photograph, here presented across three slides in Figure 9-2. The headlines of all the Act I slides are hidden in this and the rest of the examples in this chapter. Although you should keep the headlines visible through most of Act II because they guide understanding of the in-depth new information on your Explanation and Detail slides, they are not essential in Act I because here you are primarily making an emotional impact, and as always, your narration will supply the verbal information that synchronizes with your visual slides.

**FIGURE 9-2** The Setting slide introduced to the jurors a gripping story.

As Mark told an anecdote about Carol and Bob while the first photograph was on the screen, it packed the image on screen with meaning. Here the jurors could connect emotionally with Bob and Carol, because anyone could relate to the details of their life together and be happy for them. But the emotion that had been attached to the first slide was suddenly stripped away visually with the removal of the background in the second slide, signaling that something unexpected was about to happen. The third slide becomes deeply poignant when visually Carol is suddenly left alone, with only an empty outline defining the space where her husband once was. Although the photo sequence is very simple, it had a deeply profound impact. When you think of writing and illustrating your Setting headline, consider how you can use a simple anecdote and photograph to quickly orient your own audience in an equally savvy way.

# Reviewing the Act I Slides for The Trial

In an entertaining fictional story, the main character is someone an audience observes from a distance. But in a nonfiction BBP presentation, you write the Role statement in Act I to heighten the audience's interest by acknowledging their role here at the center of the action. Transitioning from the preceding photograph with a heavy black outline of Bob, shown on the upper left in Figure 9-3, Mark now "deputized" the jurors as crime scene detectives in the Role slide (upper right) with the simple phrase *CSI: Angleton* illustrating the hidden headline "You get to be like CSI detectives and follow the evidence." Mark knew that this technique would connect with his audience because many of the jurors had indicated in their written questionnaires that the popular *CSI* television show was one of their favorites. Even if all of the jurors had not seen *CSI*, they would know its premise because of the show's broad market awareness. As you write and illustrate your own Role headline, consider what words and images you can use to instantly place your audience at the center of the action in an effective way like this.

**FIGURE 9-3** The Setting, Role, Point A, and Point B slides of The Trial.

In keeping with the classical storytelling form described in Chapter 4, Mark's next step was to present the main characters with a challenge they face on the Point A slide. In this case, Mark defined the jurors' challenge in the hidden headline, "The evidence will lead you to the pharmaceutical company," illustrated with an office building similar to the one shown on the lower left. In screenwriting terms, this introduced the challenge that is built into your Point A headline—an obstacle or an event that confronts the main character and begins the action that drives the story forward. In this case, Mark defined the obstacle as the evidence these "CSI detectives" would now need to follow. But for the problem to be fully defined, Mark needed to provide the jurors with a second crucial element—Point B, or where the jurors wanted to be, which is defined in the story template with the headline "You'd like to bring justice to the situation." The image of a gavel (lower right) along with Mark's narration reinforced the problem the jurors faced: they will follow the evidence that leads them to the company (Point A), and then they want to bring the situation to justice (Point B).

The underlying structure of conventional PowerPoint presentations rarely engages audiences at an emotional level, leaving them struggling to figure out why this information is relevant to them. But with Act I of the story template, Mark's presentation efficiently adapted a story technique to make the topic personally relevant to his audience. By creating a gap between Point A where the jurors stood and Point B where they wanted to be, Mark tapped into the core element of classical story structure—unresolved tension. People do not sit comfortably with tension, and it is the quest to resolve tension that compels a main character to action. By presenting the jurors with a problem, Mark engaged the jurors both emotionally and intellectually, and he answered the toughest audience question any presenter faces: "What's in this for me?"

## Reviewing the Call to Action and Key Point Slides for The Trial

By using Act I of the story template, Mark would not leave his audience without a way to get from A to B. As described in more detail in Chapter 1, the Call to Action slide, shown on the upper left in Figure 9-4, distills the entire presentation into a single slide based on the hidden headline "Follow the three parts of the case to bring justice for Mrs. Ernst." With the three-part formula of *motive + means = death*, Mark introduced the vast amount of new information to the jurors as being as simple as 1-2-3. Just as the murder-mystery motif is a familiar structure, the jurors would also know the phrase *as easy as 1-2-3*. If the upcoming story would be as easy to understand as that, the jurors could relax as they listened to the case.

Next Mark had written Act II of his story template to divide the story of the case into three roughly equal Key Point (Case Theme) headlines that he would spend equal amounts of time explaining. Each corresponding Key Point slide carried forward the 1-2-3 numbering system along with an enlarged version of each icon from the Call to Action slide. Each image used on these slides was carefully chosen to carry the visual essence of each Key Point headline. Writing each Key Point headline in your story template distills and summarizes all of the corresponding Explanation and Detail headline to follow; here each Key Point image in the storyboard now also serves as a visual distillation and summary of all of the corresponding Explanation and Detail slides to follow.

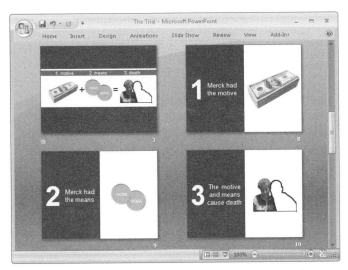

**FIGURE 9-4** The Call to Action and Key Point slides of The Trial.

As illustrated simply yet powerfully here, the ideas and images and narration you use on your Key Point slides are the most important ideas you want your audience to integrate into long-term memory. In a similar fashion, you'll want to apply a blend of your best creative and intellectual thinking to design your Act I and Key Point slides because they represent the verbal and visual essence of the most important information you want to communicate.

With this familiar story structure in place on the Call to Action and Key Point slides, Mark solved the toughest communication challenge any presenter faces—how to make it easier for an audience to understand new information. As described in Chapter 2, as much as you might hope otherwise, the reality is that you cannot pour information directly into your audience's minds and have them simply "get it." The working memory of your audience can become quickly overloaded when the audience is unfamiliar with too much of the information or if the material otherwise is not presented properly. To overcome this problem and increase his audience's ability to understand his case, Mark related the new information of the case using a story framework through Acts I and II that the audience already knew—the murder-mystery motif.

The graphics used on these slides are created using images from the iStockphoto Web site, family photographs, or PowerPoint graphical tools. This presentation is a good example of how the simple visual surfaces of BBP presentations offer few clues that there is a sophisticated verbal strategy beneath them, yet the powerful impact of the approach is very real and profound. As you apply simple visual surfaces to your own BBP verbal structures, you'll begin to tap into similar results in your own presentations.

# Keeping on Track with The Plan

The Trial example showed a range of verbal and visual techniques that you can apply to your own presentations even if you never set foot in a courtroom. The next example, named The Plan, might come in handy if you find yourself leading a team toward accomplishing a project. In this scenario, your group has a deadline to accomplish a task, but you're running into problems that might delay the project. Most of the people on your team work in your local office, so you'll present this version live to them tomorrow morning; the rest of the team works in different cities, so you'll give the same presentation tomorrow afternoon using a Web conferencing tool.

## Writing Act I of the Story Template

As you start your story template, you've done your research with your audience and know that there is a shared sense of frustration with the delays on the project, but as an experienced project manager, you also know what the basic problems are and how they can be resolved. The Setting statement, shown in Figure 9-5, affirms "We've been racing to finish the project and earn our bonuses." The reference to the bonuses establishes right away something the audience personally cares about.

| The Plan by Pat Coleman | | |
|---|---|---|
| **Act I:** Set up the story from the audience's viewpoint ("*A to B, what's in it for me?*") | | |
| **Setting** (*Where am I?*) | We've been racing to finish the project and earn our bonuses | |
| **Role** (*Who am I here?*) | But unsolved problems keep sending us back to the starting line | |
| **Point A** (*What challenge do I face?*) | **Call to Action** (*How do I get from A→B?*) | **Point B** (*Where do I want to be?*) |
| A few key hurdles stand in our way | Overcome each hurdle as we face it, and we'll win the race | We will reach the finish line if we can overcome them |

**FIGURE 9-5** Act I of The Plan presentation example.

In the storyboard sketches shown in Figure 9-6, the reference to "racing" in the Setting statement plays out as a motif on the Setting slide as a group of people running a race (upper left). Remember, introducing a motif to a BBP presentation is not a "fluffy" nice-to-have addition in the story template and slides, but rather a strategy of introducing a familiar verbal and visual framework from the audience's long-term memory to introduce new information to their working memory.

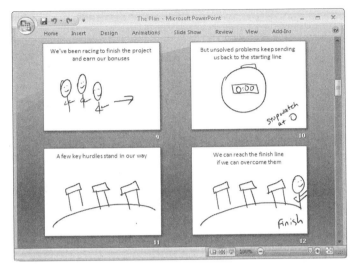

**FIGURE 9-6** Sketches of the Setting, Role, Point A, and Point B slides of The Plan presentation.

The Role statement in the story template affirms, "But unsolved problems keep sending us back to the starting line," which plays out on the Role slide as the sketch of a stopwatch set to 0 minutes to indicate the beginning of the race (upper right). The Point A statement carries the motif further and engages the audience by visually describing "A few key hurdles stand in our way" with sketches of hurdles on the Point A slide (lower left). On the Point B slide (lower right), a runner is shown on the right in the slide, past the same hurdles and the finish line, to visually illustrate the headline "We can reach the finish line if we can overcome them."

## Researching and Adding Available Graphics for The Plan

If you have a limited budget, as in this project, it's worth taking a few minutes to make a quick check of the graphical resources you have available before you commit to a motif you will use in your story template and sketches. You might have a great idea for a motif, but if you don't have the available graphics to pull it off, it won't become a visual reality. A *lightbox*, available at some stock photography Web sites, is a very useful tool in your research for available graphics. You can use the lightbox to temporarily collect photos in a single place, without committing to purchasing licenses until you are ready to use specific photos. For example, create a lightbox named The Plan Presentation at iStockphoto. In keeping with the race motif of The Plan presentation example, search for terms such as "hurdles," "runners," and "finish line," and when you see a photo you like, click the Add To Lightbox button below the photo. In the pop-up window, select The Plan Presentation lightbox, and then click Add. When you have finished your search, visit The Plan

Presentation lightbox, and you'll see thumbnails of all the images you selected in your search in a single space, as shown in Figure 9-7.

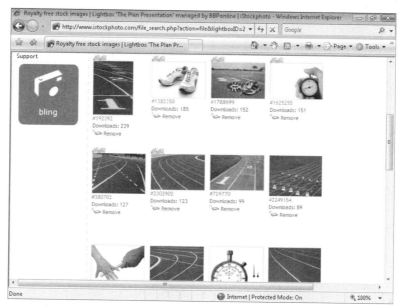

**FIGURE 9-7** A lightbox at iStockphoto.

## Reviewing the Act I Slides for The Plan

A search for the term "runners" on iStockphoto resulted in a number of good aesthetic matches with this audience, so add one to the Setting slide, as shown on the upper left in Figure 9-8, and then send the headline behind the photograph, as you'll do on the rest of the Act I slides. Then search for "stopwatch," and add the photo to the Role slide (upper right). A search for "hurdles" did not result in photos with three hurdles as the sketch described, but a single hurdle will work fine on the Point A slide (lower left). A search for "finish line" did not turn up a match for the sketch either, but a picture of a running track will work, along with a banner shape added using the PowerPoint 2007 drawing tools and showing the words *Finish Line*, as shown on the Point B slide (lower right). As these examples demonstrate, you won't always find the perfect match for your sketches, but you'll likely find something that will work.

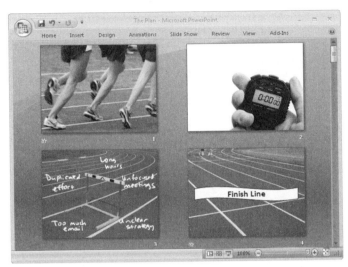

**FIGURE 9-8** The Setting, Role, Point A, and Point B slides of The Plan presentation.

As described earlier, Point A is a crucial slide on which you need to make sure that your audience feels emotionally connected with the challenge they face. To make sure that is the case, when you present the Point A slide, ask your audience, "What are some of the problems you see that stand in our way?" Then, if you have a Tablet PC, write the responses directly on the screen, such as "long hours," "unfocused meetings," or "too much e-mail," as shown on the lower left in Figure 9-8. This shifts the dynamic of the presentation because you are not telling your team what their problems are; rather, they are telling you. Instead of risking that they will be alienated by feeling that you know it all, you give your audience a feeling of ownership. When you advance to the Point B slide (lower right), you can affirm, "Yes, those are all valid problems, and we need to overcome them in order to reach the finish line."

## Reviewing the Call to Action and Key Point Slides for The Plan

Although you opened the floor to the audience on the Point A slide, you also know from your research and your experience as a project manager that you need to cover the primary obstacles defined as the three Key Points you write on the story template, shown in Figure 9-9.

| Act II: Develop the action ("1-2-3, show me only what I need to see") | | |
|---|---|---|
| Key Point (5 minutes): How? | Explanation (15 minutes): Why? | Detail (45 minutes): |
| Overcome the focus hurdle by reviewing the project plan each morning | The project plan changes periodically because of feedback from our client | Our client has been undergoing... |
| | | Just last week, the board of... |
| | | We have to be flexible in order... |
| | The project manager posts any changes each evening and sends out a reminder e-mail | The project manager keeps up... |
| | | She makes sure to follow-up to... |
| | | Each evening, she updates the... |
| | Without knowing about the changes, you may end up wasting effort | For example, the IT team started |
| | | Then they found out that the... |
| | | They could have saved two days. |
| Overcome the communication hurdle by talking to someone directly, instead of e-mailing | Many of the frustrations are coming from long e-mail messages | For example, the recent project... |
| | | A total of 63 e-mails from 33... |
| | | The final e-mail was 32 printed... |
| | It's easy to become detached from your coworkers if you only use e-mail | The situation could easily be... |
| | | Ironically, the team worked... |
| | | They finally solved it simply by... |
| | If there's a problem, it's more efficient to talk in person | When in doubt, talk to the... |
| | | Project Team Alpha managed... |
| | | Without a single e-mail, they... |
| Overcome the duplicated effort hurdle by checking off completed items on the intranet | The complexity of the project means there are overlapping tasks | Six project teams are handling... |
| | | Eight off-site firms are coding... |
| | | Together the teams manage... |
| | The intranet is designed to keep track of who is doing what | The central project site is now... |
| | | Project managers are in charge... |
| | | You can check the status at any... |
| | If you use the intranet to mark off what you do, you solve the problem | Every person is authorized to... |
| | | By simply clicking the button... |
| | | When everyone follows these... |

**FIGURE 9-9** Act II of The Plan story template.

Carry forward the race motif to your Call to Action sketch, shown on the upper left in Figure 9-10, and sketch the numbers *1*, *2*, and *3* on each hurdle. Carry through the numbering on each Key Point slide (upper right, lower left, and lower right) to indicate which hurdle in the sequence you are covering in that section of the presentation.

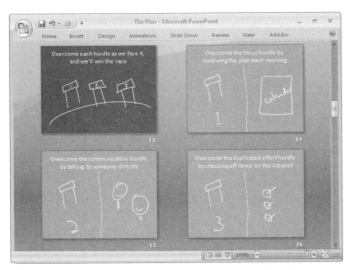

**FIGURE 9-10** Sketches of the Call to Action and Key Point slides.

Since the three Key Point slides will all share the same photograph of a hurdle, create a Key Point slide custom layout that includes the photo, as explained in the section "Tip 3: Use Custom Layouts to Add the Same Graphic to Related Slides" in Chapter 8. In this case, use the photo of the hurdle from the Point A slide, except tightly crop the photo and place it on the left side of the split-screen layout, as shown in Figure 9-11.

**FIGURE 9-11** Creating a custom layout to apply to the Act I slides.

Return to Normal view of the Call to Action slide, and add three photos of the hurdle, apply the new Key Point custom layouts to the Key Point slides, and add photographs to the Picture placeholders, as shown in Figure 9-12. If you have a Tablet PC, when you present the Call to Action slide (upper left), write on the screen with your stylus the numbers *1*, *2*, and *3* below each hurdle as you relate the headline, "Overcome each hurdle as we face it, and we'll win the race."

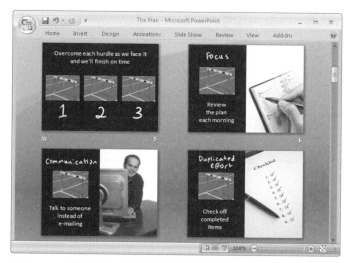

**FIGURE 9-12**  The Call to Action and Key Point slides with graphics added.

When you reach the first Key Point slide, write the word *Focus* in the blank space above the photo of the hurdle as you relate the topic to what your audience told you on the Point A slide and as you convey the message of the headline, here shortened on the slide from the original, "Overcome the focus hurdle by reviewing the plan each morning" (upper right). Then write *Communication* on the second Key Point slide (lower left) as you relate the headline, shortened on the slide from the original, "Overcome the communication hurdle by talking to someone directly." Last, write *Duplicated Effort* on the third Key Point slide (lower right) as you relate the headline shortened from the original, "Overcome the duplicated effort hurdle by checking off items on the intranet."

> **NOTE**    The headlines were shortened on the Key Point slides to leave empty space on the screen where you could write with a Tablet PC stylus to increase engagement—if you don't have a Tablet PC, insert text boxes on the screen instead.

As you sketch the rest of the Explanation and Detail slides, use the range of graphical possibilities as described in Chapter 7 to sketch the slide headlines and then to add graphics, as shown in Figure 9-13. As you saw in earlier chapters, these graphics might include photos, screen captures, diagrams, charts, or other media elements. Add a navigation bar to your custom layouts for the Explanation and Detail slides to provide a cue to the presentation's organization and also to consistently carry through the visual motif in the form of a hurdle in the lower-right corner of each slide.

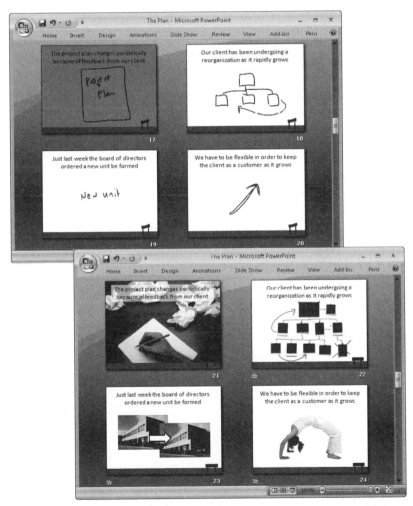

**FIGURE 9-13** Sketches and completed examples of Explanation and Detail slides.

These completed slides use photographs from iStockphoto to communicate the message of the headlines. The photo used on the Explanation slide (upper left) fills the screen, and a fill color was added to the title area to make the headline text legible. The Detail slide with the organizational chart (upper right) has additional arrows added to denote "reorganization" in the headline, and the Detail slide with the office buildings (lower left) shows the photograph of an office building duplicated and an arrow added to illustrate "a new unit." The Detail slide with the person doing a yoga stretch to illustrate "we have to be flexible" might come across as too playful to some audiences, but for this presentation to a team within an organization, it is perfectly fine to have a visual sense of humor.

**TIP**  Stock photography Web sites usually offer different sizes of graphics for licensing. For example, at iStockphoto, you can generally purchase the small size of a photograph, which has a resolution of 72 dpi that is fine for on-screen presentations, and a size that normally will fill a PowerPoint screen, which measures 7.5 inches by 10 inches. Carefully read all licensing agreements and size specifications for graphics before you purchase graphics to make sure that you are covered for the appropriate use.

## Delivering The Plan Remotely

When you deliver the same presentation to the rest of your team the next day using a Web conferencing service, you'll present using a Web browser along with a telephone or a computer microphone and speakers. In a virtual environment such as this, you obviously cannot use flip charts and other off-screen media that the audience can't see, but you can use additional tools that services such as Microsoft Office Live Meeting offer. For example, when you present the earlier Point A slide using the Live Meeting console, ask your audience the same question, except now annotate the slide by using the console's tools to insert text boxes to record the audience comments, as shown in Figure 9-14. Alternatively, use the Live Meeting console tools to create a poll that allows respondents to vote on your question, or use a text screen where you can write down the notes of your conversation for all to see.

**FIGURE 9-14** Using Microsoft Office Live Meeting to present the Point A slide with text boxes added.

BBP works particularly well in online meeting environments because it counters the lack of in-person dynamics with its visually engaging style. You will also make full use of the built-in tools to prompt engagement and involvement because you know exactly where you will use them—for example, on the Point A and Point B slides as well as the Key Point slides.

## Presenting Results with The Analysis

Now that you've had a taste of using BBP as a way to present The Plan, the next example presents a new challenge—communicating the results of market research you conducted to your company's clients with The Analysis. Your client's sales have dropped, and the client has asked your market research firm to help. This type of presentation featuring quantitative information is typically called a "data-driven" presentation.

But given the research realities presented in Chapter 2, it's ironic that many conventional PowerPoint presentations that are called data-driven actually do not have a research basis built into the foundation of the presentation approach itself. These presentations subscribe to the myth that you can simply "drive" data into your audiences' heads and they will "get" it, with no regard for the importance of respecting the limits of working memory when you present new information, synchronizing the visual and verbal channels, and guiding the attention of an audience in specific ways. BBP, on the other hand, accepts these research realities and subscribes to the idea that there is no such thing as a data-driven presentation—there are only "cognitive-driven" presentations, because ultimately the audience's minds will determine whether understanding happened, not the data.

Act I of The Analysis presentation, shown in Figure 9-15, is a good example of how dramatically different a formerly data-driven presentation looks when you restructure it using BBP. In this example, the Setting statement summarizes that your client has hired your market research firm because "Your sales dried up last year in your most lucrative market segment." Next the Role statement puts your client in its proper place as the main character of this story as "You asked us to drill into the numbers and analyze the situation." The Point A statement explains the challenge you believe the client faces, "You have tapped out your existing revenue base." Point B then goes on to confirm to your client that "You need a strategy to get profits flowing again." Now what should your audience do to get from A to B? They should "Tap into three undiscovered wells of revenue by reaching new customers in new ways," according to your Call to Action slide.

| The Analysis by Pat Coleman | | |
|---|---|---|
| **Act I:** Set up the story from the audience's viewpoint ("*A to B, what's in it for me?*") | | |
| **Setting** *(Where am I?)* | Your sales dried up last year in your most lucrative market segment | |
| **Role** *(Who am I here?)* | You asked us to drill into the numbers and analyze the situation | |
| **Point A** *(What challenge do I face?)* | **Call to Action** *(How do I get from A→B?)* | **Point B** *(Where do I want to be?)* |
| You have tapped out your existing revenue base | Tap into three undiscovered wells of revenue by reaching new customers in new ways | You need a strategy to get profits flowing again |

**FIGURE 9-15**  Act I of The Analysis presentation example.

If it's helpful to you, rename the Act II column headings for this type of presentation from Key Point to Recommendation and from Detail to Methodology/Data. As always, you end Act I of the story template with the Call to Action headline and expand on it with the Key Point (Recommendation) headlines in Act II. Then you flesh out each individual Key Point (Recommendation) headline, as shown in Figure 9-16, with further Explanation and Detail (Methodology/Data). With this approach, you know that you have applied a logical method to organize your thoughts and that you have built in scalability to present the same material in 5, 15, or 45 minutes, as described in Chapter 6, without losing the integrity or quality of your critical thinking.

Although the BBP structure might look straightforward and logical, it literally turns upside-down the most common structure of data-driven PowerPoint presentations. In the conventional structure, you normally jump right into the detailed data and the methodology and then finally make your recommendations on the very last slides. It's natural to think of structuring a presentation this way because you might think that if you start from the beginning and go one at a time through the detailed steps you took to arrive at a recommendation, your ideas will have more credibility. However, the huge risk you take when you do that is that you overwhelm the limited capacity of working memory of your clients with so much new information, as shown in Figure 9-17, that they are disoriented and confused—which, ironically, diminishes your credibility.

| Act II: Develop the action *("1-2-3, show me only what I need to see")* | | |
|---|---|---|
| **Recommendation** (*5 min.*): How? | **Explanation** (*15 min.*): How? | **Methodology/Data** (*45 min.*): Why? |
| Reach suburban commuters and increase share 22% | More than 66% of your customers travel at least one hour per day | We conducted a random survey in your three target geographies |
| | | More than 4,000 respondents completed the survey |
| | | An analysis found that two-thirds travel at least one hour daily |
| | The right mix of radio ads will help you reach them | Your customers break out into three types of listeners |
| | | You can reach them by allocating revenue based on their listening preferences |
| | | Targeted buys like this produce consistent results |
| | A $5 million investment in advertising can produce a 10% increase in sales | Company X faced a similar situation in Q1 |
| | | They invested $5 million in a similar ad buy |
| | | The result was a 10% increase in sales |

**FIGURE 9-16** The first Key Point (Recommendation) headline of The Analysis story template, with its accompanying Explanation and Detail statements.

**FIGURE 9-17** Presenting your methodology and data first before your recommendations quickly overwhelms working memory.

A symptom that overwhelm has happened in your presentation is if your client asks you to skip ahead to the end, or asks you to get to the point—which indicates that you didn't get to the point in the first place. Remember, journalists call this ineffective structural approach "burying the lead," because you put the most important information somewhere else other than at the top level of attention of your audience. The good news is that you likely don't have to create new information for your presentation—you just have to restructure what you have using the story template to ensure that you present the most important information to the audience's working memory first.

None of this is to say that you will not present detailed data or complex charts when you present the Explanation and Detail (Methodology/Data) slides. If your clients have prior knowledge of complex data structures, the slides can include those elements without overwhelming their working memory because the understanding of the structure of this information is already held in the audience's long-term memory. If the source of the data is important to have available for detailed discussion, provide that on paper or in an electronic document to accompany the presentation.

## Researching and Adding Available Graphics for The Analysis

Now that you have addressed the data that you will cover in the Explanation and Detail (Methodology/Data) columns and you have determined the priority and sequence of all the slides in Act II, you can free yourself up creatively to make the critical top level of the presentation as interesting, engaging, meaningful, and memorable to your clients as you can. Being visually creative in what is supposed to be a data-driven presentation might initially be perceived as intellectual fluff, but with BBP, you know that your creative visual surfaces rest on top of a foundation built from a rigorous critical-thinking process. If your graphics are an aesthetic match with your audience, your clients will find the images refreshing, and the presentation itself will differentiate you from the boring, disorienting, and lifeless bullet-point presentations of your competitors.

As with the preceding examples, if your budget for The Analysis is limited, you'll want to take a quick look to see what graphics are available to integrate as a motif into your story template and storyboard. In keeping with the "tapping into wells" verbal motif, a search for "oil well" in iStockphoto turns up a result shown in Figure 9-18—a series of icons including oil wells. This particular graphic is termed an "illustration" in iStockphoto, which means that it is not a photograph but instead a vector art image that can be opened and manipulated using a vector illustration software program. If you don't know how to use that type of software, most illustrations also come with a version of the illustration that you can insert on your slides and crop to use only the parts you want, as in the following examples.

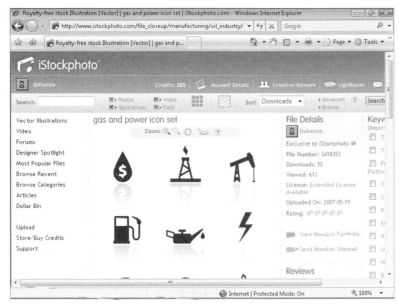

**FIGURE 9-18** Search result for "oil well" in iStockphoto.

## CREATING YOUR OWN GRAPHICS

If you can't find the illustrations you need, you can create your own or hire someone to create them using a vector illustration software program. Aim for a simple, pared-down style for the illustrations. If you export these graphics in .emf or .wmf file formats, you might be able to group, regroup, and recolor the elements using the PowerPoint 2007 graphics tools.

## Reviewing the Act I Slides for The Analysis

Following your story template and storyboard sketches as usual, set up your Act I layouts and apply them to your slides, and then add graphics. The example in Figure 9-19 features a split-screen layout, except this variation is horizontal, with a graphic at the top and a related photograph from iStockphoto below. The headlines from Act I of the story template are hidden in these slides to let the visual power of the graphics tell the story along with the narration. The Setting slide (upper left), uses a declining sales chart created from your client's data at the top and a photo of a cash register receipt below to illustrate the hidden headline "Your sales dried up last year in your most lucrative market segment." The Role slide (upper right), uses a photo of a spreadsheet below but now shows an oil well above to illustrate "You asked us to drill into the numbers and analyze the situation." The Point A slide (lower left) uses the same oil well along with a "no sale" photograph to illustrate "You have tapped out your existing revenue base." And the Point B slide (lower right) uses the same oil well with an arrow pointing upward from a cash register drawer to illustrate "You need a strategy to get profits flowing again."

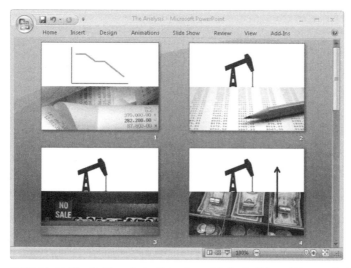

**FIGURE 9-19** The Setting, Role, Point A, and Point B slides of The Analysis presentation.

The consistent horizontal split-screen layout across the slides creates an interesting dynamic as the changing photos carry through the meaning of the hidden headlines, which you will explain verbally. To set up the custom layout for these Act I slides, add a Picture placeholder to fill the bottom half of the screen, as shown in Figure 9-20, and then change the font color of the headlines to white to make them appear invisible against the white background.

As described in Chapter 8, after you create a custom layout using a Picture placeholder and apply the layout to your slides, you simply right-click the placeholder and choose Paste on the shortcut menu to automatically crop and size the photo to fit; alternatively, you can click the picture icon to insert a graphic from somewhere on your computer. If you're good at creating custom layouts, share them with others to make their jobs easier—if you have used a Picture placeholder (not a Content placeholder) on the custom layout, all they do is click and add the photo without having to worry about designing layouts, cropping, and sizing.

**FIGURE 9-20** Horizontal split-screen custom layout for the Act I slides.

## Reviewing the Call to Action and Key Point Slides for The Analysis

The horizontal photographic layout works so well in Act I that you can apply a similar layout to the Call to Action and Key Point slides as well, except this time divide the slide into thirds horizontally and leave the headlines visible in this version. The Call to Action slide shown on the upper left in Figure 9-21 features a photo of customers, except now there are three new oil well graphics to illustrate the headline "Tap into three undiscovered wells of revenue by reaching your customers in new ways." (The headline was shorted to fit the 2-line limit of the slides.) The first Key Point slide (upper right) features a single oil well with a photograph of cars on a highway to illustrate the first well of revenue explained in the headline as "Reach suburban commuters and increase share 22%." The second Key Point slide (lower left) features a second oil well with a photo of city traffic to illustrate the headline "Reach city travelers and increase share another 15%," and the third Key Point slide (lower right) features a third oil well with a photo of an airplane to illustrate "Reach frequent fliers and increase share another 7%."

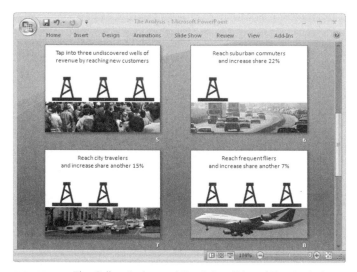

**FIGURE 9-21** The Call to Action and Key Point slides of The Analysis presentation.

Together these Act I and Key Point slides create a compelling and interesting way to present the most important information your audience wants to know. The Explanation and Detail slides that follow, as shown in Figure 9-22, along with your backup printouts and spreadsheets, will go into the rigorous detail of quantitative-based reasoning that your client expects. A small oil well icon added to the Detail custom layouts carries the visual theme through the presentation on these slides.

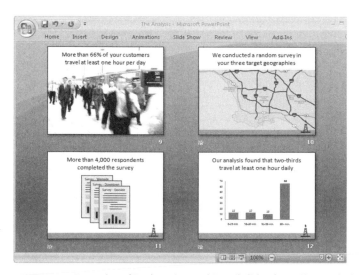

**FIGURE 9-22** Examples of Explanation and Detail slides from The Analysis.

Much more than capturing the data on the slides, you have captured the imagination of your audience so that they can literally see what your abstract recommendations will mean to them in no uncertain visual terms. And in the process, you turned a data-driven presentation into a cognitive-driven presentation, with a visually appealing result.

# Making Information Meaningful with The Report

The next example of a BBP presentation is based on a scenario in which your team recently contributed to the successful launch of Product A and you are now working on the launch of Product B. Your regional supervisor is paying you a visit and you want to let her know how things are going, so you prepare a presentation for her—The Report. You see this supervisor only occasionally, so this is your chance to meet her in person, and because this is just an update and not a set of recommendations, as in The Analysis, you initially plan to put together only an "informational" presentation to show her the facts.

Just as it's hard to let go of the myth of the data-driven presentation even in light of the research realities in Chapter 2, it's equally hard to let go of the idea of the informational presentation. You can hold on to the hope that you can present your supervisor with new "information" and she will automatically "get it," but the reality is that understanding happens only if she integrates the new information into her long-term memory. That means you must present the new information in particular ways that increase the chances that her working memory will handle it appropriately.

The phrase *informational presentation* often indicates that a presentation does not have a clear purpose. When you dig a little deeper into what people mean by this phrase, they usually say that they want to provide someone with lists of facts, typically in the form of bulleted lists of information. But without purpose or context, a list is just that—a list. If what you want to do is simply pass on facts for someone's reference, you don't need to go through the trouble of creating a presentation or having a meeting—just send the facts in an e-mail message or as a Microsoft Office Word document or Excel® spreadsheet and save yourself and your audience the time. But if you and your audience go through the trouble of gathering together, it should always be for a purpose—to make information and facts *useful*.

When you do have a reason to meet beyond just passing on facts, completing Act I of your story template is a reliable place to start your presentation, because the process of completing Act I always forces you to transform information into clear understanding that your audience finds meaningful and practical. Generic informational presentations normally lack a structure with a beginning, a middle, and an end, but with Act I as a structure, you know that you will start strong and end strong every time. With Act II as a structure, you know that in the middle of your presentation, you will elevate the most important information to the top level of your audience's attention and make sure that you cover the explanation and detail from there. Instead of listing every possible piece of information and showing *every* detail, you get right to the most important information and show only *the most important* details.

In this specific example, you might not be trying to recommend or sell your supervisor anything, but she does have something you need—her ongoing support. If your presentation fails to assure her that you are on top of your responsibilities, you can be assured you won't carry those responsibilities for much longer. And from her perspective, she wants to know that you are on top of things so that she can focus on handling problems elsewhere. With this perspective in mind, Act I of your story template for The Report takes shape, as shown in Figure 9-23. In this example, the Setting statement explains, "Product Launch A went like clockwork," and the Role affirms, "You'd like to make sure Product Launch B goes just as smoothly."

| The Report by Pat Coleman | | |
|---|---|---|
| **Act I:** Set up the story from the audience's viewpoint (*"A to B, what's in it for me?"*) | | |
| **Setting** *(Where am I?)* | Product Launch A went like clockwork | |
| **Role** *(Who am I here?)* | You'd like to make sure Product Launch B goes just as smoothly | |
| **Point A** *(What challenge do I face?)* | **Call to Action** *(How do I get from A→B?)* | **Point B** *(Where do I want to be?)* |
| You haven't had a chance since last quarter to examine how things are working here | Be assured we will meet our goals | You'd like to be confident things are working smoothly |
| **Act II:** Develop the action (*"1-2-3, show me only what I need to see"*) | | |
| **Summary** *(5 minutes):* How? | **Breakdown** *(15 minutes):* How? | **Backup** *(45 minutes):* How? |

**FIGURE 9-23** Act I of The Report presentation example.

The Point A statement summarizes the challenge your supervisor faces, "You haven't had a chance since last quarter to examine how things are working here." Where she wants to be at Point B is, "You'd like to be confident things are working smoothly." How does she get from a state of uncertainty at Point A to confidence at Point B? By following the simple Call to Action, "Be assured we will meet our goals." Instead of leaving your boss unclear about what she should do, you now have presented information in a way that ensures that she can take action on it, even if that action is to believe something new or different—in this case, to be assured of your progress.

As shown in Figure 9-23, for this type of presentation you can change the Act II column headings from Key Point to Summary, from Explanation to Breakdown, and from Detail to Backup. As you write your Key Point (Summary) headlines, you'll cover the three most important points that explain how your supervisor will be assured that you will meet your goals:

**Key Point 1** We accomplished what we said we would.

**Key Point 2** We are on track to accomplish our new goals.

**Key Point 3** We will overcome our challenges.

As you complete the rest of the story template, you'll cover the Explanation and Detail slides that include the diagrams, charts, screen captures, photos, and anecdotes that back up your appeal for her assurance. Knowing that you have covered the detailed information you need, you can be assured yourself that you can focus on making the important Act I and Key Point slides a solid visual framework to cover the rest of the meaningful information to come.

## Researching and Adding Available Graphics for The Report

If your story template and storyboard sketches call for a verbal motif of clockwork (and that motif is a match with your supervisor), a search for "gears" in iStockphoto produces the photo in Figure 9-24, which will serve as the visual motif for several of the Act I and Key Point slides.

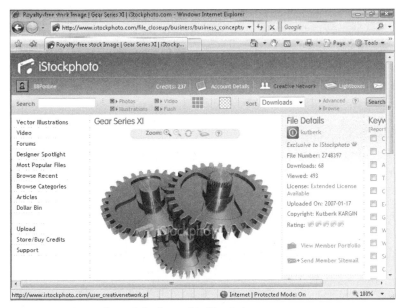

**FIGURE 9-24** A search result for "gears" in iStockphoto.

## Reviewing the Act I Slides for The Report

Although the headlines are hidden in the Figure 9-25 examples, the visual power of the images is clear. The Setting slide (upper left) features a photo of a clockwork from iStockphoto with a simple text box added that reads "Product Launch A" to illustrate the hidden headline "Product Launch A went like clockwork." The Role slide (upper right) features the same clockwork photo with a text box in the same position that reads "Product Launch B," referring to the headline "You'd like to make sure Product Launch B goes just as smoothly." Instead of the text boxes here, you could use the logos of the products.

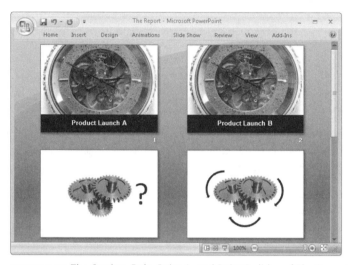

**FIGURE 9-25**  The Setting, Role, Point A, and Point B slides of The Report.

The Point A slide (lower left) features the iStockphoto graphic of three gears and a text box with a question mark to illustrate the headline "You haven't had a chance since last quarter to examine how things are working here." On the Point B slide (lower right), the same photo now includes three arrows created with the PowerPoint drawing tools to illustrate "You'd like to be confident things are working smoothly."

## Reviewing the Call to Action and Key Point Slides for The Report

Next, insert three callouts with the numbers *1*, *2*, and *3* on the Call to Action slide next to each gear and arrow, as shown on the upper left in Figure 9-26—when the slide appears, you will verbally explain that there are three reasons why your manager should

"Be assured we will meet our goals," as described in the hidden headline. Then, on the first Key Point slide (upper right), use only the photo and add one arrow to illustrate the first Key Point headline, "We accomplished what we said we would." The Act II slides that will follow this slide in the presentation will provide the breakdown and backup for these accomplishments. Then, on the second Key Point slide (lower left), add a second arrow and the second Key Point headline, "We are on track to accomplish our new goals." The following Act II slides will provide the breakdown and backup for your new goals. Then, on the third Key Point slide (lower right), add the third and final arrow and the third headline, "We will overcome our challenges." The following Act II slides will provide the breakdown and backup for how you will overcome those challenges. When you create your custom layouts for your Explanation (Breakdown) and Detail (Backup) slides, add a small version of the gears to the navigation bar to carry the visual theme through the presentation on those slides.

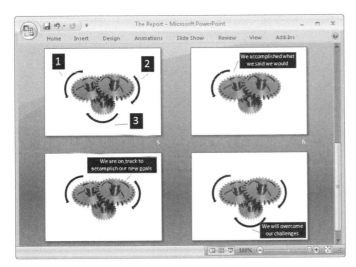

**FIGURE 9-26** The Call to Action and Key Point slides of The Report.

Because you are giving this presentation to such a small audience, try giving it in a printed form using notes pages handouts. But whatever way you go, with the BBP foundation in place, you have transformed what normally might be an "informational" list of facts into a much more meaningful and useful story that you carry forward both visually and verbally.

# Engaging Students with The Class

Beyond courtrooms and meeting rooms, BBP has tremendous potential to guide the structure of presentations used in classrooms and training rooms at every educational level. After all, the research realities described in Chapter 2 that inspire BBP are being extensively tested and applied by educational psychologists interested in improving learning using multimedia. If you use PowerPoint to teach, you'll find BBP a practical and effective method to help your students learn new information. And just as with The Analysis example, applying BBP to an educational presentation usually does not involve creating new material, but rather you will restructure existing material in a new way to make the material easier for your students' working memory to handle.

As with the other applications of BBP in other contexts, with an educational presentation, you always start with Act I of the story template. Here your aim in the first few slides of the presentation is to bring to bear the best of your ability to make the topic of your course emotionally relevant to your students and to set the framework that will guide your students' understanding of the rest of the material to follow in the class. Instead of potentially losing students' interest and motivation to learn, here you'll help them maintain interest from the first slide to the last.

In the example Act I shown in Figure 9-27, you are an instructor teaching a class on DNA, and you introduce the Setting as "DNA is one of the great scientific discoveries of all time" and then engage the students by placing them in the Role as "In this class, you will somehow get to play a role in discovering it for yourself." Next the challenge the students face in Point A is "Without knowing how to approach it, DNA seems like an unsolvable puzzle," and Point B is "You'd like to solve the puzzle to discover the big picture." So how do the students resolve the tension between not knowing how to approach the puzzle of DNA and solving it? By following your Call to Action, "Solve the DNA puzzle in three steps."

| The Class by Pat Coleman | | |
|---|---|---|
| **Act I:** Set up the story from the audience's viewpoint (*"A to B, what's in it for me?"*) | | |
| **Setting** *(Where am I?)* | DNA is one of the great scientific discoveries of all time | |
| **Role** *(Who am I here?)* | In this class, you somehow get to play a role in discovering it for yourself | |
| **Point A** *(What challenge do I face?)* | **Call to Action** *(How do I get from A→B?)* | **Point B** *(Where do I want to be?)* |
| Without knowing how to approach it, DNA seems like an unsolvable puzzle | Solve the DNA puzzle in three steps | You'd like to solve the puzzle to discover the big picture |
| **Act II:** Develop the action (*"1-2-3, show me only what I need to see"*) | | |
| **Lesson** *(5 minutes)*: How? | **Explanation** *(15 minutes)*: How? | **Detail** *(45 minutes)*: How? |

**FIGURE 9-27** Act I of The Class presentation example.

With an engaging start to the presentation in writing in Act I, the next step is to complete the Act II columns of the story template. Begin by renaming the Key Point column

heading to Lesson if you want. Often the biggest challenge for educators when completing Act II is not completing the Explanation and Detail slides, because those usually
already exist in some form. Rather the difficulty comes in distilling the Explanation and
Detail columns into an even simpler set of three Key Point (Lesson) headlines. It is essential that you provide students with only a few Key Point headlines that they will certainly
remember, which then will serve as long-term memory reference points to access your
Explanation and Detail headlines. In this example, as you write your Key Point (Lesson)
headlines, you'll cover the three most important points that you want your students to
remember from the class:

**Key Point 1** Assemble the theory.

**Key Point 2** Assemble the research.

**Key Point 3** Apply what you know.

Continue by completing the other two columns of the story template, and then create
your Act II slides from these according to the process described in the other examples in
this chapter.

## Researching and Adding Available Graphics for The Class

To visually realize your puzzle motif from the story template and storyboard sketches,
in Normal view of any slide, select the Insert tab, and in the Illustrations group, click Clip
Art. In the Clip Art pane, type the search term **puzzle**, and then click Go. When you find
the puzzle shape you want, position the mouse pointer on it, click the arrow to the right
of the puzzle piece, and choose Insert, as shown in Figure 9-28.

**FIGURE 9-28** Inserting a puzzle shape from the Clip Art pane in PowerPoint.

You might not want to use all of the elements included in this particular puzzle graphic, but you still can work with it because it is *vector art*, called "resizable" at the Microsoft Office Online Clip Art And Media site. The value of this type of graphic is that you can break it into its components using the PowerPoint graphics tools and use only portions of it on a slide. Another advantage of this type of graphic is that you can resize it without ever losing its sharp, clear lines.

Right-click the puzzle graphic you inserted on the slide, and on the shortcut menu, click Group, Ungroup. (If the Ungroup option doesn't appear on this shortcut menu, the clip art is not resizable.) If a Microsoft Office PowerPoint message box appears that reads, "This is an imported picture, not a group. Do you want to convert it to a Microsoft Office Drawing Object?" click Yes. Right-click the graphic again, and then click Group, Ungroup again on the shortcut menu, which breaks up the graphic into its parts.

**TIP** When you search for vector art graphics at the Microsoft Office Online Clip Art And Media site, you'll know that a graphic you find is vector art if the search results box includes the term "Resizable" under Dimensions.

Click and delete any pieces of the group you don't want, and click and change the fill color of any of the objects if you want. When you have deleted the elements you don't want to keep and have made any other changes to resizable clip art, right-click some-where on the graphic and select Group, Regroup from the shortcut menu—this regroups the graphic into a single unit again instead of many separate smaller pieces. To resize a piece of resizable clip art on a slide, select it to display the sizing handles. Hold down the Shift key, and drag one of the corner sizing handles to change the graphic to the size you want. Holding down the Shift key while you drag a corner sizing handle preserves the proportions of the graphic as you resize it; otherwise, the image will be distorted.

## Reviewing the Act I Slides for The Class

When you create a custom layout for your Act I slides, change the background color to black and then apply the layout to all of your slides—this will hide the headlines, as shown in Figure 9-29. Based on your story template and storyboard sketches, add a text box that reads "DNA" to the Setting slide (upper left). Animate the word so that when you click the slide, the word *DNA* slowly fades into the background as you relate the headline "DNA is one of the greatest scientific discoveries of all time." On the Role slide (upper right), add a text box with question marks that fade into the background to intrigue the students as you affirm, "In this class, you somehow get to play a role in discovering it for yourself."

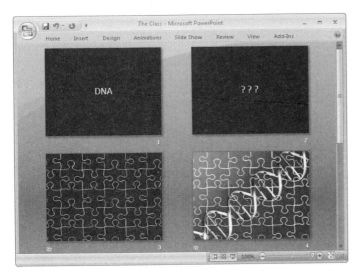

**FIGURE 9-29** The Setting, Role, Point A, and Point B slides of The Class.

On the Point A slide (lower left), duplicate the puzzle pieces so that they fill the screen, change their fill color to black, and then animate the group to fade in when the slide appears and you relate the hidden headline, "Without knowing how to approach it, DNA seems like an unsolvable puzzle." On the Point B slide (lower right), add a photograph of a DNA strand from iStockphoto, copy the puzzle pieces from the Point A slide and paste them on top of the photo, and then remove the fill color of the puzzle pieces so that only the puzzle piece outlines remain. As the DNA puzzle appears, relate the Point B headline, "You'd like to solve the puzzle to discover the big picture." These Point A and Point B slides reinforce the puzzle motif and create a visually interesting framework for the topic the students will address through the class.

## Reviewing the Call to Action and Key Point Slides for The Class

Next abbreviate your Call to Action headline to read "Solve the DNA puzzle," as shown on the upper left in Figure 9-30. Search for the term "custom puzzle" on the Web, and you'll find many companies that will create a custom jigsaw puzzle using your DNA photograph for as little as $11. If you have the budget, buy one, and now while you present the Call to Action slide as you relate the hidden headline "Solve the DNA puzzle in three steps," hand out the actual pieces of the custom DNA puzzle to the students so that they literally hold the motif in their hands. Tell your students that they now hold in their hands the puzzle they will solve, and ask them for their thoughts about how they think they can solve it.

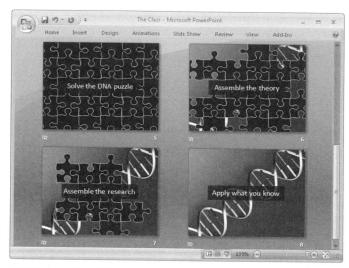

FIGURE 9-30 The Call to Action and Key Point slides of The Class presentation.

As you create your Key Point (Lesson) slides, leave your headlines visible, but delete some of the puzzle pieces from the first Key Point slide, "Assemble the theory" (upper right); delete more pieces from the second Key Point slide, "Assemble the research," (lower left); and last delete all of the pieces from the third slide, "Apply what you know" (lower right). Create the rest of the slides from the headlines of the story template, using these Key Point slides to guide you and your students through the engaging experience of solving the DNA puzzle.

## THE THREE-YEAR TRAINING PLAN

Although this presentation example of The Class is designed for a 45-minute presentation, you can use the BBP story template to plan a much longer class or even a multiyear curriculum. Consider how much time you have—45 minutes, 2 hours, 3 days, or 3 years—and write in the Key Point column the three most important lessons you want someone to learn during that period of time. Then continue working in the story template from left to right—you'll add more columns to the right of the Detail column depending on how deep you want to go into the material.

Together with your engaging story template structure, these slides add a visual dynamism and interest that increase the likelihood that your students will remember and apply the most important information you want to teach.

# Putting Your Clients at the Center in The Pitch

The last BBP example in this chapter shows one more way that BBP can unlock the verbal and visual power buried inside a presentation—this time with a sales pitch that your Internet services firm is making to a potential client. The typical outline in the old way of doing PowerPoint presentations would feature a structure with category headings like Our Company, Our Team, Our Services, Our Differentiation, and Our Clients—the message would be essentially "All About Us." Of course, each category heading would be followed by list after list of facts, without a story to be found anywhere to tie them together.

Often the origin of this type of presentation is the marketing department, where the goal of the marketers is to create a single, uniform, consistent message that they will then distribute to the sales team to deliver exactly as it is. The only problem, though, is that the typical organizational process of making the presentation uniform also makes it canned, generic, one-size-fits-all—in other words, boring. Not surprisingly, even though some companies spend millions of dollars and countless hours and untold energy in creating these presentations, the sales team ignores them. And who could blame them? After all, the canned presentations in reality would likely cause them to *lose* sales rather than win them because if they actually delivered these presentations, their prospective clients would send them packing out the door for wasting their time with a one-way, domineering recital of bullet points.

The problem is solved when the company gets the marketing and sales teams together in a room and then uses a projector to put the BBP Story Template on the screen so that everyone can work on it together, as shown in the example in Figure 9-31. Now, by viewing together the first five headlines they write of Act I, both marketing and sales can agree that the salespeople in the field need to start strong every time with a story structure that puts the company's prospective clients in the starring role of the presentation. With your Setting statement, you affirm to your client that "Your numbers have been off the mark" and in the Role that "You're under pressure to improve your game." With these two simple statements, suddenly the entire focus of the presentation has changed from "All About Us" to "All About You"—the salesperson's audience.

| The Pitch by Pat Coleman | | |
|---|---|---|
| **Act I:** Set up the story from the audience's viewpoint (*"A to B, what's in it for me?"*) | | |
| **Setting** (*Where are we?*) | Your numbers have been off the mark | |
| **Role** (*Who are we here?*) | You're under pressure to improve your game | |
| **Point A** (*What challenge do I face?*) | **Call to Action** (*How do I get from A→B?*) | **Point B** (*Where do I want to be?*) |
| Your current messages are not reaching your target | Aim for three goals, and you'll hit the marks you want | You'd like to hit the target more accurately and frequently |
| **Act II:** Develop the action (*"1-2-3, show me only what I need to see"*) | | |
| **Benefit** (*5 minutes*): How? | **Feature** (*15 minutes*): How? | **Demonstration** (*45 minutes*): How? |

**FIGURE 9-31** Act I of The Pitch presentation example.

Custom-tailoring this presentation to this specific audience continues in the Point A headline, which defines the client's challenge as "Your current messages are not reaching your target," and in the Point B headline, which defines the client's goal as "You'd like to hit the target more accurately and frequently." How does the client get from A to B? The Call to Action headline provides direction in the form of the statement, "Aim for three goals, and you'll hit the marks you want."

As your team moves to Act II to flesh out the rest of the presentation, change the Act II headings from Key Point to Benefit, from Explanation to Feature, and from Detail to Demonstration if you prefer. Now, in the Key Point (Benefit) column, write headlines that explain how aiming for three goals will help your audience hit the marks they want. By choosing to answer the question *How?* you make this an explanatory presentation rather than a persuasive one, as explained in Chapter 5, which makes this presentation feel more like a consultative educational session than a stereotypical sales pitch. But even more important, this structure defines and elevates the three most important benefits as the client sees them from the context of Act I:

**Key Point 1** Hit better sales numbers with Service X.

**Key Point 2** Hit better margins with Service Y.

**Key Point 3** Hit better customer ratings with Service Z.

Here the benefits for the audience have been tightly integrated into the wording of the headlines to bring these benefits to the top level of the audience's attention. You definitely will talk about your services throughout the rest of the Act II columns, but now each of three Key Point (Benefit) slides makes it clear how any and all of the information in the presentation is important to the audience. This ensures that from the start, your audience is perfectly clear about the answer to the continuing question, "What's in this for me?" If your service or product has more than three benefits, you can easily make the presentation modular be creating more Key Point sections and hiding the slides that do not apply or interest any particular client.

## Researching and Adding Available Graphics for The Pitch

Following your story template motif and storyboard sketches as usual, search for the term "dartboard" in iStockphoto to find a result similar to the one shown in Figure 9-32.

**FIGURE 9-32** Search result for "dartboard" in iStockphoto.

## Reviewing the Act I Slides for The Pitch

Next create and apply a custom layout for the Act I slides that leaves the headlines white so that they are hidden on the screen. On the Setting slide, include a chart tailored to your client's numbers, as shown on the upper left in Figure 9-33, showing the numbers dropping as you describe your hidden headline "Your numbers have been off the mark," and add the dartboard to introduce your motif. On the Role slide (upper right), continue the line upward so that it hits the bull's eye in the center of the dartboard as you verbally explain the hidden headline "You're under pressure to improve your game." On the Point A slide (lower left), add the photo of the dart and rotate it to point upward, off-target from a red bull's eye that you create using the PowerPoint drawing tools—here you'll relate the hidden headline "Your messages are not reaching your target." Next, on the Point B slide (lower right), rotate the dart so that it hits the middle of the bull's eye target as you explain your hidden headline "You'd like to hit the target more accurately and frequently."

**FIGURE 9-33** The Setting, Role, Point A, and Point B slides of The Pitch.

If you can pull it off, bring a real dartboard to the sales call that uses darts with plastic safety tips, and hang it on a wall or place it on a chair. When you click to the Point A slide, throw a dart and miss the bull's eye. When you advance to the Point B slide, place a dart in the bull's eye by hand. Of course, using a prop is a good way to prompt a conversation—for example, during the Point A slide, you might ask, "Do you always hit a bull's eye with your messaging?" and during the Point B slide, you might ask, "Would you like to find a way to hit the target more accurately?"

## Reviewing the Call to Action and Key Point Slides for The Pitch

When you create the Call to Action slide shown on the upper left in Figure 9-34, place the dartboard graphic at the center, and duplicate the dart twice so that you have three darts to rotate and position at the bull's eye. Leave the headline hidden as you verbally relate the point, "Aim for three goals, and you'll hit the marks you want." For the Key Point (Benefit) slides (upper right, lower left, and lower right), apply a split-screen custom layout as described in Chapter 8, using a Picture placeholder on the right half of the slides for the photographs. On the left half of the custom layout, include the dart and bull's eye to sustain that visual element through the presentation at these most important slides. The dartboard and dart are also elements that fit naturally into a navigational bar through the corresponding Explanation and Detail slides. It will be a nice touch to leave your audience with the plastic darts and dartboard, which will serve as persistent physical reminders of your motif and memorable message.

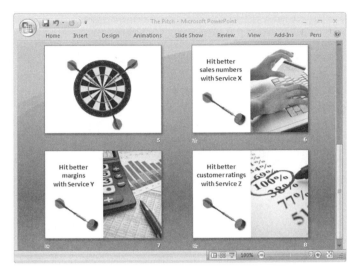

**FIGURE 9-34** The Call to Action and Key Point slides of The Pitch presentation.

You'll continue to create your Act II slides as usual, and when you reach the Demonstration (Detail) slides, you'll switch over to another application on your desktop, as described in Chapters 7 and 8, to show sections of your live demonstration of Services X, Y, and Z at the appropriate places.

With the story template as a foundation, the BBP process produces a crisp package that is easy for any salesperson to tailor and customize, using custom layouts and placeholders that do not require the salesperson to have any graphical skill in creating layouts. But perhaps most important, because the sales force is involved in the creative conception and development of this story, they will feel they own it and this will be something they really use.

**NOTE**    As mentioned at the start of this chapter, the design constraints of the examples in this chapter include a limited budget, stock photography, and graphics that can be created within PowerPoint. With a larger budget, you can hire a professional designer to create custom layouts and graphics especially for your presentation. Within your budget and time constraints, only your imagination and creativity will limit the possibilities of what you can do.

# Handling Objections to BBP

This chapter shows examples of how you can apply BBP to a wide range of presentations, yet it still offers only a tiny glimpse of the limitless range of verbal and visual possibilities before you. As you begin the process of creating a BBP presentation, keep in mind that every decision you make along the way can mean the difference between whether or not you hit the mark with your audience. Your success depends on the words you choose for your story template, the illustrations you sketch on the storyboard, the aesthetics you create across the slides with the graphics you add, and finally the way you deliver the presentation and engage your audience.

If you try BBP and it doesn't work or is otherwise not received well, the most common reasons are because the story template, storyboard, graphics, aesthetics, or delivery need more work. Sometimes the content of the story template is an intellectual mismatch with the audience, or the wording is too simplistic—or not simple enough. At times the storyboard graphics are an aesthetic mismatch, or the delivery style does not connect with the audience. If any of these might be an issue, discuss the situation with your team—and with your audience, if possible—to figure out what happened, and then return to the story template, the storyboard, the ground rules, and your audience research.

However, you might present a perfectly good BBP presentation and still find that the audience is resistant to your approach. For example, if you give your first BBP presentation to a group where there is a strong bullet point culture, their immediate response might be "Where are the bullet points that we expect?" or "This is too simplistic—where's the text?" If you expect you might get that reaction, prepare the audience in advance for what is about to come. Bring handouts of the notes pages, and pass them out while you verbally assure your audience that the detailed information is available here in printed format instead of on the slides. Assure them that you respect their time so much, you have done a great deal of advance work to identify only the most important information they need to know so that you don't waste their time.

BBP is a huge shift in thinking and action, and it can represent a threat to existing political structures within organizations. Some of the examples in this chapter demonstrate that there are deeply ingrained PowerPoint habits and cultures, and there can be a great deal of resistance to doing anything differently from what is normally done. Often the objections to BBP have nothing to do with the methodology or the content of a presentation but instead are attempts to demonstrate an audience member's power by publicly raising doubts about the presenter's credibility. In other cases, using BBP well can make others feel uncomfortable that they don't know something that you do, and so as a result, they might try to undermine you.

## EASING BBP THROUGH THE EYE OF THE NEEDLE OF YOUR ORGANIZATION

It takes leadership to ensure that BBP works, especially when working with teams and within organizations. It's not a matter of simply having an effective approach, because even the best approach in the world can be stifled by an entrenched bullet point culture. If your organization's culture cannot stray outside the narrow bounds of the conventional PowerPoint approach, it will take an organization-wide commitment from senior leadership that gives everyone permission and the resources to make a successful transition to a more effective approach. This has happened at the board of directors level of major organizations that have decided to move beyond a conventional approach that no longer works for them. For more on organizational issues related to adopting the BBP approach, visit *www.beyondbulletpoints.com*.

If you expect you might get these types of reactions, listen to the comments, and if they are valid concerns, accept them and say that you'll take them into account while you prepare your next presentation. But if the comments are more about politics than the presentation, defend your BBP foundation and explain how and why BBP works effectively to increase the audience's understanding of your material. Explain the research realities from Chapter 2, the classical story structure of Act I from Chapter 4, the logical critical-thinking structure of Act II from Chapter 5, and the way the storyboard balances verbal and visual channels from Chapters 6 through 8. If appropriate, set up a separate meeting at your organization where you use the Chapter 2 research realities to compare the old way and the BBP way side by side. When you are confident that you have effectively prepared your presentation using BBP, you can be confident that you present your clear case for how and why your presentation works.

Now that you have reviewed a range of presentation examples, it's time to move on to the next chapter and review the elements you should consider when you deliver a BBP presentation.

CHAPTER 10

# Delivering Your BBP Presentation

**THE ROOT** of the word *inspire*, spirare, means "to breathe," and that's one of the core objectives of the BBP approach—to inspire you with the confidence and tools you need to breathe deeply and relax more when you present. Most of the elements that contribute to your confidence are built into the BBP process every step of the way, but now, when you've finished your presentation, it doesn't hurt to revisit them as you prepare to bring your story to life.

Although BBP slides look dramatically different from conventional slides, the real fruit of your labor is your confident understanding of what you want to say and how you want to say it. You have expanded the capability of Microsoft® Office PowerPoint® 2007 beyond a tool for designing slides into a tool that helps your audience understand new information more effectively. Because you use the story template as a thinking tool to organize your ideas and structure a story, you can then use PowerPoint as a creative tool to express yourself with a limitless range of media possibilities. When you open your BBP presentation, you actually have a sophisticated media toolkit that blends your clear ideas and story with the delivery technology.

Now it's time to use that toolkit to bring your story to life.

# Delivering Your Presentation Using Three Ground Rules

The term *production* refers to the point when filmmakers capture the live action of actors on film. Film directors spend a great deal of time setting up scenes and filming the action many times so that they'll be able to use the best performances in the final cut. But you don't have that luxury in your PowerPoint production because you're presenting in a live environment, which means that you typically get only a single shot at engaging the audience. Managing the complex mix of elements in a live presentation can be challenging, but you already have firm control over the projected media, spoken words, and printed handouts in your BBP presentation. As you use the PowerPoint file to deliver your presentation, a set of ground rules can help keep the experience in balance.

## Rule 1: Step into the Screen

The size and placement of the screen for a live BBP presentation creates an experience very different from conventional PowerPoint presentations. In conventional presentations, often a small screen sits to the side of a presenter, where it is a nonessential visual aid that could be turned off without much impact on the presentation. Instead, the audience should perceive you as literally inside a large screen, as if it were a stage or a giant television set. Remember that you are a living, engaging presence in a presentation, and you provide the critical audio track that ties everything together. When you step in front of the large screen, you create a hybrid medium that did not exist before. The projected screen makes your abstract thoughts visible, your body keeps the presentation grounded, and your voice guides and informs the experience.

After investing so much time in creating your visual media, you absolutely need to make sure that the screen and its placement are appropriate to your presentation. Many conference rooms are not designed well, often placing focus on a chandelier or other architectural element rather than on the media experience you need to produce.  Make sure that you communicate what you need to the meeting or event planner. Never allow a screen to be placed on the opposite side of the room from where you are speaking, because this will cause a split-attention effect in which you place unneeded extra cognitive load on the audience by forcing them to continually look back and forth between you and the screen as they work to reconcile the two visual sources of information. Instead, make sure that the screen is directly behind or just off to the side of you so that the light from the data projector does not shine in your eyes.

# Rule 2: Remove the Distractions

It's easy to lose your focus on the message when there are endless things you could do to fine-tune the PowerPoint file, such as adding more graphical elements, animations, and special effects. One of the major advantages of keeping the basic format of the slides simple, which you did in Chapters 7 and 8, is that a simple design keeps you from being distracted by unnecessary details and the audience from being distracted by too much happening on the screen. Removing distractions leaves you in control of the media instead of the media controlling you.

You use PowerPoint well when people don't even notice you use PowerPoint at all. The last thing you want is for someone to compliment you on your slides—that would mean that the medium called attention to itself instead of your ideas. The most important outcome of the presentation is that the audience understands the meaning you intend to communicate. When you finish the presentation, you want the audience to talk about your special ideas, not your special effects.

Making your media transparent can be a challenge. But just as you work hard to make the story structure invisible within the flow of the story, you also need to work hard to make sure that the other elements of the production are invisible too. That means removing distractions from the entire live presentation experience, beginning when the audience walks into the room and ending when they leave it.

# Rule 3: Manage the Flow

It's important to align your PowerPoint presentation with your unique personality so that you make an authentic connection with the audience. For example, when you spend the time to carefully write the story template in your own words, you develop a deep confidence in your story that frees you to improvise your narration and tailor your words to your audience instead of being chained to reading bullet points in the conventional PowerPoint approach. All this leads to a more relaxed and comfortable approach that will make the audience feel more relaxed and comfortable too.

A presentation is not a free-for-all, however, so it's important to improvise within the constraints of a specified form. This fundamental principle is applied in many arts, including jazz, in which musicians improvise only after they've mastered the fundamental techniques of the musical form. In a similar way, you can improvise on the constraints defined in the ground rules presented throughout this book once you've mastered the basic presentation forms.

**THREE GROUND RULES FOR DELIVERING YOUR PRESENTATION**

Your single storyboard helps you manage your spoken words, projected visuals, and printed handouts. Follow these three ground rules to ensure that the rest of the live presentation experience is engaging:

**Rule 1:** Step into the screen.

**Rule 2:** Remove the distractions.

**Rule 3:** Manage the flow.

# Removing Distractions

Up to now, this book has concentrated on helping you to prepare a PowerPoint file that minimizes distractions that would otherwise overload the limited capacity of the working memory of your audience. You remove unnecessary information from the presentation by narrowing the focus of the story template. You keep extraneous information out of the slide area by following the storyboard and design ground rules. And you keep both graphics and words focused on the headlines. Now that you've removed distractions from the PowerPoint file, it's time to focus on removing distractions from the environment in which you'll present.

## Preparing the Environment

The physical environment in which you present is just as important as the story you tell. The quality of your hard work is diminished if the room is physically uncomfortable, if there are distracting noises, if you don't have an electrical outlet within reach of the projector, or if the room looks just plain shabby. Just as you have a personal responsibility for the story template, you also have a personal responsibility for the physical experience of the environment in which you present. You'll need to use your leadership and diplomacy skills to work with facilities managers or meeting planners to ensure that everything is in order.

If you have access to the room where you'll present, visit it in advance of the presentation so that you can plan for your needs. When you visit the room, review the options for configuring the physical space, and rehearse the presentation in the actual environment if that's possible. If you're not able to visit the physical location in advance, contact someone familiar with the room to find out about the room setup.

> **TIP** ✓ Lighting the room properly for a PowerPoint presentation can be a challenge. On the one hand, you want people to see the screen clearly, but on the other hand, you don't want the room to be so dark that people start to doze off. Some of the latest models of data projectors have brighter displays that allow the audience to see the images on the screen clearly without turning down the room lights. When you visit the room where you'll present, try out the projector and stand at the back of the room to review things from the perspective of audience members sitting there. Adjust the lighting so that everyone in the room can see the slides and see you clearly too. Ask a facilities manager to help if the lighting controls are not readily accessible or if you need additional lighting.

At a minimum, both you and your audience should be physically comfortable in the environment. You should have a base of operations when you present, such as a podium, and you should have the physical freedom to move around the room comfortably as you speak. If you use a Tablet PC to deliver your BBP presentation, place it on a podium or a low table out of the line of sight of your audience, and make sure that the projector cable and a power source are within reach.

When you're comfortable with the physical environment, turn to the technology you'll use to project the PowerPoint presentation.

## Checking the Technology

Stories rely on a strong beginning to set the tone and direction of the rest of the narrative. Although you have a strong beginning built into Act I of the story template, the presentation actually begins when the eyes of the audience turn to you and recognize you as the speaker. You're not off to a strong start if what they see is you connecting the projector cable to your computer, focusing the image on the screen, and searching for your PowerPoint file amid the clutter of your computer's desktop screen. Audiences are sometimes tolerant of these sorts of distractions, but you can't count on that. That's why you need to prepare for your technical needs in advance.

When you survey the room where you'll present, take the time to perform all of the steps required to set up the technology for the presentation. Plug the projector into the computer, power up the equipment, and open the PowerPoint file. Make any technical adjustments you need, and then resize the image to fit the screen and focus it. If you use a remote control device to advance the slides, try it out to make sure that it works properly. Test the Internet connection if you need one, and review any online materials you'll show on the projector during the presentation. If you plan to display Web pages, make a backup copy of them on your local computer in case you have problems with the Internet connection. If you will use the PowerPoint presenter tools in Slide Show view or on a Tablet PC, review the instructions in Appendix B on the companion CD to prepare the presentation.

If you're not able to set up the equipment and rehearse in the room in advance of the presentation, at a minimum you should set up the equipment before the presentation with enough time available to resolve any technology issues that might arise. You might also want to rehearse in a similar room beforehand.

## Planning for Problems

Even if something goes wrong, you can still produce a solid presentation experience. For example, if your speaking time is unexpectedly cut from 45 minutes to 15 or even 5 minutes, you can quickly scale the presentation to the reduced time by hiding slides, as you did in Chapter 6. If your computer crashes and you have no way to recover it, you can still cover all of the presentation points by using a printout of the story template, storyboard, outline, notes pages, or slides. If the projector bulb burns out and you have no spare, your simple slides might be clear enough to be seen on the computer screen by a small audience at a table. Your thorough preparation will enable you to carry out the presentation with confidence, no matter what problems come your way. If the presentation is particularly critical, such as the opening statement at a high-stakes legal trial or a keynote presentation to a large group at an important conference, arrange for your associates to run a second presentation in parallel as a backup, and connect both computers to a switch—that way, if something unexpected were to happen, you could switch to the second presentation without distraction.

## Rehearsing Away Distractions

In the past, you might have waited until you had finished creating the slides before you rehearsed the presentation for the first time. But with BBP, you're really rehearsing through the entire process. You get comfortable with your story when you write the story template in Chapters 4 and 5. You become acquainted with the flow and sequence of the story when you prepare the storyboard and narration in Chapter 6. And you become familiar with the visuals on screen when you sketch the storyboard and add graphics in Chapters 7 and 8. Through each of these steps in the BBP process, you mentally rehearse the core of the presentation and address a number of possible distractions such as becoming too reliant on the slides to remind you of every detail you want to present.

Now deliver an actual dress rehearsal of the presentation to remove distractions from the delivery of the presentation that come from being ill-prepared. When you check the room and technology setup, stand in the physical location where you'll present and give a complete delivery of the presentation.

During a presentation, all eyes are on you, and people will watch for cues that indicate your enthusiasm and interest in a topic. If you speak in a monotone and appear disinterested, you shouldn't be surprised if the audience mirrors your lack of enthusiasm. Instead, vary your voice to emphasize important points, and pause for effect when you want a particular point to sink in. You've been working hard on your story—let your enthusiasm come through your voice, as well as through your facial expressions. As you rehearse, you're sure to run into rough spots or things that you want to change in the presentation, so keep a piece of paper handy for jotting down revision notes to yourself as you go. Then return to the presentation to make any final changes to the slides.

Ask someone on your team to attend your rehearsal and give you honest feedback about the presentation, because you're better able to improve with the help of an outsider's perspective. People are inclined to mention only good things, so ask your evaluators not only to confirm what you do well, but also to suggest specific ways you can improve. It's a good idea to ask for a range of opinions, because each viewer will give you advice from a different perspective. Take account of whatever feedback you get, and make adjustments as needed.

## Using Notes

Presenter view, described in detail in Appendix B on the companion CD, is a great asset to a presenter and provides helpful tools to remind you of what to say. Not only does the notes pane provide cues about what to say, but so do your headline and simple graphic, as well as the thumbnails of the slides below, which serve as visual summaries of the points to come.

**TIP** One of the most common verbal distractions is the use of filler words like *um*, *uh*, *I mean*, and *you know*. Most people aren't even aware that they use these words—even some of the most experienced speakers. To reduce distracting verbal fillers, record yourself when you speak so that you can listen to yourself and count the *um*s. Or ask someone you know to count the number of filler word occurrences while you speak. The surest cure for this distracting habit is becoming aware that you do it in the first place.

Although you should be intimately familiar with the presentation at this point, it's a good idea to keep a set of speaker notes on the podium in the form of a printed story template or storyboard outline. Don't use the complete notes pages as speaker notes—the written text in the notes area might tempt you to read from the page, and you'd need to physically flip from one page to the next, which would be distracting. Instead, when you print your key PowerPoint documents, consider using as speaker notes the story template, a text outline of the storyboard, or thumbnail images of the storyboard. To print these key documents, follow these steps:

1. Open the Microsoft Office Word 2007 document that contains your story template. If you made any changes to the headlines in the storyboard, update the Word 2007 document to reflect those changes, and then print a copy.

2. To print a text outline of the storyboard, open the PowerPoint file, click the **Microsoft Office Button**, click **Print**, and in the **Print What** area of the **Print** dialog box, click **Outline View**. Then click **OK**.

3. To print thumbnail images of the storyboard, in the **Print What** area, click **Handouts** and select **6** or **9** in the drop-down list. Leave the **Print Hidden Slides** check box selected, and then click **OK**.

4. To print handouts from notes pages, click **Print**, and in the **Print What** area, click **Notes Pages**. If you used hidden slides, clear the **Print Hidden Slides** check box, and then click **OK**. You can also print the individual slides one per page, but you should have enough material with just the thumbnail images of the storyboard and the notes pages printouts.

5. While you're at it, print any additional handouts you'll reference during the presentation, such as Microsoft Office Visio® 2007 diagrams or flow charts, Microsoft Office Excel® 2007 spreadsheets, and detailed charts and graphs.

Once you've printed all of the documents, assemble them in a folder so that you have them in a single place for reference.

| TIP ✓ | To customize your speaker notes using thumbnail-size images of the storyboard, go to the View tab, and in the Presentation Views group, select Handout Master and make adjustments there. |

# Developing a Dialog

When you make the audience the main character of your story in Act I of the story template, you make the story *all about them* instead of *all about you*. So rather than the presentation being a performance in which you're the star who entertains an adoring crowd, you're part of the supporting cast in the service of the audience. This is a shift from seeing the primary function of PowerPoint as *speaker support* to a new view in which PowerPoint serves as *audience support*.

A presentation isn't a one-way street; it takes the interaction of presenters and audiences to create a dialog. You just happen to be the first one to speak, and because you're the presenter, you're the one who is in charge of getting the interaction started.

## Being Authentic

The dialog you create with the presentation begins with you—after all, the audience is granting you their time to listen to what you have to say. An audience will be more likely to give your presentation a fair hearing if they know that you're being authentic. You communicate your authentic personal credibility in a number of ways, beginning with the introduction you planned in your storyboard in Chapter 7, continuing with the clarity of your ideas and the crispness of your message, and then carrying through with the visual credibility of your slides and the verbal credibility of your narration.

Adding your name to the byline of the story template when you begin writing the script establishes your personal responsibility for the presentation process from start to finish. The biggest benefit of being so closely involved is that the presentation eventually becomes an extension of who you are.

As you work on focusing the story in Act I and boiling down your ideas to three main points in Act II, you become increasingly confident in your message. And making creative choices for the design of the storyboard makes the PowerPoint presentation start to feel like an extension of your personality.

One of the biggest obstacles you can impose on yourself when you speak in public is the idea that you need to be someone you're not. This problem becomes magnified if you're handed a generic corporate PowerPoint file with the same overstylized but boring look that everyone else uses. Although these presentations might look slick on the surface, they're often lacking the heart and soul that only the personality of a unique human being can bring.

You can break out of this trap by using the new PowerPoint file you've created, which should reflect your character and personality in the choices you make for the story and visuals. Now you can expand on that personal beginning by delivering a presentation that expresses your original voice. Audiences will always prefer a presentation that's imperfect and a little rough around the edges—but still authentic—over a perfect and flawless presentation that has no soul.

When you present, never be afraid to be yourself, because that's what people really want you to be.

## Working Confidently with Your Slides

For many people, the thought of public speaking inspires fear, not confidence. The fear often comes from speakers not being comfortable with their story, with themselves, or with their level of preparedness. You remove the elements that create fear by securing a strong story, extending your personality through the story, and rehearsing thoroughly along the way. Your confidence comes shining through most clearly in the way you use the projected slides you designed.

After working with the PowerPoint file in Notes Page, Normal, and Slide Sorter views, you should be very comfortable with the material. When you advance to a new slide in the presentation, that slide's headline will prompt you about what to say next. The headline also addresses the audience in a conversational tone, making them feel relaxed and helping them to easily understand what you want to convey at that point.

Next on the slide is the graphical element. One of the benefits of the BBP simplified design approach is that the slides are free of bullet points and excess clutter; instead, you show a meaningful headline illustrated by a simple graphic. The goal of simple slides like these is to inspire interdependence between you and the audience. By showing less on screen, you pique the audience's curiosity.

Next you answer the audience's questions about the slide with your spoken words, which you developed fully in the written explanation of each slide in the notes area. You explain the meaning of the headline and graphic to the audience in your own natural voice.

These three basic elements—headline, graphic, and your voice—work together to create an implicit dialog that engages the audience. When you finish the thought at hand, you advance to the next slide and repeat the process in a steady flow that naturally continues the dialog.

With the new PowerPoint presentation, you'll gain the focused attention of the audience through your relaxed approach, interesting story, and engaging visuals. Scan the room as you speak, making direct eye contact with audience members in every part of the room. Watch their faces to see how they're responding to the presentation. If people are fidgeting or restless, you might need to turn up your enthusiasm and speaking level.

# Handling Q & A

If you've done your work well in the story template, you anticipate questions by tailoring the presentation to the audience and addressing the questions they're wondering as you complete each of the acts and scenes. Opening the floor to Q & A is important—even if you've covered everything, people who are making decisions will still want to ask questions so that they feel like they've participated in the experience. Depending on how you planned it into your storyboard, you might open up the floor to conversation from the very start in Act I, at the end of the first and second Key Point sections, or after you conclude your prepared remarks and invite audience comments. In some instances, you might even want to purposely leave a few questions unanswered so that the audience will be sure to ask them and engage you in the Q & A. If you're speaking to a large audience and take a question, restate the question before you answer it to make sure that everyone in the room hears it.

If someone asks a question about a particular slide, refer to the printed storyboard for the corresponding slide number, and then type the number of the slide and press Enter to go directly to that slide. If you want to show a slide that relates to a general question from one of the Act II scenes, type the number of whichever Act II slide corresponds with the question and press Enter. If you have extra material that didn't fit into the Act II slides but you think you might still be asked about it, add the extra slides to the end of the presentation and refer to them if some questions relate to them.

| TIP | As an advanced technique, use the PowerPoint storyboard on screen as a navigational aid. Before you start your presentation, go to Slide Sorter view and display the storyboard at a size that lets you see all of the slides at once—say, 33 percent. Leave the presentation in this view, and when you're ready to present, press F5 to begin. At the end of the presentation, press Esc to return to Slide Sorter view. This creates an interesting visual, and because you know the storyboard so well, when someone asks a question about a slide, you can click the slide to go directly to it. |
|---|---|

# Improvising Within Constraints

Because your new PowerPoint file is such a versatile platform, you can try endless improvisation with it as long as you follow the basic BBP approach and stick to the ground rules. Following these rules keeps the presentation firmly rooted while leaving your creative options open to try new things.

## Keeping Control of Your Story

Because of your relaxed approach, you might find that people ask you questions during the presentation or offer stories of their own experiences. This is a good sign that the audience is feeling comfortable with your speaking style, and it is perfectly fine if that's the way you planned the presentation in the storyboard. The danger is that these queries can also cause you to head off on a tangent that throws off your timing and story structure. Handle questions graciously by quickly answering them if you can, or by acknowledging them and if necessary deferring them to the Q & A session at the end of the presentation. If you don't know the answer to a question, admit that you don't know, and offer to follow up on the matter later.

It's essential to stay on course with your story; if you don't, you can easily lose control of the situation. The goal of the BBP approach is to create a compelling story that's tailored to the audience and anticipates their questions so that they're completely absorbed to the very end. If you missed the mark and your story wasn't a good fit for the audience, spend time after the presentation reviewing the story template so that you can improve the next story you write. Pay particular attention to the Act I scenes to ensure that the story engages the audience fully.

If you need flexibility, you can always jump ahead to any point in a presentation by typing the number of a slide and pressing Enter. At a minimum, you should present the 5-minute version of the presentation described in Chapter 6, which includes all of Act I, the first slide in each scene in Act II, and all of Act III, which together form the essential structure of your story.

## Preparing for Different Contexts

The BBP approach is based on a time-tested classical story structure that should appeal to anyone, so you should be able to use the same approach for audiences of different sizes.

For most audiences, a large screen is ample for projecting a presentation; for large audiences, the screen needs to be large enough for the people in the back row to see the slides clearly. A large audience size usually prevents you from getting feedback while you're presenting, but that doesn't prevent the experience from being an implicit dialog, as described earlier in this chapter.

For an audience of one or two people, you can give the presentation using a laptop with a large screen, printouts of the slides, or even a handheld computer. In each of these cases, you lose the power of a large projected image, but you gain in terms of a more casual and conversational approach and the immediacy of starting right away with little or no need to deal with technology setup.

## Handing Out Handouts

Many presenters find it best to provide handouts after the presentation to prevent distractions. On the other hand, many audiences ask for handouts because they like to make notes on paper during a presentation. Try both approaches to see what works best for you and your audiences. One compromise is to print and hand out in advance a one-page version of the story template so that the audience has a basic road map of where you're going. You can mention at the beginning of the presentation that you'll provide comprehensive handouts at the end, and at that point provide sets of handouts in the form of printed notes pages.

# Presenting Without Being Present

If you can't present in person, you obviously miss out on the kind of communication that happens only in a live environment. But that doesn't have to stop you from presenting when you're not physically present—you just need to configure the PowerPoint presentation differently.

## Sending Your Notes Pages (Not Your Slides)

When you add graphics to the presentation in Chapter 7, you know that the slides prepared using BBP don't make much sense unless you look at them in Notes Page view. The same holds true if you send the PowerPoint presentation to someone who couldn't attend the presentation in person, so never send just the slides—always send the notes pages.

Handouts in the form of notes pages offer quick reading as a printed document. Readers quickly understand the main idea of the document by skimming headlines and visuals from page to page, and they can also spend more time reading narrative detail in the notes area if they want.

An effective way to send notes pages is in PDF file format, as described in Chapter 9. When you e-mail the notes pages in this format, the audience has access to all of the information you want to present but not access to the original PowerPoint file where you keep the graphical materials and editable text you might not want to make available.

## Producing an Online Presentation

When you can't be there in person, you can instead display the presentation in a Web browser. As described in The Plan presentation example in Chapter 9, BBP presentations will work well in the Web browser context because the same engaging story structure is there. The same simple visuals that support interdependence with your spoken words are there too, as well as the same evenly sized pieces of information, the same even pacing, and the same even flow.

### BBP CHECKLIST: DELIVERING YOUR PRESENTATION

Before and during the presentation, do you:

❏ Prepare the environment, check the technology, and properly rehearse in advance?

❏ Use your physical presence and voice to bring the experience to life?

❏ Engage your audience both implicitly and explicitly?

❏ Use the tools and techniques of BBP to manage the working memory of your audience?

The simplest way to put a presentation online is to post a PDF file of the notes pages on a Web site. Or you can convert the presentation to an online format using a conversion tool that allows you to record your narration as you display the slides. With most of these tools, such as Microsoft Office Live Meeting, the slides are displayed in a browser, and you use a microphone to record what you've written in the notes area. When the audience views the slides, they hear your spoken narration through their computers. Some online technology solutions also make the notes area viewable, in case people prefer to quickly scan what you're saying and skip ahead.

# And Now, Presenting . . .

You should now be ready to present to your audience. With the thorough presentation you've prepared using BBP, you're sure to persuade the audience with your focused, clear, and engaging story.

As you apply this system to other presentations, keep this book handy, and visit the companion Web site for this book at *www.beyondbulletpoints.com* to get a steady supply of ideas and inspiration.

Now that you've seen why and how BBP works, it's time to get started on your own presentations. As you begin your own presentations using BBP, use this book to guide you through the process step by step. Find others in your organization who are willing to help. As you apply the approach and get good results, you'll quickly create a momentum that will propel clearer and more effective communications throughout your organization. As you start to live a life *beyond bullet points*, there's no turning back—you're on your way to a much more engaging way of presenting.

# 10 Tips for Enhancing Your Delivery

You now have a flexible and robust system for bringing your ideas to life using PowerPoint. Before you give a presentation, review the following 10 tips to find ideas to spark your imagination or inspire you to try something new.

## Tip 1: The Living Brand

In the conventional bullet points approach, it's common for presenters to place a logo on the Slide Master in an effort to ensure that the visual stamp of an organization is on every slide. But based on the research realities in Chapter 2, BBP keeps extraneous visual information off every slide and instead uses a different set of techniques to ensure that an organization's identity is carried through presentations. Eliminating the logo from the Slide Master increases the amount of screen real estate available for presenting information and opens up the many creative options that an empty screen allows. And keeping the screen clear of a logo removes an obstacle that would stand in the way of the audience becoming completely absorbed in a story.

But beyond those reasons, in a live presentation context, the concept of a visual stamp on a slide diminishes in importance because all eyes are on you, and you are actually *living the brand*. The high quality of your ideas, the compelling story, the interesting visuals, and the high level of engagement all contribute to an experience that the audience will not soon forget. And just in case the audience does forget some of the details of the experience, they'll always have the handout, which includes your logo on the notes pages.

## Tip 2: Toastmasters

If you're not a member of a speaking club, you should be. Any speaker can benefit from attending a regular meeting with the sole purpose of learning and improving a full range of speaking skills. Toastmasters International, at *www.toastmasters.org*, is a good choice because it's inexpensive and all clubs are run by the volunteer efforts of their members. When you join, you'll participate in speaking exercises during meetings and give a series of prepared talks according to a sequence in a training manual.

The biggest benefits will likely come from simply attending regularly. As you're exposed to more speaking opportunities in a supportive environment, you'll develop skills to manage your nervousness, and your confidence will increase not just in public speaking but in all aspects of communication.

Many clubs haven't yet embraced the use of presentation technologies. If your local club doesn't yet use PowerPoint, bring a data projector and introduce some of the ideas you've picked up in this book to blend projected media and solid speaking skills.

## Tip 3: Stretch Yourself

A live presentation draws on the full spectrum of communication skills, but almost no one is good at everything. You're probably better at one part of the BBP process—for example, writing your story, editing your headlines, distilling your ideas to their essence, checking your reasoning, creating visuals, or actually speaking and presenting. When you know your strength, pick a different area to work on improving. For example, if you're good at writing, learn graphics, or if you're good at graphics, work on your public speaking. Only by stretching can you keep on growing.

## Tip 4: Innovative Handouts

Try creating an unconventional note-taking handout by including only the three Key Point slides on a single piece of paper. As the audience members see each Key Point slide on the screen, it will cue them to the corresponding image on the handout and reinforce the top-level visual-verbal message you want to communicate.

## Tip 5: Got Gobo?

Many standard meeting rooms feature fluorescent lights and ordinary tables, but with inexpensive lighting tools, you can change the atmosphere of the room to remove the distractions of a shabby presentation environment. For example, a simple way to light up the presentation environment is with a *gobo*, which is a partial screen with the cutout of a pattern that's placed over a light. When you turn on the light, it projects the image of the pattern onto a surface. You could use a gobo to project a subtle pattern to cover up an uneven wall or to add a soft color to make glaring lights less obvious. As with all of the visuals you've prepared for the presentation, any visual effects should be transparent and never distract from the message. If you've "got gobo," or any other special lighting, keep in mind that people should remember the message and not the lighting.

## Tip 6: Visual Mnemonics

Having problems trying to remember what you want to say? Try using the graphics on your slides to trigger your memory. For example, if you display a particular image on a slide and you plan to make certain points when you narrate it, associate each point with an element on the photograph. When you use an image on a slide as a visual mnemonic, you can make your ideas, as well as the presentation, memorable.

## Tip 7: Make the Conversation High Voltage

In *Moving Mountains* (Crowell-Collier Press, 1989), Henry M. Boettinger wrote, "Presentation of ideas is conversation carried on at high voltage—at once more dangerous and more powerful." This is one of the best definitions of presentations because it packs so much meaning into a brief sentence, which becomes even more meaningful when it's broken up into pieces:

- You're presenting *ideas*. Not your ego.

- A presentation is a *conversation*. There are at least two people involved.

- A presentation is *high voltage*. It's not boring.

- A presentation is *dangerous*. It's risky.

- A presentation is *powerful*. It has strength.

The next time you speak, keep Boettinger's wise definition in mind to stay focused on the meaning you pack into your presentations.

## Tip 8: Magnify Intimacy

One of the most powerful techniques in film is magnifying the face of an actor to give the audience a feeling of intimacy with that person. Although you won't see that technique in most presentations, new technologies continue to transform the presentation landscape.

For example, in some presentations, an IMAG image magnification camera will zoom in on a presenter's face while he or she is speaking at a live event. The image is often featured in a split-screen format next to the speaker's PowerPoint slides on a wide screen. If you have the chance to have your face magnified on a screen, embrace the opportunity—you're giving the audience a chance to see you up close. But before you do, rehearse using a live camera similar to the one in the presentation along with the event producers, who will arrange for lighting and makeup to make sure that you look good on the big screen.

## Tip 9: Flip Through Flip Charts

If you use paper flip charts along with your screen presentation, when you walk over to the flip chart, write out a headline in a complete sentence that corresponds to the point you want to make on that slide in the storyboard. Writing out the headline on the flip chart keeps your point persistent, stays visible to the audience, and reminds the audience of and reinforces your point. The headline on the flip chart will stay visible after you return to the screen media, so make sure that it's a point you want to make visible through the rest of the presentation—otherwise cover what you wrote with a blank sheet.

## Tip 10: Predesign Media Tools

If you work with a Tablet PC or flip charts, consider predesigning parts of the slides or printed pieces before you use them. For example, you might have the background scene of a slide set up and then write over it using the Tablet PC. You can do this with scanned documents, screen captures, and just about any other type of media so that when you start sketching, you already have a visual beginning point.

> **NOTE**    Be sure to review the companion CD where you'll find a bonus Chapter 11, the Appendixes, and a copy of the BBP Story Template and Storyboard Formatter

# Index

# What do you think of this book?

# We want to hear from you!

Do you have a few minutes to participate in a brief online survey?

Microsoft is interested in hearing your feedback so we can continually improve our books and learning resources for you.

To participate in our survey, please visit:

**www.microsoft.com/learning/booksurvey/**

...and enter this book's ISBN-10 number (appears above barcode on back cover*).
As a thank-you to survey participants in the United States and Canada, each month we'll randomly select five respondents to win one of five $100 gift certificates from a leading online merchant. At the conclusion of the survey, you can enter the drawing by providing your e-mail address, which will be used for prize notification only.

Thanks in advance for your input. Your opinion counts!

**\* Where to find the ISBN-10 on back cover**

ISBN-13: 000-0-0000-0000-0
ISBN-10: 0-0000-00000

00000

0 000000 000000

Example only. Each book has unique ISBN.

*Microsoft*
*Press*

No purchase necessary. Void where prohibited. Open only to residents of the 50 United States (includes District of Columbia) and Canada (void in Quebec). For official rules and entry dates see:

**www.microsoft.com/learning/booksurvey/**